The Aesthetics of Education

The Aesthetics of Education:

Theatre, Curiosity, and Politics in the Work of Jacques Rancière and Paulo Freire

Tyson E. Lewis

continuum

KH

Continuum International Publishing Group
A Bloomsbury company
80 Maiden Lane, New York, NY 10038
50 Bedford Square, London, WC1B 3DP

www.continuumbooks.com

© Tyson E. Lewis 2012

ISBN: 9781441157713 (hardback)

Library of Congress Cataloging-in-Publication Data
A catalog record for this book is available from the Library of Congress.

Typeset by Fakenham Prepress Solutions, Fakenham, Norfolk NR21 8NN
Printed and bound in the United States of America

6/28/13

Contents

Acknowledgments

There are many people I would like to thank for their assistance with this book. First and foremost, I would like to acknowledge Gert Biesta who has supported my project from the beginning and has given me generous feedback on several chapters of this book which appeared as separate articles in his journal *Studies in Philosophy and Education*. Also, my Belgian colleagues, Jan Masschelein, Maarten Simons and Joris Vlieghe have been instrumental in providing insight into many of the ideas presented in the following pages, and their imprint on this manuscript cannot be underestimated. It is also important to recognize Eduardo Duarte, Daniel Friedrich, Megan Laverty, Rene Arcilla, David Backer, and Mike Schapira who all participated in a Rancière reading group at Teachers College. In particular, Megan inspired me to take a closer look at the Kantian dimensions of Rancière's writings, Eduardo provided persistent skepticism of several of the claims that formed the backdrop of my project, Daniel remained a constant source of insight into Rancière's work, and Rene provided me with a set of challenges which I hope to have met. Finally, my graduate assistant, Olivier Michaud, helped me track down obscure references and provided help with the translation of several French sources.

This acknowledgement would be incomplete if I did not recognize my wife, Anne Keefe, and her infallible editorial advice and her keen eye for the turn of a phrase and the power of a metaphor for unlocking the poetics of my own writing. But most importantly, I would like to end with an acknowledgement that is also a dedication. Before reading Rancière's book *The Nights of Labor*, I had already been introduced to its basic thesis. In fact, the book seemed to be a shockingly simple and elegant affirmation of something that my father, Steven Lewis, had taught when I was a young child: that nights are not for sleeping but for dreaming, creating, and thinking. As a man with only a high-school education, my father refused any predetermined role as a mere laborer whose nights should be spent sleeping in order to replenish his labor-power for the following day. Instead, he spent his nights singing in bands, writing songs, and teaching himself various instruments. With little formal education, he denied the predictions of cultural habitus and took up reading novels, critical theory, and political analyses. Indeed, my father is one of those unlikely individuals who has consistently challenged the divisions of labor that scar our society: divisions between the hand and the mind, the night and the day, the literate and the illiterate. As such, the pages of this book are infused with the spirit of my father. Thanks, Dad.

Introduction:

The Aesthetics of Education

The development of man's capacity for feeling is, therefore, the more urgent need of our age, not merely because it can be a means of making better insights effective for living, but precisely because it provides the impulse for bettering our insights.
—*Fredrich Schiller,* On the Aesthetic Education of Man

In the novel *The City and the City* by China Mieville (2010), the reader follows the Kafkaesque journey of Inspector Tyador Borlu through the labyrinthian political conspiracy set in two politically autonomous yet territorially overlapping cities: Beszel and Ul Qoma. Although "grosstopically" interwoven like topographic doppelgangers, the two cities are perceived as distinct political and cultural territories. Even as citizens from the two cities intermingle on divided streets, live in buildings where different floors exist in different cities, and children climb on trees territorially split ("crosshatched") down the center, they must learn to "unsee" and "unnotice" one another. The major role of education is to teach children the peculiar skill of literally unseeing what one is seeing—a paradoxical gesture which demands both seeing and not seeing simultaneously. For instance, Ul Qoman drivers must avoid collisions with oncoming Beszel traffic all the while "unseeing" the cars they must avoid. Looking out the window of Senior Detective Qussim Dhatt's house, Ul Qoman detective Borlu summarizes this startling situation:

> From their living room I saw that Dhatt and Yallya's [Dhatt's wife] rooms and my own overlooked the same stretch of green ground, that in Beszel was Majdlyna Green and in Ul Qoma was Kwaidso Park, a finely balanced crosshatch. I had walked in Majdlyna myself often. There are parts where even individual trees are crosshatched, where Ul Qoman children and Besz children clamber past each other, each obeying their parents' whispered strictures to unsee the other.
>
> (Mieville 2010, 195)

To move from one city to the other is an experience of unseeing what one is unseeing—not so much a physical journey as a *perceptual shift*. As Tyador Borlu experiences when traveling between cities, the re-education process is a painful redistribution of what can and cannot be seen, what can and cannot be heard, what can and cannot be acknowledged. When his investigation into the murder of a young graduate student takes him from Beszel to Ul Qoma, he literally must train his eye to perceive what years of habituation had taught him to ignore. Borlu narrates, "Mostly, as with our own equivalents, the course [an orientation to life in Ul Qoma] was concerned to help a Besz citizen through the potentially traumatic fact of actually *being in* Ul Qoma, unseeing all their familiar environs, where we lived the rest of our life, and seeing the buildings beside us that we had spent decades making sure not to notice" (Mieville 2010, 133). This "acclimation pedagogy" uses complex computer simulations to work directly on the field of perception. Again, Borlu describes the acclimation apparatus: "They sat me in what they called an Ul Qoma simulator ... on which they projected images and videos of Beszel with the Besz buildings highlighted and their Ul Qoman neighbours minimized with lighting and focus. Over long seconds, again and again, they would reverse the visual stress, so that for the same vista Beszel would recede and Ul Qoma shine" (Mieville 2010, 133). Here education is an education in and of perceptual alteration—a learning to see, hear, smell, taste differently.

Any evidence (even a momentary glance across the divide, any acknowledgment of the disavowed "other" that lives across the perceptual divide) can be held as evidence of a "breach" which is the worst crime imaginable in the two cities. The breach breaks with the division of the sensible that maintains the borders of the cities. In other words, a breach establishes a new field of vision, confusing or disfiguring the distribution of what can and cannot be sensed. This crime against perceptual censorship is an even worse offence than murder because it challenges boundaries that maintain the ordering of bodies, spaces, and gestures, throwing the fragile political structure underlying the stability of Beszel and Ul Qoma into chaos. As such a special, secret police force is needed. Called the "Breach," these shadowy officers exist between the two cities and are fully "invisible" to either set of citizens. In this paradoxical location both inside and radically outside the two cities, Breach officers search for those in violation of the law of "unseeing." In this sense, they are the sovereign force that exists outside particular national laws and yet are the supplemental force necessary for these laws to remain in operation.

In order to understand the weird worlds of *The City and the City* and thus to provide a justification for this strange detour through science fiction as a viable opening to a book ostensibly concerning education and aesthetics, I need to turn to the work of Jacques Rancière. As Rancière has recently argued, societies are structured according to a particular "distribution of the sensible" (2006c, 12). This distribution of the sensible "reveals who can have a share in what is common to the community based on what they do and on the time and space in which this activity is performed" (Rancière 2006c, 12). In other words, there is an aesthetic partitioning at the heart of social life—an aesthetics that defines the spaces, places, and modalities of visibility, audibility, and so on. Sensitivity (to sensation) and sensibility (the appearance of logical or reasonable accord) are therefore closely connected, the former a precondition for the latter. The result is a society that is composed of certain sensory inclusions and exclusions defining the field of what counts as community.

Opposed to the naturalization, ossification, or institutionalization of certain sensible hierarchies, politics is, for Rancière, "aesthetic in principle" (1999, 58). The aesthetic principle of politics, according to Rancière, "always defines itself by a certain recasting of the distribution of the sensible, a reconfiguration of the given perceptual forms" (2006c, 63)—a "heterology" that disturbs the meaningful organization of the sensible. The rupture that defines politics is always an aesthetic disfiguration of conventional distributions of who can speak and think, what can be seen, and finally, what can be heard. In other words, what genuine political and artistic acts share is a creative labor to introduce new forms of speech and activity that challenge the distribution of allotted roles in a given society. Mieville's weird fiction clearly presents a fantastical version of this fundamental thesis. Beszel and Ul Qoma are separated not by geographic distance or physical barriers but by a particular partitioning of the sensible which organizes what can and cannot be sensed. The political crime par excellence is a breach of this partitioning. Stated differently, those who are caught breaking the perceptual divide are engaging in a political practice that "reconfigure[s] the map of the sensible" (Rancière 2006c, 39). If for Rancière, the major function of the police within a community is summarized in the phrase: "Move along! There is nothing to see here!"(2010c, 37) then this motto equally applies to the officers working within Breach. The Breach maintains the certainty of national identity and the solidity of national boundaries through a policing of glances, gestures, and speech acts that potentially see what must remain unseen or acknowledge that which must remain unacknowledged. In other words, they maintain a certain partitioning of the sensible by enforcing the law of the "unseen." The "acclimation pedagogy" described in the book is therefore a form of education that must work on the training of the senses so that they conform to a predetermined field of the visible and audible.

Although Mieville's weird fiction is perhaps too surreal for some, the connections between unseeing and education cannot be easily reduced to mere fantasy. Is it not true that we all teach ourselves and our children to "unsee" certain realities that would otherwise challenge our fundamental beliefs were they to be openly acknowledged? For instance, we must learn to unsee homeless individuals, stray animals, pain and suffering, exploitation, and ecological disasters if we are to maintain the ability to function as productive workers within a post-industrial economy. Or we must unsmell trash, noxious fumes and other disagreeable odors which would indicate the decay of our environments. Likewise, some teachers might practice the art of "unseeing" struggling students in their classrooms or surprising appearances of creativity and ingenuity for test scores and standardized goals. Thus the first lessons of education are always on the level of the senses themselves. Before cognition, there is *already an aesthetic partitioning of the sensible*. As Joseph Tanke argues, the aesthetic dimension in Rancière's formulation "operates upon the transcendental conditions [space and time] that structure the distribution of the sensible and thus the subjects that inhabit it" (2010, 12). If as Aristotle once argued, *philia*, or the feeling for living with one another (*Nicomachean Ethics* 1155a, 21–2), is the primary affect of a political animal, then this sensation is an aesthetic *problem as much as it is a political and transcendental one.*

Rancière argues that the greatest political journey is more often than not the shortest distance from our homeland—an aesthetic journey across the perceptual divide that separates and hierarchizes, that includes and excludes. In his book *Short Voyages to the Land of the People*, Rancière writes, "This book is about voyages. Not so much to far-off isles or exotic vistas as to those much closer lands that offer the visitor the image of another world. Just across the straits, away from the river, off the beaten path, at the end of the subway line, there lives another people (unless it is, quite simply, the people) ... More than the analysis of oppression or the sense of duty toward the oppressed, the core political experience of our generation may well have been to go on such a voyage, discovering for ourselves this recognizable foreignness, this shimmering of life" (2003c, 1–2). A political voyage is a "goodbye" to the sensible distribution of affects that tie us to particular places, experiences, and identities predetermined by the allotted roles in a society. It is a goodbye to a certain aesthetic configuration of the self and an openness to mixing and disfigurement under the sudden arrival of new sights and sounds, smells and tastes that have no fixed coordinates in the order of things. Breach is a political act in *The City and the City* precisely because it opens up an "atopia" (a literal placeless place) which throws off pre-constituted political modes of seeing and acting, belonging and identifying internal to the order of both Beszel and Ul Qoma. For Rancière, "atopia" is a space and time marked by a fundamental incommensurability between sensation and taken-for-granted cultural values, and the "atopos" is "someone who is dis-placed, an extravagant" (2003c, 122) living within this breach—a subjectivity without an identifiable subject position. In this sense, the political act is not demystification through ideological critique but rather an aesthetic displacement of allotted roles and identities—a poetical redistribution that calls into question the fundamental coordinates of time and space that organize the feeling for living with one another. *The City and the City* might be a work of fiction, but it is an accurate depiction of the fiction which weaves together aesthetics and politics both in society and in education.

In the rest of this book, I will explore Rancière's basic thesis that politics is aesthetic in principle but with a twist. While Rancière's work has concentrated on the aesthetics of politics and the politics of the arts of the aesthetic regime, he has paid significantly less attention to the aesthetics of education and in turn, the politics of this relationship. Indeed, it is the exact nature of politics, education, and the arts that Rancière fails to completely conceptualize, thus creating a gap that mysteriously separates and yet conjoins these three relatively autonomous fields. Although Rancière argues that "aesthetics has its own politics, just as politics has its own aesthetics" (2009f, 285), this does not mean that political practice is identical to artistic practice or that politics collapses into a form of art. Rather it demonstrates that the political and the aesthetic domains exist in a certain relation of interpenetration and tension. One of the key tensions involves the issue of scale. The aesthetic dimension of politics, for instance, operates through the construction of a people that institutes a disagreement within a community. Democracy is fundamentally poetic for Rancière because it concerns the sudden "appearance of the people" (1999, 99)—a people that no longer remains in their "proper space" within the sensible boundaries and borders of the community. Rancière writes, "Appearance is not an illusion that is opposed to the real. It is the introduction of a visible into the field of experience, which then modifies the regime of the visible" (1999, 99). Appearance is affective and effective, engendering profound disruptions of distributed bodies, voices, and gestures. As Rancière argues, "the aesthetics of politics consists above all in the framing of a *we*" (2010c, 141) and thus "continuously interferes in politics and contributes to weaving the fabric of the political, its words, images, attitudes, forms of sensibility, etc." (2009e, 122). Because the political mark of the emergence of a "we" is always in a space where it should not be, the intervening production of the people is an invention, a *fiction*—a subjectivation that exists precisely where it does not and when it does not. The appearance of a fictitious "people" that speaks in the name of the community of which it is not a part is inherently democratic in that it verifies an underlying claim to equality through a perceptual reconfiguration of *philia.*

The political dimension of the arts of the aesthetic regime on the other hand does not form a "*people*," and thus "its population is not the *demos*" (Rancière 2009f, 284). Instead, the arts function to define communities of sense that are political because they do not hold "democratic flags" or "shout out egalitarian mottos" (Rancière 2009f, 284). For instance, "literarity"—as a function of modern literature—forms "an imbalance in the relationship between signs, things, and bodies" (Rancière 2009f, 278), disrupting hierarchical orders distinguishing between "refined" and "prosaic" subject matter and challenging predetermined ways of speaking and using language. Rather than the annunciation of a claim (the proclamation of a new logos under the sign of equality), the politics of literarity announces a new balance between pleasure and pain, a new passion, a new distribution of sensible subjects and objects. Rancière summarizes: "What literature endows the workers with is not the awareness of their condition. It is the passion that can make them break their condition, because it is the passion that their condition forbade" (2009f, 278). In other words, passion builds a new sensory world that is not reducible to mere delusion, but is itself a refusal to accept the rules that bind certain affects to certain times, places, activities, and modes of annunciation and production. This is precisely the production of poetic freedom as a translation of sense across preestablished coordinates of space and time. Simply put, the political valence of literarity is predicated on a "fraternity of the subterranean drives or impersonal rhythms and intensities of collective life" (Rancière 2009e, 122) that move across boundaries that separate *pathos* from *logos.* Summarizing this distinction, Rancière makes a distinction between political and literary forms of dissensus:

Literary dissensus works on changes in the scale and nature of individualities, on deconstruction of the relationships between things and meanings. In this, it differentiates itself from the work of political subjectivation which configures new collectivities by means of words. Political dissensus operates in the form of subjectivation procedures that identify the declaration by the anonymous that they are a collective, an *us*, with reconfiguration of the field of political objects and actors. Literature goes in the opposite direction to this organization of the perceptual field around a subject of utterance. It dissolves the subjects of utterance in the fabric of the precepts and affects of anonymous life.

(Rancière 2011c, p43)

For Rancière, there cannot be a strict equivalence between these two types of equality (literary and political). One valence of equality works on the level of "we, the people" in order to redefine *philia* in terms of a poetic fiction, and the other valence works on the level of pre-personal senses in order to continually interrupt any notion of *philia*. As Raji Vallury aptly summarizes, "Political dissensus is the construction of a sensible [a people], while literary misunderstanding is a deconstruction or even an invalidation of its coordinates" (2009, 236). The sensorium unleashed by the politics of literarity cannot constitute a community without betraying its own logic of immanence. While Vallury argues that Rancière misses the connection between the two precisely because he does not allow "for the entry of aesthetic modes of individuation into the field of the aesthetic possibilities of politics" (2009, 237), I would argue that Rancière does allow for a certain form of "permeability" (Lewis in press). This permeability is the work of democratic equality within the aesthetic arts and within political wrongs, both of which challenge inequality but in their own domains and with their own strategies and tactics.

If the relation between the aesthetic arts and political disagreements has caused some confusion in Rancière's work, then the relation between art, education, and politics is perhaps more perplexing. For instance, in the secondary literature concerning Rancière and education we see a conflation of education with the arts of the aesthetic regime. Perhaps one of the most dramatic examples of this conflation is seen in the work of Cath Lambert whose article "Psycho classrooms: Teaching as a work of art" (2011) utilizes Rancière's insights into the politics of aesthetics to theorize the juncture of art and pedagogy, ultimately dissolving any distinction between the two through her theory of the pedagogical function of haptic architectural spaces. On the other side, we see a conflation of education with political subjectivation in the form of the "ignorant citizen" (Biesta 2011). This concept shifts our understanding of education from a process that socializes newcomers into existing social and political orders to education as an event that constitutes new political subjectivities. These new subjectivities are, for Biesta, ignorant citizens precisely because they have no predefined identity and are ignorant of the specific content defining "good citizenship." As distinct from political subjectivation, Maarten Simons and Jan Masschelein have argued that "pedagogic subjectivation" is not the verification of a "we" (even if this we consists of ignorant citizens) or a radical desubjectivation of the passions but rather the verification of an "ability to" or the "will to" (2010, 601). In the act of mutual teaching, Rancière writes, "each ignorant person could become for another ignorant person the master who would reveal to him his intellectual power" (1991, 17). What is important in this quote is the emphasis on ignorant *person* which is not reducible to either the concept of the citizen who refuses any specific pre-defined civic identity (a new people which lacks an allotted place within the polis), nor to a passionate deterritorialization. Rather the ignorant person is the one who first and foremost is, as Simons and Masschelein argue (2008), the subjectivation of a will which enables him or her to break with the logic of the "will to learn" that forms part of the current neo-liberal and entrepreneurial "learning apparatus." While such a reading is perhaps the most faithful to Rancière's project, this strict autonomy of the educational sphere seems to equally miss the particular aesthetic component of emancipatory education.

As an intervention into these debates, my book is an attempt to think the nature of this conjunction of domains as a space of *playful study* between affect and identity, between the subjectivation of a people and the pre-subjective realm of affective intensities—a paradoxical space that most directly expresses Rancière's fundamental thesis: "the figure of subjectivation itself [is] constantly unstable, constantly caught between the work of symbolic disincorporation and the constitution of new bodies" (Rancière 2003b, 197). Indeed, education is the precise location of Rancière's *atopos* or exceptional individual who is neither here nor there, neither this nor that, but rather studying these various positions with a certain curious disposition and a will to experiment, perform, and play. And the educational community is neither simply atomized wills nor is it a defined collectivity (a "we"), but rather a "community of dis-identified persons" (Rancière 2009c, 73) who are studying what they shouldn't and who are dis-placed from their proper places.

In this sense, Mieville's triangulation between politics, aesthetics, and education is perhaps a more convincing model of analysis, and in certain ways helps us to further advance Rancière's own work. For Mieville, politics, aesthetics, and education form a complex, overdetermined unity that is internally differentiated. The links which Rancière does not adequately articulate in his philosophy are therefore given a poetic form through Mieville's weird fiction. Moving between Mieville's novelistic intuition and Rancière's philosophical analysis, it is my assertion that all democratic education is likewise an aesthetic experience that teaches us to redistribute the relationship between what can and cannot be seen as well as what can and cannot be heard. This means that an aesthetic dimension does not have to be added onto education (in the form of arts programs), but rather that it is immanent to democratic education as such. This also means that aesthetic experience is not simply an experience of the beauty or imaginative expression of art (as it is often discussed in educational theory), but is, as Rancière describes, first and foremost "a certain disconnection from the habitual conditions of sensible experience" (2006d, 1). Democratic education thus must first and foremost work on the level of the senses themselves, on the level of sensuous intuition (Kantian transcendentalism) and of *philia* (Aristotelian social affect) without simply becoming yet another form of literary or aesthetic experimentation. Key here is the underdeveloped relationship between four themes which I will investigate through the various chapters of this book. First, there is the need to articulate two important concepts in Rancière's work: curiosity and will. If curiosity is a passionate affliction specifically related to aesthetic experience, and will is a faculty of empowerment verified in education, then the aesthetics of education must determine their relation and mutual interconnection. It is my contention that if education is the subjectivation of the will, our understanding of the will remains incomplete without an attending appreciation for the aesthetic passion of curiosity which jumpstarts and orients the attentive nature of the will. Second, there is the question of the aesthetic metaphors that inform teaching practices. Although Rancière draws explicit connections between theatre and politics, a similar relation between theatrical performance and education remains under-theorized in his work. Rancière's connections between the emancipated spectator and the subject of universal teaching offer an entry point for further exploring the unique and vital roles that acting and staging have in the educational relationship. By focusing on the pedagogical dramaturgy of universal teaching, I will, in turn, be able to reevaluate the relationship between educational equality—a theme stressed not only by Rancière but also in the secondary literature—and the much more marginalized issue of individual freedom. And lastly, there remains the specific educational function of the arts, and in particular of visual images in relation to curiosity and will. If Rancière is suspicious of the pedagogical function of the arts, it is my goal to redeem this function, but with significant revisions and qualifications.

In sum, rather than a mere application of Rancière's thought to the field of education, this book will attempt a philosophical and practical extension of Rancière's aesthetic project in ways not anticipated by his own reflections on education. In particular, I move beyond his principal writings on education, including the classic text *The Ignorant Schoolmaster: Five Lessons in Intellectual Emancipation* (1991) in order to center aesthetic concerns as fundamental for an understanding of what he describes as "universal teaching." Although *The Ignorant Schoolmaster* has proven to be the key text referenced in the ever-increasing literature on Rancière and education—enabling philosophers to rethink emancipation (Biesta 2010), sociology of schooling (Simons and Masschelein 2010; Pelletier 2009), the practice of educational philosophy and research (Bingham 2009; 2010), and resistance to educational inequalities (Cho 2005a)—this book increases our appreciation for the aesthetic dimension of multiple modes of education, each of which either remains faithful to the promise of dissensual aesthetics or betrays this promise. In turn, an analysis of the internal aesthetics of education will enable us to once again return to the question of the unique politics of education: the moment when students suddenly demand to struggle for the time and space to study through the proclamation of "we, the students."

Verifying Equality: Rancière and Freire

At the outset, it is important to differentiate this program from certain strands of critical theory influencing education today. While authors such as Daniel Friedrich, Bryn Jaastad and Thomas Popkewitz (2010) and Gert Biesta (2008) have utilized Rancière to call into question several major assumptions of critical pedagogies—the seemingly inescapable and predetermined reproduction of inequality, the citizen as a pedagogical project, and the institutionalization of democracy—my project is perhaps more radical in its orientation. Rancière offers not simply another form of critique, another form of critical discourse that can be absorbed into the umbrella of critical pedagogy. Instead, as Rancière argues, "The true philosophical or critical task is to do away with that so-called critical trend ... It is to do away with the prophetic tone and with the plot of decadence that is only the reversal of a former trust in the sense of history and to focus on the existing forms of intellectual, artistic, and political intervention" (Rancière 2008a, 188). The problem with critique is that it always *defers* equality, positing it as a goal to be achieved rather than an axiom to be verified. The "prophetic tone" of critique relies on a "plot of decadence" which views the present as a totality that must be negated in order to ensure equality in the future. For the present, the oppressed must remain dependent on the expertise of the philosopher, critical sociologist, or critical pedagogue who orients them toward their true, revolutionary vocations. What is missed in this model is the verification of the unanticipated ruptures of equality that are always already happening within and against existing hierarchies. This is not to deny that such hierarchies exist, or that exploitation and subjugation are "distant memories." If hierarchies exist it is not despite equality but rather because of an underlying equality—an equality that enables the slave to understand the commands of the master, or that allows the worker to perform the tasks described by the factory boss to his or her specifications. It is this underlying, always already present equality of intelligences that can, at any moment, rupture the given distribution of labor and the given partitioning of the sensible defining a given social order. Rather than offer yet another model of critique, Rancière's reflections on emancipation open up the space for a type of thinking that replaces critique with performance, temporal displacement with contemporary verification, and imaginative vision with sensorial redistribution.

Similarly to Rancière, Michel Foucault in the lectures collected under the title of *The Government of Self and Others* (2011) presents an unusual reading of Kant's article "What is Enlightenment?" that challenges the privilege of critique as a model for politics. As is well known, the brief newspaper article written for *Berlinische Monatsschrift* in 1784 argues that enlightenment is man's way out from his self-incurred tutelage and thus grounds the courage to dare to think for one's self. In this sense, the project of enlightenment autonomy is a question of education, of daring to think and speak the truth on one's own without recourse to dependency on a tutor or master. Summarizing Kant, Foucault writes, "If men are in this condition of tutelage, if they are subject to direction by others, it is not because these others have seized power, or that it has been handed over to them in an essential, founding and instituting act. He says it is because men are unable or do not wish to conduct themselves, and others have obligingly come forward to conduct them" (2011, 29). In particular, there are three forms of tutelage which bother Kant: books come to take the place of understanding, spiritual directors take over ethical judgment, and doctors become responsible for philosophical/aesthetic concerns. While Foucault finds a point of commonality with Kant's quest for an ontology of the present (i.e., what is the present moment?), Foucault points out that Kant's own solution is largely inadequate for the job at hand precisely because his work is indirectly implicated in his critical analysis. "It seems to me," Foucault states, "that this analysis of tutelage should be read in terms of the implicit and underlying presence in this text of the three *Critiques*" (2011, 31). In other words, if critique attempts to create the groundwork for enlightenment autonomy and speaking the truth, it only creates the very dependencies which block such progress. The result is the political tutelage of the people under Fredrick of Prussia, and ultimately, the tutelage of all under the enlightenment of the philosopher, the critical knowledge of the sociologist, or the political vision of the critical pedagogue. While Kant might have approached the question of freedom in his essay "What is Enlightenment?," he nevertheless retreats from the full implications of this public use of freedom, thus "taming" freedom through a "judgmental ethos of obedience" (Masschelein and Simons 2011, 169).

As an alternative to the dialectics of freedom and dependency found in Kant's critical project, Rancière's book *The Nights of Labor* (1989) reveals the secret lives of workers in the aftermath of the July Revolution of 1830 in France. Whereas leftist intellectuals assumed the existence of a unified "class culture" which was submersed in labor and thus had little time for anything beyond the replenishment of labor-power, Rancière discovered that many workers were not using their nights for sleeping. Rather, they were busy experimenting with a variety of scholarly and artistic pursuits that effected a radical redistribution of the sensible divisions between intellectual and manual labor, night and day, amateur and expert, and so on. Instead of dependency on the philosopher to provide political orientation through critique of existing relations of production, what the workers revealed was a certain militant refusal of the locations, activities, gestures, and passions assigned to them by both capitalists and leftist intellectuals. They present a work on the self by the self that redistributes knowledges, discourses, and practices often reserved for various "gate-keepers" interested in maintaining a strict division of labor. This redistribution of *pathos* and *logos* found in the nights of labor verified the equality of all even within the most unequal of circumstances. Here the limits of critique are reached: if critique relies on a subtle form of tutelage, then a militant practice of dissensus breaks with intellectual dependency by asserting the abilities of all to think, speak, and act differently on their own accord.

In order to test Rancière's hypothesis of equality against the theoretical assumptions posited by critical pedagogy, the privileged interlocutor throughout most of this book will be Paulo Freire—a key figure in the genesis of critical theory's educational cousin, critical pedagogy. This choice is far from arbitrary. As Kristin Ross has argued, Rancière's intervention into education with the "untimely" publication of *The Ignorant Schoolmaster* resembles, "however slightly" (2009, 16) the earlier interventions of Freire. As opposed to Ross, Charles Bingham (2010) draws a clear delineation between Rancière and Freire, arguing that the latter's theory of truth remains mired in the paradox of explication antithetical to the ambiguity of educational truth. Bingham further argues that Freire's conceptualization of the student as a psychological subject in need of educational psychoanalysis in order to achieve political emancipation forecloses on Rancière's fundamental model of the student as a political subject whose existing emancipation merely needs to be verified (Bingham, Biesta, and Rancière 2010). Agreeing in part with Bingham and Ross, it is the rather tantalizing phrase "however slightly" that most directly concerns me in this text—a phrase that speaks to a shared space of overlap but also of profound differences. Perhaps I could even argue that "however slightly" suggests a "grosstopic" relation between the two, or an overlap that conjoins and separates simultaneously. Certainly Rancière's emphasis on the politics of literariness—the relationship between the availability of the written letter and democracy—and Freire's practice of empowerment through literacy share many conceptual overlaps and in certain ways complement each other. Yet it is this very overlap that also highlights divergences in how the democracy of writing operates for Rancière and Freire, differences that are not simply political or pedagogical, as outlined by Sarah Galloway (in press), but also aesthetic. In sum, "however slightly" suggests a space wherein we can not only utilize Rancière to think differently about Freire but also where we can utilize Freire to think differently about Rancière. This will resist transforming either figure into a "master" who can "explain" the flaws in his rival theorist. It will also avoid either simple synthesis or simple polemic. Guided by my inquiry into the aesthetics of education, I hope to defamiliarize certain taken-for-granted interpretations of Freire's work which either romanticize his project (and thus place him above reproach) or dismiss him as nothing more than a Eurocentric colonizer.

As such, the following chapters will not simply be summaries of what Freire said about art or aesthetics but will be an *active* translation of his work in order to probe the latent potentiality of his thought for further educational experimentation. In this sense, my book is part of a larger trend which repositions Freire in relation to major political thinkers such as Peter McLaren's (2000) rehabilitation of Freire's Marxist Humanism or Raymond Morrow and Carlos Alberto Torres's (2002) interpretation of Freirian dialogue as a form of Habermasian communicative action. While perhaps methodologically similar, my book stands resolutely opposed to these other texts which, in their own ways, demonstrate how critique itself always displaces the political (and perhaps the educational) onto another scene. While reuniting Freire with the question of political struggle, McLaren's comparison of Freire with Che Guevara could be characterized as a "metapolitical"(Rancière 1999, 81) appropriation of Freire—a reading that substitutes the principle of politics for another principle, in this case Marx's economic determinism. As McLaren writes, "Freire warrants his reputation as a pre-eminent critical educationalist in the way that he was able to foreground the means by which *the pedagogical* (the localized pedagogical encounter between teacher and student) is implicated in *the political* (the social relations of production within the global capitalist economy)" (2000, 160). Here politics becomes displaced (repressed) by economics. The result of this metapolitical glissade is that political disagreement itself is reduced to nothing more than a false appearance of a deeper truth which the teacher (in this case the economy itself) unveils. McLaren's attempt to revolutionize Freire by reconnecting him with historical materialism (via Che Guevara) in the end precisely misses what is political in Marx's own writings. As Rancière argues, Marx indicates, "a revolution of the forms themselves of the sensible life, an aesthetical revolution in the strongest sense" (2009d, 464).

Alternatively, Morrow and Torres's Habermasian Freire results in a "parapolitics" (Rancière 1999, 70) which reduces the scene of dialogic disagreement to mere misunderstanding within a rational linguistic exchange preventing provisional consensus. Morrow and Torres defend their Habermasian Freire by arguing against naïve interpretations of the ideal speech act as excluding conflict. Opposed to utopianism, the consensus of the ideal speech situation is an "empirical counterfactual" that "people act as if this were a real possibility" (Morrow and Torres 2002, 51). Yet this is not Rancière's claim. For Rancière, consensus is full of disputes and conflict, yet what is missed is that these conflicts themselves are already identified as part of the common. In other words, Habermas and his theory of the ideal speech act is problematic because it erases the contest over what counts as speech, reducing disagreement to the regulation/ negotiation of pre-given parts without disturbing the distribution of the sensible (the visual and verbal) that forms the terrain of contestation. Simply stated, there is no room for "the dispute over the existence of the dispute and the parties confronting one another" (Rancière 1999, 55). The scene of politics is already defined by the procedural norms of communicative action and the parties involved in the dispute already recognize one another as actors in a specific dispute. Habermas empties the political of politics precisely because he misses the aesthetic dimension of rupture that undoes the terms of the debate, the common ground of the conflict. This danger is replicated in Morrow and Torres's treatment of Freire.

The political glissades of these authors fold back on Freire's educational theory, producing what I would call metaeducational and paraeducational effects. In terms of the former, McLaren increasingly equates participation in economic struggle with education as such—hence his turn from life in schools to reflections on large-scale social movements. In this sense, he allows economic revolution to do the job of education by other means. The political displacement that McLaren enacts replicates itself in the form of an educational displacement. In such a model, the authoritative knowledge claims of the teacher are not erased, but rather projected onto the economic master who is absolute and tells the only historical lesson worth memorizing. As with the metapolitical appropriation of Freire's work, the parapolitical reading also results in a paraeducation where the administration of communicative speech acts between teachers and students replaces the radical break with the logic of inequality that is universal teaching. In the end, both of these readings simultaneously miss the political *and* educational possibilities of Freire's theory—possibilities that only become recognizable when reconceptualized in relation to Rancière's project.

What follows is not so much a critique of Freire (although at times I might take a rather polemical stance on some of his philosophical and educational formulations), but rather *a redistribution of the sensible that has become "Freire"*—a radical change of *mise-en-scene* that allows us to hear and see a different Freire—in order to challenge certain orthodoxies within various forms of critical pedagogy that result in para- and metapolitical appropriations. What I hope to produce is an atopic space of thought that resides in a gap that both separates and conjoins the two in relation to key educational, political, and aesthetic questions. In order to shed light on these resemblances and differences, my analysis of the aesthetics of emancipatory education will focus on five interconnected questions:

1) What is stultifying pedagogy? Here I will turn to Rancière's analysis of his former teacher Louis Althusser—an analysis that shares many features of Freire's depiction of "banking education" (or an educational practice that institutes strict hierarchies of knowledge and ignorance, activity and passivity between teachers and students). It is my contention that while Rancière rejects Althusser's project on multiple levels—thus revealing the inscription of stultification within every claim to emancipation—we

can use Rancière's method of equality in reverse order to verify how in every moment of stultification there is a faint inscription of equality. This heretical reading will demonstrate a new genealogical point of entry for thinking education, the opening to which is found in Althusser's late comments on the contingencies of materialism and what he describes as a "swerve" effect. In Chapter One of this book, I will pick up on this swerve effect in order to swerve Rancière's own reading away from polemic denunciation and toward a poetic project of building an "uncertain community" between himself and Althusser. In other words, I will attempt to enact a translation of Althusser's work which does not deny its problems while also affirming the axiom of equality at work in the most unlikely of places.

2) What are the possibilities and limitations in constructing analogies between the teacher and the artist, between art forms and forms of education? In particular, I want to look at the work of Freire and his strategic deployment of this analogy. I will argue that Freire was correct in that the role of the pedagogue is like that of the artist (a point of intersection with Rancière's own reflections on the subject), yet his understanding of this role is fixed within the classical regime of art and must be challenged on four accounts: the harmony of beauty over the dissonance of the sublime, the passivity of the spectator/ student, the hierarchy between word and image, and the intentional fallacy underlying the meaning of images. These limitations to Freire's understanding of the aesthetics of teaching and the use of images in problem-posing dialogue undermine the centrality of his commitment to equality and emancipation, demonstrating how critique once again rests on the prophetic vision of the educator who defers liberation for a future yet-to-come at the expense of verifying the axiom of equality in the present.

3) What are the affective dimensions of learning? While Rancière focuses on the shift from intelligence to will as a central methodological facet of universal teaching, Freire's educational problematic rests on the movement from spontaneous curiosity to epistemological curiosity. Here I suggest that both theorists are largely incomplete and that a synthesis that moves beyond both Rancière and Freire is needed. On the one hand Rancière is correct when he shifts registers from intelligence to will, yet he does not see how the emphasis on curiosity in his aesthetic interventions fits into his overarching educational reflections. In this respect, Freire is helpful in constructing this missing link in Rancière's project. On the other hand Freire's model of curiosity remains within

the framework of epistemology and of scientific understanding and thus misses Rancière's more insightful connections between curiosity and aesthetic redistribution of the sensible. Holding true to the question of curiosity and its role in the aesthetics of education is productive for helping to reconstruct democratic education as an act of perceptual alternation rather than critical consciousness raising, thus enabling us to recognize how equality is not simply a project to be achieved but is the production of new ways of seeing, being, hearing, and interacting within the present.

4) How are we to verify the aesthetic politics of education? More often than not, art in education is used to transform the imagination (Greene 1995; Baldacchino 2008), yet my emphasis in this book is slightly different. Agreeing with Davide Panagia (2009), education begins with a rupture of the partitioning of the sensible, the transcendental dimensions of space and time that form the basis of imaginative constructions. If the politics of literature outlined above focuses on a shift in the passions, then playful study rests between affective passions and the arrival of a name (a name of a people). As such, we must pay careful attention to passion in education, not in order to reduce education to the alteration of the passions but rather in order to understand how education exists in the moment of an uncertain community poised between passion and *logos*—this is the space necessary to verify what I refer to as the "theatrical will" as a will to act "as if …". In Chapter Seven, I will argue that laughter is a particular redistribution of pleasure and pain that breaks with the affective void in contemporary schooling practices. As such, laughter becomes a verification of the joy of democracy and in turn opens a space for new forms of curiosity to emerge. Inverting Rancière's thesis in *The Flesh of Words: The Politics of Writing* (2004a), I argue that laughter is an instance where the flesh (passion) has yet to be translated into words, opening a space of dissensus within the standardized classroom.

5) How can emancipation be a practice that involves both equality and freedom? If Rancière focuses almost exclusively on the question of equality, then in Freire's work we see an almost exclusive emphasis on the question of freedom. Reading the two theorists together will help us understand emancipation as a more complex operation which exists in the dynamic tension between equality and freedom. Without this tension, Rancière's equality becomes a form of voluntary servitude, and Freire's call to freedom becomes a call for benevolent authority. The result of the fracture within emancipation therefore results in certain limitations for both Rancière and Freire—limitations which can only

be overcome by once again returning to the question of aesthetics in education.

6) What is the connection between history, literature, and death? In the conclusion of this book I will suggest that we need to return to Freire's critique of necrophilia and his attending practice of biophilic pedagogy of emancipation. Drawing on Rancière's analysis of history as the name for the intersection between time, words, and death, I suggest a more positive and life-affirming role for death than is granted in Freire's analysis. It is ultimately in the distance afforded by and through death that the space of the laugh becomes possible and in turn the passion of education becomes realized.

These investigations will problematize three dimensions of Freire's work which have formed the backbone of most contemporary critical pedagogy and have in turn led to the para- and metaeducational effects discussed above.

1) Teaching as a beautiful act (pedagogy)
2) Epistemological curiosity (learning)
3) Consciousness raising as emancipation (politics)

Together these presuppositions rely on a certain partitioning of the sensible that repeatedly misses its political mark. As an alternative, the aesthetics of democratic education (a) focus on teaching as a sublime act that ruptures the harmony and mutual recognition of beautiful symmetry, (b) reconnects learning to its aesthetic foundation in the experience of the sublime, and (c) troubles the assumed relationship between critical consciousness raising and emancipation. As Rancière argues, his methodology concerns "horizontal distributions" of what can and cannot be seen, heard, or sensed rather than vertical distributions of "the hidden beneath the apparent" (2006c, 49). Vertical methodologies of critique that have so dominated the field of critical pedagogy both in terms of metaphor (Freirian consciousness "raising") and in terms of methodology (ideological criticism) are always, in the first instance, linked with practices of expertise and thus presuppose the forms of inequality which they are attempting to move beyond. The key to overcoming this hidden form of inequality that lies at the heart of critical pedagogy, we must take *appearance* seriously, and in turn pay closer attention to the aesthetic dimensions of teaching and learning. On the ground of the poetics of educational performance we can once again renew the commitments to emancipation that have fueled critical pedagogy and create a new genealogy of democratic education against the critical theory tradition. Throughout the following chapters, I hope to create a new philosophical stage for thinking about Rancière and Freire, and in turn gesture toward a new vision of the relation between aesthetics and education not recognized by either theorist.

In short, the aesthetics of democratic education represent the true suspension of the law of what Mieville called assimilation pedagogy in the name of a fundamental breach between sense and sense. Educational philosophy must become a "weird fiction" of its own in order to promote the practice of that which has no home, of that which has no place within the order of things: democracy. This does not mean that educational philosophy must become a fable (forever deferred through the impossibility of "a long time ago") or a science fiction (perpetually locked in a future-yet-to-come), but rather that it must live a precarious life where there can be no well-defined boundaries between methods of science and methods of literary theory (Rancière 2006d). Thus educational philosophy must become a practice that embraces a certain form of ignorance, actively ignoring disciplinary divisions and demarcations in order to construct fictions of teaching and learning that dispute canonical readings, disciplinary hierarchies, and taken-for-granted practices of "progressive" lineages and conservative backlashes. Here fiction refers to the "material reorganizations of signs and images, of relations between what one sees and what one says, between what one does and what one can do" (Rancière 2000a, 9). Educational philosophy should become an experiment in such aesthetic reorganizations, and in turn come to embody democracy as the quintessential weird fiction that is beautiful just as much as it is sublime.

But what is a possible model for this aesthetic gesture? Here I would like to briefly return to Mieville's novel. The crime around which the plot of the *The City and the City* takes place is a large conspiracy orchestrated by Doctor Bowden, an anthropologist working closely with transnational corporate interests to undo the partitioning of the two cities in order to establish a certain mythical unity between the two halves. In the climax of the novel, Borlu confronts Bowden as he tries to walk out of the country unseen in broad daylight. He remains unseen yet not in breach either. The anthropologist, an acute observer of national customs, walked and acted between cities without transgressing any borders. Borlu describes his gait as "strange, impossible. Not properly describable, but to anyone used to the physical vernaculars of Beszel and Ul Qoma, it was rootless and untethered, purposeful and without a country" (Mieville 2009, 296). Because no one could recognize his gestures—neither familiar nor unfamiliar, and thus properly uncanny—no one knew if they could see him. Bowden's walk, which is unidentifiable and thus paradoxically invisible in its visibility, is simultaneously in Ul Qoma and Beszel while being radically outside of them. In violating all laws of custom and behavior (all specific mannerisms that create unique forms of the gesture), Bowden's gesture is a true profanation, a gesture that is neither this nor that, here nor there, visible nor invisible. Yet at the same time, he had not "officially" crossed over from one country to the other and thus had not committed the crime of breach. This gesture is perhaps best thought of as an indescribable *stumble*—not a fall off the map into complete and utter incomprehensibility but rather a slight adjustment within the map that nevertheless renders the gesture strange to itself, and in the process, suspends the very parameters of the map itself. In other words, he was in breach of Breach! This is the real state of exception—the true no-man's-land, an atopic stage opened for a strange new performance. This is where identity is held in suspension between the unseen and the seen, opening a new *mise en scene* that is strange precisely because it suspends the taken-for-granted logic of sense that separates Qoma from Beszel. Bowden is most dangerous in this atopic zone because his body is a body that has lost its proper gesture, and thus is a whatever gesture unrecognizable even to the avatars of Breach. It is this final twist that makes us realize that there is a zone of indistinction beyond even Breach, beyond the strict allocation of parts to this or that specific national location. Thus in the last analysis, it is not breach that is the atopic scene of politics, but rather this nameless place that even the Breach cannot properly demark or fix. Certainly Bowden is the criminal of the book, producing a series of unforgivable crimes including murder and smuggling, yet it is this final, ambiguous move within yet decisively beyond the logic of acclimation pedagogy that defines the city and the city that is his most dastardly deed. For it is here—in the place that is not a "here"—that his strange movements become profane gestures loosed from any identity to be this or that citizen, and thus create a community without preconditions of recognition or belonging—a community of aesthetic play. It is as if Bowden's final resignation indicates that he could not face the magnitude of his own gesture of refusal, as if the potentiality of his strange movements escaped him and exhausted him. When Borlu offers Bowden the opportunity to see what really lies between the cities (Breach), Bowden gives in. Borlu narrates the scene: "Nasty broken man.... He sagged, with some moan: apology, plea, relief" (Mieville 2009, 303). What exhausted him so was not the guilt of his various petty crimes and masterful scheming, but rather the rootless and untethered gesture of his walk—a gesture that produces a new notion of *philia* without recourse to predefined roles, places, or even languages.

What I am suggesting is that while Bowden is not a redeemable character, his gesture is a model for the gesture that defines the work of educational philosophy which remains attentive to the moments in education when acclimation pedagogy is breached by the aesthetic principle of democracy. If a pedagogy emerges from the disorienting and disruptive effects of aesthetic play, it is a criminal act against the partitioning of the sensible naturalized through acclimation pedagogy, and educational philosophy in turn becomes the weird fiction produced from and in dialogue with this perceptual redistribution. As such, nothing could be more criminal than the heretical aesthetics of educational philosophy as it opens a space for curiosity within an atopia of profane gestures and asks "Did you see that?"

Chapter One:

From Stultification to Emancipation: Althusser *avec* Rancière

Fundamentally, Althusserianism is a theory of education, and every theory of education is committed to preserving the power it seeks to bring to light.
                                                                                 —*Rancière,* Althusser's Lesson

Warren Montag (2003) begins his book on the infamous French Marxist Louis Althusser with an overview of the uses (and abuses) of Althusser's work in the social sciences and in literary studies. In the former, there is an avoidance of Althusser's actual writings for cursory summaries that reduce his positions to mere caricatures. In terms of the latter, there is a certain anxiety concerning Althusser's pre-Deleuzian rejection of totalization beyond temporary historical conjunctions. Montag's overview is insightful, and we can easily extend his critique of Althusserian scholarship into the discipline of educational theory as well. In this field, Althusser is also reduced to a representative of structuralist criticism which lacks a clear theory of agency (Giroux 2001) or to a totalitarian theorist of state control (Hill 2005). Thus education, like the broader field of social sciences, has not read Althusser "to the letter." In this chapter, I will turn to one of Althusser's most ardent critics, his former student Rancière, in order to evaluate his philosophical and pedagogical polemic against Althusser. This reading will allow me to reposition the relationship between Rancière and Althusser in a way that sheds light on the radical break between the student and his former teacher as well as certain continuities that tie them together. If Rancière's denunciation of Althusser is part political and part pedagogical, it is precisely Althusser's later focus on the aleatory event as well as theatre that enables us to read them together not as combatants but rather as strange travelers on the unfamiliar road of democratic events. Rather than a simple break with Althusser, a more nuanced understanding of the complex relationship between former student and former teacher reveals how (a) stultification is not monolithic but rather highly complex and differentiated, containing important fissures where a democratic excess emerges awaiting to be verified, and (b) even the most stultifying of discourses reveals a certain opening to democratic possibilities. In conclusion, a reevaluation of this particular relation between student and teacher will enable us not simply to further Rancière's own project but also to provide a new role for Althusser in educational philosophy.

Althusser's Pedagogies

In an interview on politics and aesthetics with Peter Hallward, Rancière reflects on his relationship with his former teacher. Here Rancière makes two interesting observations concerning Althusser as a teacher: a) "Althusser was seductive" (2003b, 194) while at the same time "Althusser taught very little" (194). The obvious question becomes: if Althusser taught very little, what exactly made him so seductive? Obliquely, Rancière seems to argue that it was not Althusser's philosophical expertise that seduced but rather his pedagogical tact—his ability to create a certain passionate attachment to *expertise itself*. Rancière remembers: "Our roles as pioneers put us in a position of authority, it gave us the authority of those who know, and it instituted a sort of authority of theory, of those who have knowledge in the midst of a political eclecticism" (2003b, 195). In sum, during his tutoring sessions and graduate seminars, Althusser overtly taught very little content, but he was nevertheless highly seductive, teaching a certain distribution of the senses and of the passions surrounding the myth of philosophical expertise. Students, at least according to Rancière, were taught to organize the sensible around the fulcrum of the authority of theory, thus producing a new partitioning between *logos* and *pathos* that conferred a certain aura of knowledge to the work of the academic scholar. Unlike Rancière's theory of universal teaching which creates a passion for equality, Althusser's pedagogical practice creates a passion for hierarchical divisions of thinking and speaking. Stated differently, this is a contest of two passions: a hierarchical passion that institutes inequalities versus a democratic passion that interrupts the institution of inequalities.

What is interesting to note is that Althusser's pedagogical practice does not completely coincide with Rancière's depiction of the master explicator. For Rancière, the master explicator's main function is to "transmit his knowledge to his students so as to bring them, by degrees, to his own level of expertise" (1991, 3). The act of the master explicator thus revolves around the question of distances which he "deploys" and "reabsorbs" "in the fullness of his speech" (Rancière 1991, 5). Once this distance is introduced between teacher and student, an intolerable paradox is introduced whereby all explication transforms into stultification. The result: "... the child who is *explained to* will devote his intelligence to the work of grieving: to understanding, that is to say, to understanding that he doesn't understand unless he is explained to. He is no longer submitting to the rod, but rather to a hierarchical world of intelligence" (Rancière 1991, 8). The explicator speaks, and it is his/her emphasis on the control of speech that creates the hierarchy of intelligences upon which expertise rests. Thus the explicator functions to institute a difference of intelligences through the incantation of esoteric knowledge that only he/she has access to and which testifies to a gap or distance between expert and student that can never be fully overcome. The result is an intellectual dependency on the master explicator for the answer. This dependency produces a *grieving* period on the part of the student who will perpetually see him or herself as inferior, as a mere lack or gap. As Rancière summarizes, in Althusser's criticism of "the old materialists" (such as Bentham or Owen), he actually embodies their pedagogical logic: "its was the point of view of a superior class that takes in charge the surveillance and the education of individuals by reserving for itself the ability to dictate every determining circumstance: the use of time, the distribution of space, the educational planning" (2011b, 5). In other words, Althusser's goal is more educational than political: "the restoration of the 'old materialism,' the materialism of educators, of those who think for the masses and who develop theses for 'scientific understanding'" (2011b, 11).

Yet in Rancière's depiction of Althusser's pedagogy, he says very little (i.e. there is silence instead of speech), and the students are left to construct the answers for themselves. In this sense, the classroom Rancière sketches might at first blush resemble a form of "universal teaching" wherein "each ignorant person could become for another ignorant person the master who would reveal to him his intellectual power" (1991, 17). Etienne Balibar also remembers the care which Althusser took with his students in preparing them for the *aggrégation* and the "intellectual freedom" (2009a, n.p.) of his famous seminars. Because of this intellectual freedom, his students were given the opportunity to utilize their own wills in order to realize their individual powers. If this process involved grieving on the part of the student, Rancière and Balibar give no evidence. In fact, it would seem the opposite. The students were actively encouraged to use the wills to produce something new and thus to empower themselves. While such a situation might initially appear to resemble a horizontal equality of intelligences, this is not the case. Indeed, Althusser's students were given certain freedoms, but this denies the education of the passions, the aesthetic dimension of Althusser's pedagogy, which fosters an attachment to expertise rather than equality through a subtle form of seduction— seduction for the allure of theory as a tool for maintaining a hierarchy of intelligences. Rancière recalls, "Treated like heirs to the throne by our professors, we had no objections to the 'pedagogic relation'; the winners of a fiercely selective competition, trained to compete from very early on, we could not but look upon the critique of individualism and the calls for collective work groups as the reveries of illiterate minds" (2011b, 41). While there is an equality of intelligences assumed here, this is not an equality of all for all, but rather only for those who have a certain relation to theory. Thus Althusser remains an expert without being an explicator (he said very little), and in turn, his pedagogy is a form of universal teaching that nevertheless operates under the sign of inequality *through* the equality of intelligences. The result is not grievance through dependency but rather passion through seduction. If Rancière's book *The Ignorant Schoolmaster: Five Lessons in Intellectual Emancipation* argues for the overturning of intellectual inequality in the master's practice through acts of universal teaching, then his own analysis misses another problematic, one which is extremely subtle but which nevertheless reinforces inequality all the same: the seduction of the student by the allure of expertise itself. Thus there is perhaps room for a sixth lesson here: a lesson that shifts the problematic from intelligence to will, and from will to aesthetic passions. In short, equal intelligence is not enough to secure universal teaching—it must be accompanied by a redistribution of the passions.

But this is only one side of Rancière's critique of Althusser. The other side deals more directly with his written pedagogy. It is Althusser's words (what he *said* rather than what he *did not* say) that concerns Rancière. And it is here that Rancière's caricature of Althusser begins to approx- imate his depiction of the master explicator. Rather than seduction and passion for expertise, Althusser's words operate to constitute intellectual hierarchization by "correct questions" which are written and controled by the expert. In the chapter titled "Althusser, Don Quixote, and the Stage of the Text" in his book *The Flesh of Words: The Politics of Writing* (2004a), Rancière performs an ingenious deconstruction of Althusser's symptomal reading method. In particular, he highlights a passage in the text in which Althusser argues that symptomal reading exposed the suppressed "dotted lines" of a text (the absent signifiers that structured the text in their very absence). It is worthwhile summarizing Rancière's analysis of the metaphor of the dotted line in full:

> Dotted lines or ellipses, we know in fact to what genre of books they belong: elementary textbooks. In these books, the dotted lines are there for the missing words, words that the student must restore in a sentence left incomplete. These dotted lines that summon the right answer themselves assume the place of another procedure of knowledge: that of the answer to the teacher's question. They are there to verify that the student knows his lesson and knows how to apply what he has been taught. This is a pedagogical procedure that is more elegant than asking questions. The teacher puts the finishing touches to his work by disappearing into dotted lines. If he can disappear into them, of course, it is because he knows all the questions and all the answers. Thus he can absent the word, the word to be found that says that the pedagogue knows and that the student will know. Dotted lines are, strictly speaking, the presence of the teacher in his absence ... (2004a, 134)

If the project of symptomal reading is to reveal gaps or epistemological breaks in the text, the metaphor of the dotted line drawn from elementary school reveals instead a continuity that is secured by asking the right questions at the right time in order to reveal the correct answer. Scholarship as the production of new concepts becomes conflated with a simplistic model of pedagogy wherein the teacher tests the student through fill-in-the-blank exercises that have certain predetermined answers. This method of scholarship as pedagogy "rules out answers to questions never asked" (Rancière 2004a, 135), reducing the task of reading to simple verification of existing questions that are latent within the text. Such verification remains dependent on the teacher who orchestrates the production of knowledge through a control over the appearance of "proper questions." What is created is a specific community of scientists, a community encircled by a specific field of knowledge defined by the dotted lines of the pedagogue. This is a community of inclusion and exclusion, a community grounded in the principle of consensus where every dotted line has a proper place and a corresponding proper answer to be verified by the expert who knows in advance.

This depiction of Althusser's project as an elementary-school pedagogy masquerading as scholarship is echoed throughout many of Rancière's texts, including *The Ignorant Schoolmaster*. It is not a great leap from the depiction above to Rancière's notion of the master explicator who stultifies students by creating a perpetual distance between ignorance and intelligence. What exactly does the master explicator stultify? The production of new questions, questions unanticipated by the teacher who controls the reading of the text by inserting dotted lines where they did not previously exist for the sole purpose of testing the intelligence of the student. As Rancière summarizes, "An opinion, the explicators respond, is a feeling we form about facts we have superficially observed. Opinions grow especially in weak and common minds, and they are the opposite of science, which knows the true reasons for phenomena. If you like, we will teach you science" (1991, 45). Instantly in the erection of science, the explicator creates a hierarchy of knowledge about the world as well as a structure of dependency between student and teacher. Science submits language to the rule of law by providing an answer key to our questions. The offering "If you like, we will teach you science" is thus deceptive. In the pedagogical invitation to liberate the self from the veil of opinion, the master explicator produces a new dependency, a new distance that can never be fully overcome. In fact, the gesture of "goodwill" is actually a paranoid attempt to verify the superiority of the expert over those ruled by mere opinion. The first lesson learned concerns the inferiority of some and the superiority of others, and thusly, the need to overcome inferiority through reliance on the expert.

The same aporia of goodwill is found in Althusser's famous seminar titled "Philosophy and the Spontaneous Philosophy of the Scientists" from 1967. As Pierre Macherey argues, the general intent of the course was to open philosophy up to a wider audience beyond the exclusivity of professional philosophers, or to use Macherey's phrase, to effect a "displacement [of philosophy] onto new terrains where it would become accessible, and in the first place audible, to non-specialists" (2009, 14). For Macherey, the discontent with academic elitism led Althusser and his cohort of students to undertake a "pedagogical form of a discourse of initiation" (2009, 15) that would liberate philosophy from its own field by reaching out across disciplines to a wider audience of non-philosophers and scientists. The result would be a new notion of philosophy as a tool for demarking "'true' sciences from would be sciences and to distinguish their *de facto* ideological foundations from the *de jure* theoretical foundations" (Althusser 1990, 92). Although this is a pedagogical form of a discourse of initiation which opens philosophy up to a non-philosophical audience, we must remember Rancière's worry: it is in the very gesture of *initiation* into science that the distance between student and teacher is produced, and that inequality manifests in the very gesture of equality that initiation signifies. As William S. Lewis aptly points out (2005), while Althusser's seminars as well as his complex and highly sophisticated writings open themselves up to charges of Leninist vanguardism, Althusser engaged in public lectures and wrote texts put together explicitly for popular audiences. It is in his intentionally *public* pedagogy that Althusser's stultification takes on another valence. Here, the problematic of initiation is that it appears as a form of non-hierarchical teaching that teaches nothing but inequality through the dependency it fosters in the master. In *The Ignorant Schoolmaster*, Rancière calls this the Republican paradox of "public pedagogy" (1991, 131). Republicans believe in equality but not in the equality of intelligences. Through time and patience, public pedagogy will "little by little, progressively, attenuate the deficiency caused by centuries of oppression and obscurity" (Rancière 1991, 131). The problem is precisely a perpetual "infantilization" or dependency of the public on professional explication in the very gesture which is meant to affirm equality.

So what is Althusser's fear? Rancière speculates "Althusser's enterprise, however, is marked through by the dread of the Marxist intellectual, the dread of the intellectual fallen prey to politics: not to make 'literature'; not to address letters without addressee; not to be Don Quixote, the fine soul who fights against windmills; not to be alone, not to be the voice of one crying out in the wilderness, an activity by which one loses one's head, literally as well as figuratively" (2004a, 137). To avoid the madness of Don Quixote and thus the madness of literature, Althusser "must protect the communal cloth, the thick cloth of knowledge made of questions and answers that insures that in the final analysis, the questions asked by the 'Marxist' are the right questions to which the 'Communists' put up with being the orphan answers, one must protect the cloth against any tear, any dropped stitch" (Rancière 2004a, 137–8). A pedagogy of initiation protects the expert's community by ensuring a certain consensus that gathers around fixed questions and answers determined in advance by the one-who-knows. The point is not to ask new questions but rather to extend the familiar hand of particular questions to the unanointed or uninitiated. To insure the connection between flesh and word, pedagogue and student, intellectual and audience, Althusser's texts become overtaken with what Rancière calls "Brechtian pedagogism" (Rancière 1991, 141) in the form of personified concepts and concepts that speak. In other words, his texts become dramatic stagings modeled on Brechtian theatre. These pedagogical-theatrical characters (SPS, PPI and PP2, etc.) function to fill the stage of theory with prescribed conflicts masquerading as "spontaneous" manifestations of a "real life" drama between classes. The goal of this pedagogical-theatrical performance is, as Rancière observes, "to prevent any exit from the stage before the denouement, and also to keep people from coming onstage at the wrong time, people we're supposed to meet only at the denouement. Cordoning off the (wrong) exits is the condition for theater to use the logic that can open the right one. That is the second consequence: symptomal reading becomes a movement that closes the ways out to liberate at last the only way out, the encounter with reality" (1991, 143). In a paradoxical twist, it is in the very movement of denouncing the myth of ideology through symptomal reading that this very process reintroduces the myth of the "great book of history" (1991, 144). In other words, the very struggle against madness through the dramaturgy of the text results in a kind of madness wherein the symptoms that symptomal reading attempted to dispel return with full force. The result: the master becomes mad, the student full of grievances, and the world effectively stultified.

Although Rancière's reading is decisive, there is an interesting detail with which he does not directly deal—a detail that creates an interesting asymmetry between Althusser's oral pedagogy and his written pedagogy. For Rancière, Althusser's pedagogical project of initiation concerns the paradoxical move wherein equality of intelligence must be presupposed in order for infinite dependency on the expert and his/her discourse to be assured. Thus the problem lies with the question of the equality or inequality of intelligences between the explicator and the pupil. Yet this misses how Althusser himself frames his pedagogy. Interestingly, rather than a question of intelligence, symptomal reading is first and foremost a pedagogy of affective rupture and redistribution. In this sense, it is concerned with the aesthetics of perception rather than questions of intelligence. Indeed, the central question of *Reading Capital* revolves around the issue "what is it to read?" (Althusser and Balibar 1979, 15). Here reading cannot be reduced to the mere cognitive acquisition of the various complexities of *Capital.* Reading is not simply a question of intelligence. More properly, "to read" means to read via Marx's own strategy of reading. Key to Althusser is understanding the relation between Marxist literacy and the pedagogical question of how to teach others to read. As Althusser writes, "our age threatens one day to appear in the history of human culture as marked by the most dramatic and difficult trial of all, the discovery of and training in the meaning of the 'simplest' acts of existence: seeing, listening, speaking, reading—the acts which relate men to their works, and to those works thrown in their own faces, their 'absence of the works'" (Althusser and Balibar 1979, 17). In other words, symptomal reading opens up the possibility of a fissure between sense (the common sense of the subject) and sense (as the sensation of difference beyond the sensory perception of the subject). Symptomal reading is first and foremost an affective shift or disorganization of the field of sense and thus functions on a pre-subjective, pre-individual level.

I can now summarize my general line of inquiry. First, I have emphasized several texts by Rancière which provide different analyses of different pedagogies. The first, Althusser's oral pedagogy, the pedagogy of the classroom, redistributes the roles between teacher and student in terms of intellect ("he had little to teach" so students constructed knowledge themselves) yet maintains a passionate attachment to expertise. The pre-subjective realm of affect does not rupture the order of the stultifying world but is rather fully implicated in its logic of inequality. Here we see a small, tentative, and incomplete appearance of Rancière's guiding hypothesis: democracy assumes the equality of intelligences. The stultifier, as Rancière argues, gives explanations, and "every explanation is a fiction of inequality" (2007c, 83). When Althusser teaches very little, he remains silent, withholding the explanation, thus withdrawing from the position of the master explicator. Yet as quickly as this hypothesis appears in Althusser's practice, it is withdrawn by the overwhelming passionate attachment to expertise that his seduction produces. In other words, a critique of explanation is not enough to counteract the emergence of pre-subjective passions that fix the subject to subjugation in the pedagogical relationship. The second pedagogy, the pedagogy of the text or of the written word, redistributes the senses (between seeing, thinking, and reading) yet maintains a hierarchy of intelligence between those who do and do not have access to the correct questions. As with the first pedagogy, Rancière's emphasis on aesthetic redistribution appears on the stage only to be taken back by the overly paranoid drive to instill a principle of unequal intelligences between teachers and students. Thus there are two pedagogies, each containing the kernel of democracy and yet each betrays its arrival—a lag time between pedagogy and democracy is introduced in both cases. Adding to the list, we find "initiation pedagogy" or a public pedagogical practice that maintains inequality under the guise of a universal teaching open to all and accessible to all. Here the passions are not appealed to so much as an intellectual mission to liberate philosophy and in turn enlighten the masses.

Graphically, this analysis can be summarized as follows. With a knowing wink, I here use A1, A2, A3 to refer to Althusser's speaking pedagogy (A1, A3) and his written pedagogy (A2). A1 produces the intellectual experience of equality yet only through a passionate attachment to theory.

A3 seems to reject expertise, but only at the cost of an initiation pedagogy that produces the effect of inequality between those who speak in the name of theory and those who are given over to their "spontaneous" and thus ideological mere beliefs. And A2 is the classic example of stultification where the most deleterious effects of A1 and A3 are fused together to produce a hierarchy of intelligences that perpetuate individual grieving and social stratification. With reference to the graph, it becomes clear that stultification is far from a monolithic practice (as Rancière often describes it), and instead is a complex set of processes that produce a variety of possible effects. Rancière makes a guest appearance as (R):

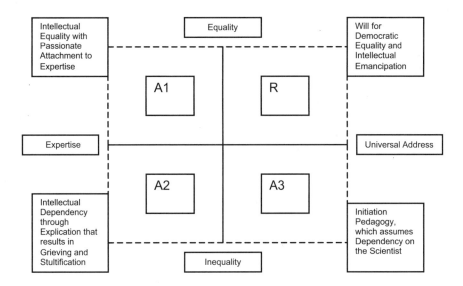

My point here is that in Rancière's denunciation of Althusser, he misses *how his own method turns against itself*, producing the very effects which he blames Althusser for: never letting the stage go silent, never letting on actors who do not belong there. To stay true to Rancière's method, we must allow for slippages that call for translation and reinscription of those moments within stultification which produce democratic slips. As Rancière observes, it would be too simple to dismiss discourses such as the Declaration of the Rights of Man or the Bill of Rights as merely ideological texts that conceal an underlying inequality and exploitation in the world. Emancipation begins not with ideological demystification of the hidden world beneath the veil of ideology but when the workers verify an inscription of equality within these discourses. Thus the Declaration of the Rights of Man is not "merely a façade designed to mask the reality of inequality" (Rancière 2007c, 46) but is rather "the grounds for a claim" or the "space open to dispute" (47) between those who count and those who do not count within a community. If equality is truly presupposed by every form of inequality, then we have to read for the inscription of democracy within even the most stultifying of discourses and practices—and then verify this existence through a dispute. In other words, we have to act as artists and poetically translate words. Likewise we cannot simply dismiss Althusser's theoretical-theatrical-pedagogical machine as mere explication and stultification. Rather we have to find within it the fleeting trace of equality in order to de-classify Althusser as this or that enemy of all. In this way Althusser can become a sign of something different—a discursive site to make a claim to democracy. How can we let Althusser back on stage in order to assume a role that was perhaps not written for him, that challenges the dogma that surrounds him as Leninist vanguard, as explicator, as stultifier? How can we read Althusser to the letter without once again assuming the existence of the dotted line? In this sense, I hope to demonstrate that Rancière's project is not the death of Althusser but rather brings together these missed opportunities in order to create his own theory of democracy. His is not a break from but rather a *seizing hold of* the appearance of democracy even within the most undemocratic of discourses—a gathering together of (a) the redistribution of the senses and (b) the critique of inequality in order to formulate a new theory of political disagreement with (c) a public or universal teaching. It is only in this combination of elements that a new, democratic education emerges as a possibility.

Theatrical Encounters: Verifying the Democratic Moment in Althusser's Work

The appearance of democracy in Althusser's work is perhaps best captured in his late theory of the encounter—a belated arrival perhaps, but an arrival nonetheless. The essay begins with a simple observation: "It is raining" (Althusser 2006, 167). A materialist observation to be sure, but importantly, an observation that suggests a very different opening to discourse than the dotted line suggested by Rancière above. Rain falling unpredictably from the heavens suggests dots on a page, but these dots are in constant motion, moving at different speeds, subject to different forces, and whose trajectories are largely unexpected. There is not a linear trajectory of dots uniformly wedded to the page by a particular subject supposed to know, who remains in control of the dots, their order and their sequence. These are dots that defy such principles. Rain as it falls becomes the principal example of what Althusser calls "a *materialism of the encounter*, and therefore of the aleatory and of contingency" (2006, 167). The difference between dots of rain and dots of the elementary-school test become clear through Althusser's reading of Epicurus. According to Epicurus's metaphysics, at the origin of the world, there existed only atoms falling parallel to one another inside of a void. Then, unexpectedly a clinamen intervenes producing an "infinitesimal *swerve*" (Althussei 2006, 169) that ruptures the orderly parallel distribution of atoms. A series of encounters akin to a chain reaction occur because of this swerve effect leading to the birth of the world. What is important to note in this reading is that (a) the swerve is not created by Reason or by the agency of a subject and (b) it cannot be predicted in advance. Unlike the parallel dots on the elementary exam, the materialism of the encounter does not convey the hidden presence of the teacher in the void of the ellipsis. The void is simply that: a void without agency or without cause. There is no intentionality behind the void, nor any line of inquiry that can trace back to its ultimate Cause (i.e., the stultifying powers of the master). And the appearance of the swerve cannot be predicted. In fact, no explanation can be given for its arrival, and no formula can be devised for its increasingly complex set of overdetermined effects.

What is the role of philosophy in this materialism of the encounter? Simply put, it is to verify the existence of contingency, of aleatory encounters as such. Here Althusser points to Machiavelli as an exemplar. Machiavelli's thought concerns the conditions for inducing a certain swerve effect to unify Italy. Yet his conclusions are shocking: "... unification will be achieved if there emerges some nameless man who has enough luck and *virtù* to establish himself somewhere, in some *nameless* corner of Italy, and, starting out from this atomic point, gradually aggregate the Italians around him in the grand project of founding a national state" (Althusser 2006, 172). As Althusser summarizes, "This is a completely aleatory line of reasoning, which leaves politically *blank* both the name of the Federator and that of the region which will serve as starting point for the constitution of this federation" (2006, 172). In other words, a void is posited, but this void is not fixed to this or that location in the order of things, and will only appear in a nameless and contingent place. The answer given by Machiavelli is not an answer that presupposes the expertise of the explicator, but rather the scientist who pays attention to the sudden appearance of an unknown man in an unassignable place, and thus awaits an encounter that may or may not happen given the contingency of elements necessary to produce the swerve effect, the results of which—"gigantic pile-up and collision-interlocking" atoms (Althusser 2006, 191)—constitute the world. In a sweeping gesture that stakes out a new materialist horizon for understanding contemporary thought, Althusser summarizes "We shall say, then, that the materialism of the encounter is contained in the thesis of the primacy of positivity over negativity (Deleuze), the thesis of the primacy of the swerve over the rectilinearity of the straight trajectory (the Origin is a swerve from it, not the reason for it), the thesis of the primacy of 'dissemination' over the postulate that every signifier has a meaning (Derrida), and in the welling up of order from the very heart of disorder to produce a world" (2006, 189–90). The philosopher is the one who is *sensitive* to the situation in which contingent elements—atoms independent of one another—collide with one another through the induction of a non-teleological swerve effect to produce a certain world (a world that has no necessity and thus could have been different). This peculiar notion of philosophy undoes the knot of expertise which binds dots to determinate places and voids to prede-termined meanings, and questions to predetermined answers. In other words, the aleatory encounter is precisely the encounter with democracy where no atoms are privileged over any others creating a field of equality where effects of disruption can be induced into the social field from any direction.

Like the dots of rain, the event of democracy cannot be contained by the dots of the elementary school test. Aleatory dots *puncture* and *interrupt* the field of the page, blurring letters, words, and sentences beyond the control of the master. They are dots that do not mind their place, that are always found where they are not wanted. Likewise, as Rancière will argue in his later political writings, democracy is a type of political clinamen that induces a swerve effect into the polis. In fact, Rancière states "Genuine participation is the invention of that unpredicatable subject which momen-tarily occupies the street, the invention of a moment born of nothing but democracy itself" (2007c, 61). Democracy in this description is a contingent, sporadic encounter between sense and sense that divides the community against itself. It is a particle collision of atoms that does not unify but rather acts to declassify subjects and suspend the illusion of social naturalness. The corresponding space opened is non-teleological and thus perpetually open-ended. This is a polemical community where individual atoms no longer fall in their "proper" places according to rectilinear ordering. Rather the swerve of democratic revolt induces a dis-organizing/ dis-ordering chain of encounters and thus a new partitioning of the sensible. The resulting political subject is not the individual who has finally found his/her voice or "become aware" of a true identity, but is rather an operator that "decomposes and recomposes the relationships between the ways of *doing*, of *being*, and of *saying* that define the perceptible organization of the community, the relationships between the places where one does one thing and those where one does something else, the capacities associated with this particular *doing* and those required for another" (Rancière 1999, 40). In other words, there is no expert subject who acts as cause and bearer of reason—democracy emerges out of nothing but itself, out of its effects. There are only processes of political production through various collisions of atomized ways of being, doing, and perceiving. Here Rancière and Althusser once again meet within the space of atopia that defines democracy—a nameless space with unknown actors, performing a script that is only written as it is performed on an improvisational stage.

It is at this point we must return back to the question of theatre. For Rancière, Althusser created a pedagogical-theoretical-philosophical machine for ordering perception according to the intentions of the master explicator. The master explicator determines the answers as well as the questions in advance thus controlling the stage of education and of politics in order to avoid the "madness" of democratic dissensus. The result of A1, A2, and A3 is stultification—in its various manifestations. On the one hand, this appropriation of theatre—and Brechtian theatre in particular—produces a type of inequality of intelligences and a hierarchical ordering of relations between those who know and those who do not know, those who watch/listen and those who recite/teach/act. In this sense it is the theatrical dimension of teaching that we would assume Rancière rejects in Althusser's project. Then again, Etienne Balibar argues that it is precisely the theatrical which Rancière inherited from Althusser. In his emphasis on the polemical staging of discourses, Rancière inherited from Althusser a "Brechtian insistence on the reciprocity of perspectives between theater and politics, which allows one to understand how political agents can distance themselves from their own representations in history or actively produce new ones" (2009b, 322).

Although Rancière offers a cutting polemic against Brecht (see Chapter Two)—a polemic in whose shadow we find Althusser—Balibar's comments are insightful in the sense that there is something in Althusser's reading of Brecht that creates a space for the emergence of democracy and in turn, a theatricalization of philosophy.

In the essay titled "The 'Piccolo Teatro': Bertolazzi and Brecht," Althusser argues that the characters in Bertolazzi's play, *El Nost Milan*, shift from a "false" dialectic of consciousness to a "true" dialectic of social relations, and in turn, this shift is to be continued by the audience after the play has finished. Althusser summarizes, "the play is really the production of a new spectator, an actor who starts where the performance ends, who only starts so as to complete it, but in life" (1969, 151). And this is precisely what Althusser does: his own essay is nothing more than the continuation of the play: "are not these few pages, in their maladroit and propping way, simply that unfamiliar play *El Nost Milan*, performed on a June evening, pursuing in me its incomplete meaning, searching in me, despite myself, now that all the actors and sets have been cleared away, for the *advent* of its silent discourse?" (1969, 151). The play produces a new consciousness in the spectator who, as in Althusser's case, formulates its silent discourse in the realm of theory and practice. In this essay, Rancière pinpoints what he calls Althusser's "theatrical impulse" which functions by "setting the stage" and by the "assignment of roles" (2004a, 141) in order to define a "community of science" that "leaves no void available" (138). Rancière finds this perspective troubling because "we [the audience] leave, new actors, actors of another kind, produced by the play" (2004a, 139). In other words, the play presupposes distinctions between false and true consciousness, passivity and activity, and its pedagogical function is one of transformation through an alienation-effect. The completed cycles end with the audience overcoming their passive acceptance of mythological consciousness and their active intervention in real life.

If Rancière wants to argue that Althusser's reading of *El Nost Milan* is the quintessential model of Althusser's "dramaturgy unique to the philosophical text" (2004a, 141), then I would say that his generalization is perhaps too reductive. Althusser's dramaturgy and its political effects extend beyond this one, perhaps too convenient, example. The fragment "On Brecht and Marx" (see Montag 2003) cannot complete the cycle that Rancière highlights between artist, stage, and audience—it cannot interpellate the audience through its pedagogy precisely because this pedagogy lacks a specific end. It is cut off prematurely and thus left dangling. The abrupt stop is not the fill-in-the-blank of the elementary-school test, which ensures the proper set of questions and answers according to the stultifying teacher. Rather the (implicit) dots at the end of "On Brecht and Marx" form an elusive ellipsis. This ellipsis suspends the pedagogical function attributed to Althusser's theoretical dramaturgy and thus opens a space that cannot guarantee the set relation between question and answer, or between play and the new consciousness of the spectator. The unfinished nature of the text is not some sort of perpetual deferral *à la* Derrida but is rather a model of aleatory interruption and intervention into the order of things by an (unknown), historical contingency. Here the stage of the text exposes itself to something that cannot be controlled, cannot be orchestrated: the forces of atoms colliding to produce unexpected results. If the audience is hailed to this or that subject position, the hailing chokes itself at the moment of its arrival, leaving behind the activity of the reader to determine his or her course of action. In short, the dramaturgy of *this* essay is not equivalent to the dramaturgy of "Le Piccolo, Berolazzi, and Brecht." The alternative staging of theory as an aleatory break or rupture that cannot be completed or sealed by the master's true knowledge of the social dialectic is the democratic moment that needs to be verified. If there is an inheritance here, as Balibar would argue, it is not simply the theme of theatre in Althusser's work, but rather the dramaturgy of a text that is open to the clash of atoms rather than sealed by the scientific community's stamp of approval. Here theory butts up against the materialism of history which leaves its ultimate trace: a radical interruption of philosophical speculation. In this moment, words do not become flesh or flesh words but rather the two enter a kind of dissensus, a disagreement, that can only be "solved" by the reader.

Bearing in mind the democratic possibilities of the aleatory event of theatre, we can perhaps end with a provocative new role for Althusser to play in education. According to Alain Badiou (2005), Althusser made a clear distinction between science (which has no subject, only the object of the economy), ideology (which has a subject and no object), and politics (which is a subjectivity without a subject). But how do we think the category of a subjectivity without a subject? What is the content of this subjectivity beyond the interpellated subject? It is here that education must be added to Badiou's list, for education is a practice (a) whose raw materials make up the subject's world, (b) whose practice is a redistribution of these things (a work on and through perceptual transformation), and (c) whose product is a subjectivity without a subject (dis-identification with all assigned roles). In this equation, education is an "encounter" between subjects and raw materials in such a way as to introduce a radical destabilization of the self and its perceptual field—a new mode of seeing, listening, speaking, and reading as Althusser would say. The result is a subjectivity stripped of any identity allotted to him or her within the community. The faculties of perception are here freed from the limits of a subject bound to the law and the immediacy of common sense—open to a new sensorial distribution of time and space, a new *philia*. Since the swerve of the aleatory encounter is never predictable and never reducible to the knowledge of the teacher, it is something that emerges *from the clash of atoms (students, teachers, curricula, various historical contingencies, etc.) in the classroom itself.* It is here that we open up to a new theory of education that moves beyond Althusser's overt pedagogies (A1, A2, or A3) through the implicit verification of equality that lies in the margins of his work—not as its repressed, latent content, but as its ever-present necessary pre-condition. It is an atopic zone—a zone that emerges when the names Althusser and Rancière are grosstopically situated within the problematic of education, theatrics, and politics. And it is from this vantage point that we can see how the precise questions of Rancière's *Five Lessons in Intellectual Emancipation* emerge:

1) If education is a process of subjectivity without a subject, what is the role of the will in this process? How is the subjectivation of the will the missing component in Althusser's formulation?
2) What is the role of the educator in this process? How can the educator verify the process of subjectivation of the will without recourse to explication or initiation?
3) What is the dramaturgy of pedagogy beyond relations of inequality or hierarchical relations of expertise?
4) And finally, how is it that the development of the lesson of contingent encounters moves us from critique to a new practice of democracy?

In the next chapter, I will argue that Rancière's theatricalization of politics and education does not signal the death of Althusser so much as the *verification* of the democratic kernel in his theoretical-theatrical-pedagogical machine. The event of Rancière's work is a *restaging of Althusser*—an Althusser that does not agree with our assumptions or with our stereotypes. Thus I want to use Rancière in order to provoke a swerve effect in our reading of Althusser's texts, and in turn open up the possibility of a new theory of materialist education that emerges from this despised or (perhaps worse) forgotten figure.

nineteenth-century France. In particular, Rancière charts the waves of regulation and revolt concerning the rise of the *goguette* (where the worker could aspire to be an artist), the theatre (where bourgeois pleasures could ignite dreams of worker revolt), and popular songs (where the illiterate worker could refashion him or herself as a lyricist and music-lover). Each form of popular culture represented an atopic space or destabilizing zone of imitation, mixture, and spontaneous/improvisational performance. As opposed to Marxist histories of working-class revolt, Rancière argues that "the problem lay less in the existence of hideouts of popular autonomy and indiscipline than in the cross-cutting between circuits of work and circuits of leisure, in the proliferation of those trajectories, real or ideal, by which workers moved in the space of the bourgeois and let their dreams wander there" (2011d, 178). The theatre proved to be politically unsettling precisely because it opened up a cultural space in which "passageways between classes proliferated" (Rancière 2011d, 179) producing new desires, new pleasures, and new sensations that cut across class divides and complicated simplistic narratives of countercultural resistance from below, the purity of working-class morality, or the objective science of class consciousness. The real drama of the theatre was therefore the peculiar mixing of sights and sounds that produced "genuinely dangerous classes" composed of "migrants who moved on the boundaries between classes—individuals and groups who developed within themselves the abilities that were useless for the improvement of their material life, but suited to make them despise this" (Rancière 2011d, 182). This spontaneous and improvisational nature of popular culture proved to be a revolt that could not be contained by the police order which continually attempted to crack down on the unnerving slippages in the correspondence between social roles, economic jobs, and aesthetic tastes. In short, the political event of the theatre was three-fold. First, workers were exposed to that which they were not supposed to hear or see, taking pleasure in that which they were prohibited from feeling. Second, they began to take an active interest in that which was not their business—in the dramas of a life that was explicitly denied them. Third, the theatre promoted a habit of being where you are not supposed to be, in "uncertain spaces" where the drama of class contact and conflation was never scripted in advance and could not be controlled by either the state or the working-class intellectuals who desired to maintain the telos of revolution. These disorderly spaces of the café-concert, the popular song, and the theatre existed before the commodification, professionalization, and state-sanctioned rise of the cultural industry. If the "pedagogic vocation" of the cinema and gramophone was the "model performance of the star artist" (Rancière 2011d, 226), then the pedagogic vocation of the popular arts was the opposite: the inappropriate performance of the amateur.

Rancière's analysis of the politics of theatre has, as Peter Hallward argues (2006), greatly shaped his political theory. For instance, Rancière argues that politics is a "theatre" which "connects the unconnected" through the performance of actors that resist inscription into prefabricated identities determined by the order of things (1999, 88). Political subjects in this sense are not fixed bodies with accompanying, predetermined interests but are "fluctuating performers who have their moments, places, occurrences, and the peculiar role of inventing *arguments* and *demonstrations*" (1999, 89). Rancière proposes a theory of role-playing, invention, and theatrical staging, shifting the political question from ontology to the centrality of appearances which is analogous to the production of a play through the "construction of a stage, the design of sets and costume, the creation of gripping characters, the invention of catchy phrases and slogans" (Citton 2009, 130). For Rancière, "Democracy is closely linked to tragedy" in that both rest upon "poetic dialogue" in the form of "improvisation by unprogrammed actors" (2007c, 102–3). In fact, Rancière argues that his work is not a reconstruction of a political theory so much as a "drama-turgy of politics" (2009e, 119) within particular contexts and in relation to particular polemical interventions. In *Disagreement* (1999), Rancière summarizes this thesis as follows: politics is always "performing or playing, in the theatrical sense of the word, the gap between a place where the *demos* exists and a place where it does not" (88). Through theatrical staging the expressiveness of all people and things undermines the authority of any one particular interpretation or decision concerning the nature of political life.

To reiterate, the theatricality of political events is, as Rancière writes, "the invention of that unpredictable subject which momentarily occupies the street" and is thus "versatile, sporadic" (2007c, 61). Here I want to emphasize the unpredictable, aleatory features of political events, which cannot be narrativized in terms of preordained actors, locations, or strategic methods/forms of organization. Thus Rancière's dramaturgy stands in stark contrast to Aristotle's "representative poetics," with its rules for artistic production, representation, and hierarchies of subject matter as well as the established social order with its similar hierarchical inequalities. In sum, I will now present the constitutive elements in Rancière's dramaturgy—the various gears and pistons that combine to form the theoretical-theatrical-pedagogical machine.

Space

As Michael Ostwald argues (2008), although Rancière only mentions architecture in passing (favoring poetry, literature, and theatre as privileged aesthetic objects), his own political analysis is more often than not couched in spatialized metaphors. Thus, for instance *On the Shores of Politics* is organized around a fundamentally architectural argument that pits the organization of the city in Plato's work against the disorganizing principle of the sea. Furthermore, Rancière (1998) speaks of the architecture of the book (which provides narrative organization) and its internally contradictory relationship with the sudden appearance of a literary, archaic impression (which disrupts this architectural framework). The truth of literature becomes the constitutive relationship between unity and separation, between form and impression. In other words, literature *stages* an agonism of continuity and rupture, of opposing and conflicting principles that are constantly threatening to pull apart. In this sense, architecture is part of the internally productive dialectic of literature.

Turning to Kojin Karatani's analysis of the Western "will to architecture" perhaps we can further tease out this architectural dimension of Rancière's dramaturgy. For Karatani (1995), the will to architecture is first and foremost exhibited in Plato's philosophic attempt to ground, stabilize, and organize society through recourse to the solid edifice of the Idea in *The Republic*. Karatani summarizes: "In the metaphor of architecture Plato discovered a figure that under the aegis of 'making' is able to withstand 'becoming'" (1995, 6). Since this faithful move, Western thought has become defined largely as a relentless drive to formalization in mathematics, sociology, and linguistic theory. The ultimate problem with this will to architecture is that it is self-referential and solipsistic. The solidity of the Idea is not simply a break with the productive tension between expressivity and mute speech but rather a fundamental denial of literarity as such, creating a self-enclosed world. Even critiques of formalism ultimately fall prey to the very same problem. Thus in mathematics Kurt Gödel demonstrated the self-referential drive of mathematical formalization. And in philosophy Jacques Derrida likewise demonstrated the inherent slippage and undecidability in all attempts to ground knowledge. Yet this critique of the will to architecture is ultimately the reassertion of this will, for deconstruction in all its guises is possible only as a result of the practice of formalism itself.

Here Karatani gestures toward Wittgenstein—and importantly his theory of teaching—for an alternative. In *Philosophical Investigations*, Wittgenstein introduced the presence of the irreducible other into the solipsistic

monologue of formalism and its deconstruction. Without attention to the
other, all attempts at dialogue become a monologue where "those who
reject the dialogue are considered irrational, no matter how profound
or how vigorously argued their truth" (Karatani 1995, 113). When we
confront the other, we cannot assume shared values, codes, or rules for
speaking and interacting. As such, the other cannot be seen as a mere
extension of the self as in solipsism. In Wittgenstein's model, communication with the other disrupts the internal circularity of formalism through
an asymmetrical exchange. The contingency of the other produces a crisis
in the architecture of thought precisely because it undermines its claims to
transparency and universality.

Bearing in mind Karatani's archeology of the will to architecture, we
must remember Rancière's critique of political consensus (1999). For
Rancière, consensus is an ordering principle within society—a will to
architecture which organizes the *polis* by providing a place and station for
all of its citizens so that no one is left uncounted within the count of the
community. Within this order, those who do not abide by certain performative rules are excluded as irrational, their voices reduced to mere noise.
Thus consensus has a certain quality of self-referentiality described by
Karatani. As opposed to the making and preserving of ordered perceptual
space, Rancière describes democratic politics as largely disordering, disfiguring, and disrupting—an aleatory encounter that collides and piles-up the
perfectly ordered atoms of the community. A political act never assumes
a common language game (shared rules). It is an act of becoming—of
annunciating an unanticipated and unexpected "we" irreducible to the
preexisting community or to fixed identities—and is thus materiality
oriented toward the process of continual subjectivation and dis-identification. In other words, dissensus demonstrates the self-referentiality of all
architectural systems, political or otherwise, and in the process introduces
the asymmetry between the count and no-count into the community. This
is a contingent encounter that forces a repartitioning of spaces, voices, and
activities.

Rather than privilege making over becoming, the artifactual staging
of political events reveals its own lack of foundation in any preordained
"natural order" precisely because it is a collectively built platform which
is only sustained through a contingent opening to the other—the learner,
the spectator, the immigrant, the refugee, and so on. In this sense, the
architecture of the stage is never a specific place (as in Arendt's political
philosophy (1998) where the social and the political must be separated),
but always an atopic space without any predefined use or clientele. Here

we might think of Fredric Jameson's notion of "dirty realism" (1994) as an example of the theatrics of staging. Originally a term used by Liane Lefaivre to describe the architectural styles of Gehry and Koolhaas, Jameson's expanded notion of dirty realism focuses on the imaginative architecture of cyberpunk, in particular the futuristic, urban landscape of *Blade Runner* (1982). The architecture envisioned in the film decomposes (*not* deconstructs) sanitized formalism with its dichotomies of inside and outside, self and other, private and public. Jameson writes, "Dirty here means the collective as such, the traces of mass, anonymous living and using" (1994, 158) that challenge all forms of architectural hierarchization or sanitization/immunization. The dirty in dirty realism speaks to unforeseen contaminations, collective uncleanliness, openness to otherness, and the general confusion of the polis wherein voices, sights, smells, and tastes mix to form unexpected sensations. Dirtiness is not outside the polis (a perfect utopia) but rather is an internal excess, a certain disruption of space from inside space that sets up new relations between actions and locations, activity and passivity, public and private, etc. Democratic politics necessitate the architecture of theatrical staging in order to proclaim its heretically dirty lesson against inequality.

Time

The time of the theatre is always the time of improvisation and interruption. If the time of Brechtian theatre is always a time oriented toward the future—when passivity will be overcome by activity, when equality will be realized against the rule of inequality—then Rancière's theatricality is always located in the time of the now, in the kairotic time of events that are always already happening, of new sensations that do not defer the axiom of equality but rather (inappropriately) verify its appearance. In other words, the time of the theoretical-theatrical-pedagogical machine is out-of-joint, a dynamic interruption of the flow of time with the abrupt punctuation of equality. "Emancipation," writes Rancière, "can be neither the accomplishment of a historical necessity, nor the heroic reversal of this necessity" and thus must be thought of in terms of a "multiplicity of forms of experimentation of the capacity of anybody, yesterday and today" (2010b, 179). The time of the now is particularly theatrical precisely because it is a *spectacular, public* NOW that emphatically enunciates the urgency of the present for verifying an equality that *cannot wait* for a future moment of arrival. Theatrical temporality is impatient, insistent, and ruptural.

The sequence of puncture holes left in the homogenous time of any given social order—so many aleatory dots—cannot be reassembled into a chronological unfolding or telos, cannot be arranged so as to provide empirical "confirmation" of any master narrative of communist revolution. What is at stake here is the distinction between a theory of temporal unfolding (the latent becoming manifest through time) versus a theory of temporal rupture/interruption (in the now of kairotic staging). This is a key distinction between Rancière and other theorists of the political moment such as Michael Hardt and Antonio Negri. As Hardt and Negri write, "The contemporary cooperative capacities through which the anthropological characteristics of the multitude are continually transcribed and reformulated, cannot help revealing a *telos*, a material affirmation of liberation" (2000, 395). In the book *Multitude: War and Democracy in the Age of Empire* (2005), Hardt and Negri pose the question, "Can new organizational forms of resistance and revolt finally satisfy the desire for democracy implicit in the entire modern genealogy of struggles?" (79). To answer this question, the authors write a novel of historical struggle that progresses from class struggle to guerrilla forces to a "network organization" of the multitude that produces the commonwealth on a global scale through immaterial, affective labor. Each form pushes the democratic possibilities of the previous forms to higher and higher levels of amplification and intensification, culminating in the unprecedented contemporary opportunity to finally achieve global communism. Certainly Hardt and Negri are careful to avoid any type of historical determinism in their argument. If, as Hardt writes, "... the conditions and weapons of a communist project are available today more than ever," then we are still left with the decisive task of "organizing it" (2010, 144). Revolution is not guaranteed by transformations in the economic base; there are only historical tendencies which must be intensified and extended by the labor of the multitude in the name of their democratic desires. But these tendencies are grounded in a historical narrative of revolutionary progression oriented toward a communist future that already exists in its nascent form within our very ontological desires. In fact, Negri (2011) argues that, given the particular historical moment, it is possible to at last write a "new grand narrative" that approaches a "concrete utopia" wherein biopolitics, the commonwealth, and the artistic sublime merge into one multitudinous project of becoming communist. As opposed to such grand narratives, Rancière writes that this vision of "the increasingly immaterial forms of capitalist production concentrated in the universe of communication are, from this moment on, to have formed a nomadic population of 'producers' of a new type; to have constituted a collective intelligence, a collective power of thought, affects and movements of bodies that is liable to explode apart the barriers of Empire" (2006b, 96) has to be renounced as a deferral of democratic equality to the climax of historical teleology. Rather than another historical plotline to reinvigorate the Left, what is needed is the meticulous plotting of aleatory points of time wherein the predictive promises of theoretical projections—on the right and left—are rendered inoperative, left speechless in the face of equality that is never *where* it is supposed to be or *when* it is supposed to be. This is the spontaneous and impromptu nature of theatrical timing that always responds to the particular context of its staging despite tendencies, despite the best predictions made by political theorists. If theatrical staging is a becoming, this becoming is always resistive to master explication, and as such, can never be fully organized into a five-act play of progressive liberation.

Performance as Theatrical Subjectivation

Rancière's theory of subjectivation clearly draws inspiration from his reflections on popular theatre and improvisational performance. As Joseph Tanke outlines (2011), the process of subjectivation is composed of two interrelated moments. First, there is the necessary rejection of allotted subject positions given within any order. Second, there is the productive staging of new names "belonging to no one in particular because they are not simply the reiteration of policed identities" (Tanke 2011, 67). Here we can articulate Rancière's theory of theatre with his insistence on democracy as a hypothetical axiom "as if ..." In recalling the story of a French worker during the 1848 Revolution, Rancière argues that the moment of freedom arrives when the artisan begins "ignoring the fact that the house [which he is working on] belongs to others, and acting *as if* what was being enjoyed [the view] by the gaze also belonged to him—this is an operation of an effective disjunction between the arms and the gaze, a disjunction between an *occupation* [laborer] and the *aptitudes* [aesthetic taste] which correspond to it" (2006d, 5). The aesthetics of politics are structured in terms of the theatrical "as if ..." of sensual disruption and disjunction, where the subject is a subject in excess of prescribed names, and thus an actor that wears the mask, performs the gestures, suffers from pains and pleasures which are the exclusive properties of others.

It is the will that acts "as if ..." and thus verifies equality on the stage of the present, in the moment of the now. In fact, I would argue that the will—a faculty or capacity so central to Rancière's work on emancipatory education (1991)—could be recast as a *theatrical will* which always plays the roles that have not been assigned to it. Behind the mask is not a fixed individual but rather a singular will to become otherwise than. It is this theatricality of the will that enables political actors to take up words that they were not meant to speak, or sights they were not supposed to see, or pleasures they were not supposed to feel. The theatrical will is a *creator of material fictions*—fictions of the senses that challenge the order of things. The theatrical will is a will that parodies the world through displacements that defamiliarize the relationships between roles, gestures, and locations. The prefix "para" does not imply an identity between subject and object (or actor and role), yet presents nothing other than the object to be parodied—an object or role that is now out-of-joint. In other words the theatrical will is always the performance of intimate distances between actor and role—an entanglement that both unites mask and subject and separates the two in the moment of performance. In this sense, there is no essence to the theatrical will beyond the masks that it displays (hence it is theatrical all the way down) while at the same time there is no necessary connection between any one mask and any one will (hence all performances are parodic). The resulting material fictions are not merely reiterations of existing identities out of context (a dis-identification); parodic appropriation is also a creative construction of a subject who is always becoming other than any one particular name, always *interrupting* and *disorganizing* a field of codified elements through the *risk* of the event of enunciation. Although Rancière has expressed some reservations about the politics of aesthetic forms of parody (2008a), Solange Guénoun (2011) has rightly pointed out how parody can become a form of aesthetic dissensus. Turning to Michel Journiac's performance titled *Mass for a body* (1969), Guénoun argues that parody is not simply a tautology (as Rancière suggests), but is rather "a 'presence' that undoes itself and a representation that denounces what sustains it" (2011, 14). Parody is, in other words, the slightest difference that makes all the difference: an opening for disagreement from within the very forms and rituals which are repeated.

Script

The script of the theatrical performance of political staging is improvisational and composed of multiple voices (see Hallward 2006). This script is therefore never written in advance of its performance. Rather than embodying the authorial voice of the playwright, the multiple voices of the theatrical script create a surplus of roles, plotlines, and gestures that cannot be fully mastered into a standard five-act drama. In this sense, theatrical scripts are properly *literary*, which Rancière defines in terms of a productive tension between the "mute-loquacious letter" and the "mute speech" of things (Rancière 1998; Ross 2011). Literarity for Rancière is a kind of mute speech in two senses. On the one hand, words are deprived of the living speech of the master and thus cannot account for themselves or explain themselves. These written words are, in this sense, "mute." On the other hand, mute letters are too talkative. They drift anywhere and everywhere without restrictions. The explicator is not present to guide or control the movement of these written words. Literariness is therefore the sudden availability of the letter which is open to free use by anyone. As such, there is something radically democratic about the "orphaned letter" (Rancière 1998) which both says too much and not enough. But there is another kind of muteness that also concerns Rancière: the mute speech of all things. Expressivity refers to the belief that all objects in the world are full of meanings and significance, thus undermining any hierarchy existing between "noble" and "base" or "high" and "low" subject matter. Suddenly everything speaks and needs deciphering—even the smallest, most "insignificant" details of everyday life become hieroglyphics. While such meaning exists in excess, the muteness of the Book of Life testifies to the recalcitrant nature of these objects in the world to reconcile flesh and word. While stones might manifest the poeticity of the world, such material also resists the signification which they embody. In other words, the expressivity of language shows and hides, and in this dialectic, reveals that no determinate meaning is possible, no conclusive interpretations can be drawn. Mute speech guarantees that no description of any object is perfect, that there is no certain connection between words, things, and actions, thus challenging any claim to expertise in the writing (or interpreting) of the world. If the teleological script offered by Hardt and Negri embodies the radical equality of expressivity (the most basic aspects of life itself are fundamentally biopolitical signifiers of a larger struggle between multitude and Empire), then they simultaneously miss the muteness of speech (reducing the expressivity of politics to a single teleological narrative that unites all movements under the sign of historical tendencies). Rancière, on the other hand, emphasizes that the script of the multitude is never totalizing, always splintering, precisely because of the tension between enunciation and silence. Thus rather than interpretations or theoretical prognostications, Rancière only offers *translations* of performances across multiple voices, gestures, and sensations.

The push and pull between expressivity and muteness defines the central statements that compose the script of political dramaturgy. For instance, inscriptions such as "We are all German Jews"—a key reference for Rancière (2007c)—or "We, the people" both offer themselves up for democratic dissensus. On the one hand, "the people" is the expressive site of a collective voice, and on the other hand the inability of "we" to signify any stable or determinate identity resists any definitive or absolute attempt to fix boundaries of "the people." These phrases are democratic precisely because of their literariness—"we" is an orphaned letter that circulates beyond the control of any explicator. To be more precise, it is the poetic work of deictic words that is at stake here. A word is deictic when it has a fixed semantic meaning but a contextually specific denotational meaning. Thus, pronouns such as "he" or "she" are deictic in that their denotational meaning is dependent upon the variables of time and space. In Rancière's work, we find deictic words in almost all of his texts. For instance, "We are all German Jews" opens to a politically dissensual script precisely because of the deictic nature of the pronoun "we" which is a place holder that can be occupied by anyone regardless of their personal identity. In other words the pronoun "we," is *a role* empty of specific content and thus creates a universal equivalence (not as the performance of a specific identity but as the invention of a name without predicates). In the case "We are all German Jews," the stage is set for a dispute over the very classification systems that created criteria for who was included and who was excluded, who would count and who would not count. This is not a linguistic theory based on the iterative qualities of language or shifting nature of signifiers (where meaning remains deferred) but rather on the irrefutable, material fiction of equality inscribed within a fixed order of appearances as a specific location for a theatre of dispute and creation. Thus the script of democracy is a script that is written only through the performance of a dispute over the *loquacious-muteness* of deictic words and their ability to always interrupt the order of things, suspend masterful interpretations, break down closed communities, or challenge the intentions of authors.

Deictic words always open themselves up to poetic translations. Emphasizing Rancière's notion of "interdiscursive" translation as a philosophical method, Claudia Ruitenberg argues, "Rancière describes translation as recasting, the exercise of seeing something *in terms of* something else, where the something else is not a linguistic system such as English or French but rather a discourse or language game" (2010, 110). For Rancière, this means that translation enables him to recast workers' writings as literary and philosophical products and to see these authors as more than mere workers but also as philosophers in their own right. Translation enables new metaphors to appear through the collisions of atoms that have suddenly fallen off course and tumbled into one another. If translation is a philosophical method, then theatrical performance is its social and political equivalent. Or, perhaps we can think of the two operations working in unison: translation creates the script for political performance to emerge and announce a wrong. Politics, as cited earlier, is a "theatre" which "connects the unconnected" (Rancière 1999, 88) through translations that loosen subjects and predicates and through performances of actors that resist inscription into prefabricated identities. The power of deictic words enables actors to connect the unconnected ("we" opens up the gap within the people for the no-count to appear and split the count in two) and thus perform democratic dissensus.

The Dramaturgy of Universal Teaching

In teaching courses in educational philosophy, I often ask students to describe how they see themselves as future teachers, and in turn, how they would describe the particular work of education. In such exercises, students turn to metaphor to find images that enable them to capture (a) who teachers are and (b) what teachers do. In particular, many students employ a host of artistic metaphors to describe their future profession. Thus, I am used to hearing statements such as "I think of the teacher as an artist" or "education is an art form—a creative, passionate craft." More specifically, a large number of my students argue that teaching is like "acting on stage" or that the teacher must "perform" for students. While Rancière is, as outlined above, suspicious of the pedagogical model of the arts—and theatre in particular—nevertheless this does not mean that the determinate aesthetic dimension of universal teaching is not theatrical performance. If such connections are explicit in my students' comments, they remain more elusive in Rancière's own analysis of universal teaching.

In his description of universal teaching, Rancière notes that it is composed of several interconnected elements: "learning, repeating, imitating, translating, taking apart, putting back together" (1991, 68). While the poetics of translation, taking apart, putting back together, speak to a wide variety of the aesthetic arts, it is the emphasis on imitation which most directly links universal teaching to theatrical performance. As I have been arguing, performance is a kind of parody of names, gestures, and sensations that are not one's own, that were meant for others unlike one's self. It is an imitation that does not simply repeat but actually creates a new subject position through the de-contextualizing effects of performance according to the axiom of equality. In universal teaching this means that anyone can teach anything even if they are ignorant of what they teach. Such a movement democratizes teaching, liberating it from the discourse and practice of the schoolmaster and undermining any claim to hierarchical expertise. Furthermore, education, like politics, is linked directly with the theatrics of improvisation. Rancière writes, "We know that improvisation is one of the canonical exercises of universal teaching" (1991, 64). There is no pre-fabricated script for universal teaching, nor are there certified actors/virtuosos who are destined to play leading roles. This is a script always in the making, composed by actors who are ignorant of what they teach, what specific skills they need to play certain roles, and so on. All parents can teach their children and thus do not have to wait for the expert or for institutional certification. As such, the time of universal teaching is always now rather than later. All that parents need is the stage, or mediating material object which exists between student and teacher and acts to cross-check the manifestation of the will—a "third thing" that is "alien to both [parent and child] and to which they can refer to verify in common what the pupil has seen, what she says about it and what she thinks of it" (Rancière 2009c, 14–15). For Jacotot, this was a French copy of *Télémaque* given to students in order to translate and imitate. Thus Rancière writes, "There is nothing beyond texts except the will to express, that is, to translate" (1991, 10). It is this will to express, to translate the skills, gestures, and roles that are prohibited that makes this expressive will also a theatrical will. This theatrical will does not hide anything beyond its own manifestations—no hidden wellspring of intellectual genius or essentialized ego animating the will. There is only the will, which is both distinct from its performances and indistinguishable from them at the same time. In short, the aesthetic event of universal teaching is also a theatrical event *par excellence*.

And thus, in the end, isn't Rancière's own *The Ignorant Schoolmaster* (1991) a type of educational/philosophical performance in its own right? This book is not simply an interpretation/explanation of the writings of Joseph Jacotot—a theoretical point of mastery over the words of the other. Nor is the text a simple re-telling of Jacotot's intellectual and pedagogical adventures as Yves Citton (2010) or Charles Bingham and Gert Biesta (2010) suggest. Rather, the book is a *theatrical staging*—a performance of Jacotot by the actor Jacques Rancière. Like all acts of universal teaching, Rancière's philosophical performance is both an act of imitating (Rancière and

Jacotot's two voices become so intimately interwoven that they ultimately become inseparable), translating (in light of recent historical intellectual and educational trends), taking apart (through the use of performative citations of Jacotot's work), and putting back together (a script of citations that collectively compose the five lessons in intellectual emancipation). The book as a stage and writing as a performance: this is the theoretical-theatrical-pedagogical work of the text. As the stage of a dispute, the book erupts on the contemporary scene through the anachronistic return to the obscure texts of Jacotot. The result is a text that performs its intervention, whose theory is a gesture as much as a sentence, and whose sentences provoke images of strange adventures/short voyages to the land of the people as much as philosophical conceptualization.

The spontaneous, improvisational, contingent, multiple aspects of theatre are precisely why the theatrical metaphor has been repressed in educational philosophy. It is well known that in *Emile, or On Education*, Rousseau argues that Emile should not be exposed to theatre until late in his life. In fact, Emile should be taught a useful trade, which promotes self-sufficiency rather than the arts (which can lead only to vanity, opinion, and false prejudices). Rousseau writes, "I do not want him [Emile] to be a musician, an actor, or a writer of books ... I prefer him to be a shoemaker to a poet, that he pave highways to making porcelain flowers" (1979 [1762], 197). A "decent trade" must be one that is useful and proper for one's sex and age, and its ultimate goal is not simply to earn a living but rather to cultivate a respect for simple things (as opposed to the arts which ignite our insatiable desires). Such trades teach that imitation is a form of corruption of human nature, and thus resist false performances for honesty, utility, and sincerity. Rousseau goes on to warn that the arts mix the masculine nature of men with the effeminate nature of women, producing an unnatural contamination. In fact, Rousseau goes so far as to argue, "If I were sovereign, I would permit sewing and the needles trades only to women and to cripples reduced to occupations like theirs" (1979 [1762], 199). The arts are for cripples and women only, and therefore unsuitable for masculine natures which desire hard, decent work outdoors and away from the corruptions of poetry and theatre. In the end, only after Emile has traveled the world over, learning to become a self-reliant, reasonable, and sensible citizen can he then be allowed to go to the theatre without the worry of incensing his passions and his vanity.

Rousseau's critique of the theatre is perhaps best captured in the famous *Lettre à M. d'Alembert sur les Spectacles* (1758) in which Rousseau argues against the establishment of the theatre in Geneva. In this letter, Rousseau takes a radical stance against the theatre on several counts: theatre produces immoral pleasures; it ignites the imagination beyond simple, natural living; and finally, acting itself inevitably leads to seduction and deception. The irony is that while the theatre is censored from Emile's general education until late in life, Emile's entire education up to that point is nothing more than pure theatrical performance. The Tutor repeatedly stages various experiences for Emile which Emile remains completely ignorant of. In fact, Emile does not recognize that his world is staged and that his encounters are following a predefined script written by his Tutor on nature's behalf. As Rousseau states, "Let him [Emile] always believe he is the master, and let it always be you who are. There is no subjection so perfect as that which keeps the appearance of freedom" (1979 [1762], 120). Such use of manipulation seems to fall dangerously close to the seduction and deception of theatre which Rousseau detests. Here Rousseau is caught in an uncomfortable paradox: in order to teach against deception and seduction, he must seduce and deceive. Rousseau writes, "Up to now you got nothing from him [Emile] except by force or ruse. Authority and the law of duty were unknown to him. He had to be constrained or deceived to make him obey you. But see how many new chains you have put around his heart. Reason, friendship, gratitude, countless affections speak to him in a tone he cannot fail to recognize" (1979 [1762], 316). Even if this pedagogical theatre is intended to teach proper moral lessons according to nature, Rousseau fails to listen to his own criticism of the theatrical model, which seems to inevitably introduce unnatural mixing, imaginative leaps, and unintended deceptions into the most sincere and consciously upright and decent of all performances. By separating Emile from knowledge of his role in this pedagogical staging, Rousseau has unfortunately separated theatre from politics, transforming it into a beautiful teleological unfolding according to nature's intended path wherein sense and sense correspond perfectly. If theatrical staging collapses into the expression of nature's intended trajectory, then there is no room left for dissensus—no room for Emile to disagree with the staging of his education, no room to disagree with the script he has been given (and likewise, no room for the citizens of Geneva to take the risk of exposing themselves to the unnatural mixing of pleasures found in theatre). If Emile is unaware of his performance as a performance, then education becomes nothing more than an instrumental and predetermined teleology which leads inevitably to the ends assigned by the Tutor/director acting on behalf of natural necessity. Rousseau therefore creates a paraeducational misappropriation of theatre that transforms it into a simple unfolding of "natural man" as citizen subject. To maintain this fable, the very man who professes authenticity as a virtue must rewrite himself as a character (Jean-Jacques the Tutor) whose authenticity is doubtful precisely because his virtuous wisdom places him at an insurmountable distance from humanity as such. In short, the disrupting and spontaneously dissenting qualities of theatrical staging and performing are lost in this educational translation.

Thus Rousseau, like Plato before him, finds theatre overtly dangerous to consensus/harmony. But what is missed when the relation between education and theatre is severed or denied is the *particular politics* of education. Here we must hold true to *The Ignorant Schoolmaster* which does not hide its theatricality but rather exposes itself as an imitation, a translation, a taking apart, and a putting together. It is this very staging and acting that in turn functions as the aesthetic event of universal teaching. The political dimension to the text is not the staging of a "we" but is rather the staging of a theatrical will (before any particular political subjectivation as this or that kind of citizen): a will to theatre as a will to perform the roles that have not been assigned by the order of things, to think the thoughts that have been reserved for "others," to speak the words that are not one's own. The theatrical will, as opposed to the architectural will, is a will that acts "as if ..." and thus denies the structure of being its solidity and its permanence. This is the political moment internal to universal teaching as a theoretical-theatrical-pedagogical machine.

Chapter Three:

The Beautiful and the Sublime in the Pedagogy of the Oppressed

... the sublime flashing forth at the right moment scatters everything before it like a thunderbolt.

—*Longinus* on the Sublime, I, 4

Paulo Freire once wrote, "For me education is simultaneously an act of knowing, a political act, and an artistic event. I no longer speak about a political dimension of education. I no longer speak about a knowing dimension of education. As well, I don't speak about education through art. On the contrary, I say education is politics, art, and knowing" (1985b, 17). It would seem that Freire agrees with Rancière in that the politics of education are firmly grounded in the pre-conceptual world of sensations and perceptions. Here aesthetics is located at the very heart of pedagogy which is *simultaneously* politics, art, and knowing, yet what exactly does this rather cryptic formulation entail? How is education simultaneously political, artistic, and epistemological? Which aesthetic metaphors underlie Freire's pedagogy of the oppressed? In other words, what metaphors give shape to the artistic event of Freirian pedagogy? Which model of aesthetic "performance" does Freire utilize to explore the analogy between artistic production and teaching?

Along with Rancière, Freire specifically highlights the poetics of theatre as important for thinking through the artistic event of education. In an interview with Ira Shor, Shor states that Freire's work is most accurately described as a "performance" on a "stage" (1987, 116) that involves visual and auditory dimensions. Here the pedagogy of the oppressed is a stage of sorts, which repartitions the divisions between who can speak and think, opening up a theatre of new actors to enter the world of politics. Problem-posing dialogue is simultaneously the event of the play and the stage of the play—it has both temporal and spatial dimensions and thus undermines the coordinates of our sensible intuition that determine *when* and *where* it is appropriate to speak.

Yet, while Freire's gesture toward theatre creates an opening for thinking through his relationship with Rancière, the particular way he conceptualizes the theatre of the pedagogy of the oppressed is highly problematic and ultimately misses precisely what is political in Rancière's theatrocracy (in this sense replicating the Brechtian failure of Althusser to realize the democratic politics of theatre). If Freire and Rancière agree on the centrality of the theatrical form for emancipatory education, there is a profound difference in how they conceptualize theatre. This chapter will analyze the similarities and differences between their competing visions of educational dramaturgy. In the end, I will suggest that what is at stake is the difference between the beautiful and the sublime. If Freire champions the former over the latter, then Rancière offers the reverse argument (or at least a subversive reading of the sublime from *within* the beautiful). Using Rancière as a theoretical reference point, I will problematize the pedagogical and political implications that Freire's pedagogy of the oppressed faces when it models dialogue on the aesthetics of the beautiful. In particular, I provide a critique of Freire's emphasis on educational solidarity and class suicide by demonstrating its pre-conceptual, pre-rational dependency on the harmony, order, and form of beauty versus the formlessness of the sublime. In sum, my examination will create a productive space of reinvention wherein Freirian-inspired pedagogy shifts its aesthetic commitments from the beautiful to the sublime, and, in turn, Rancière's own reflections on pedagogy become grounded in a practice poised between the moment of rupture and the fixity of an institutionalized curriculum.

Exporting Dialogic Education

First, we have to see how aesthetics have been displaced in the secondary literature concerning Freire and the arts. Freire's insistence on education as an "aesthetic event" might sound shocking to some, considering, as David Swanger has argued (1983), that Freire never developed a practical *or* theoretical role for aesthetics within a radical educational tradition. Alternatively, it might sound rather banal. Moacir Gadotti (2002), for instance, easily explains such a statement in relation to the creative component of Freire's particular form of radical constructivism.

Here Gadotti focuses on the *result* of dialogic education which, as Freire writes, "is not *to transfer knowledge* but to create the possibilities for the production or construction of knowledge" (1998, 30). Further supporting Gadotti's position, Freire has argued that "Even if we are not conscious of this [aesthetics] as educators, we are still involved in a naturally aesthetic project. What can happen is that, being unaware of the aesthetic aspect of education, we become very bad artists, but artists of a kind nevertheless, to the extent we help the students enter a process of permanent formation" (Shor and Freire 1987, 118). In such passages, Freire equates aesthetics with a constructivist process leading to a critical version of "life-long learning." Although Gadotti's analysis seems to offer more possibilities than does Swanger's, we must ask if such a reading truly hits the heart of the matter. When Freire proclaims that he is a teacher "proud of the *beauty* of my teaching practice [emphasis added]" (1998, 95) it would seem that we can dismiss Swanger's oversimplification and complicate Gadotti's reading. Freire does provide a location for aesthetics within his pedagogy (no matter how obscure this location might at first appear), and the beauty of pedagogy/literacy/teaching seems to indicate that the aesthetic dimension is not solely in terms of the results (production of new knowledge/new subjectivities) but in the very *practice* of education itself.

In the literature that deals exclusively with Freirian pedagogy and the arts, these questions have been largely sidestepped. For instance, Sherilyn Ottey (1996) has convincingly argued for an articulation of critical pedagogical principles and contemporary proponents of dance education. Against "banking education" as a dominant pedagogical strategy in the performance arts, Ottey sees in dance a moment of subversion through which the creativity of the student is engaged and divisions between cognitive, psychomotor, and affective dimensions of learning are deconstructed and reconstructed in a mediated fashion. Yet in the end, Ottey merely *applies* critical pedagogy to dance education in the form of problem-posing, co-development, thematic options, critical dialogue, de-socialization, and democratic authority. In other words, while advocating a new notion of dance, any simple, one-way, unilateral application of critical pedagogical practices into the material world of the dancing body risks reducing the aesthetic dimension of dance to yet another site for critical consciousness raising. Such an application of Freire's work runs against the quote cited above in which Freire explicitly stated "I don't speak about education through art" but rather about education itself as an aesthetic event.

Likewise, the work of Christine Morris (1998) focuses on how Freire's basic problem-posing methods function as the basis for community arts programs. Morris charts the various ways in which Freire used visual arts to stimulate critical dialogue and the inspiration other art activists have drawn from his example. Thus she focuses on how to teach literacy, reading, and writing to children and adults using art as a tool in a critical curriculum. The result is what she describes as a "triangular methodology of art teaching" which in many ways is a reconstruction of the pedagogy of the oppressed designed specifically for art teachers, focusing on the production of art as well as a critical reflection on the meaning of visual culture. Notice the order of operations for both Ottey and Morris. Dialogic pedagogy is a ground upon which an arts-based education is constructed. To use Marxist terminology, Freire is the foundation/base upon which a curricular superstructure is built out of artistic activities. In other words, dance and community art programs become the sites of critical pedagogy as a cognitive process of critical-consciousness raising. Yet Freire's comments seem to suggest that education itself is always already an artistic event above and beyond any regional application or exportation of critical pedagogy to this or that artistic practice.

The third and final example is perhaps the most famous and the most rigorously philosophical: Augusto Boal's *Theatre of the Oppressed* (2002). Unlike those above, Boal is concerned not so much with applying Freire's method to aesthetic education as he is with creating a new pedagogy of the oppressed out of and through theatre. Here theatre acts as a new method of problem-posing education—a distinctly aesthetic form of pedagogy akin to Brecht's epic theatre which, as Fredric Jameson (2000) has demonstrated, is most importantly a new type of educational experience. Arts are not content to be articulated through a pedagogical form that remains largely external and unchanged by this transaction. Rather theatre and pedagogy merge, each transforming the other in a complex sublation. As Boal writes, "We tried to show in practice how the theater can be placed at the service of the oppressed, so that they can express themselves and so that, by using this new language, they can also discover new concepts" (2002, 121). Here theatre itself emerges as a language and ultimately as a discourse through which a critical literacy of the body, the world, and the word emerge. And yet, Boal does to take his reader to the furthest-reaching conclusions of his theatrical pedagogy. Could we not argue that at its base, what is revealed by Boal is not a new form of the pedagogy of the oppressed but rather the inherent aesthetic event that lies at the very heart of critical pedagogy as such? Stated differently, is it not possible that the pedagogy of the oppressed is always already a kind of educational theatre?

Here it is also important to emphasize the centrality of aesthetics in Freire's own philosophical and pedagogical writings. As Peter Mayo emphasizes (2004), critics who argue that Freire suffers from a fetishization of rational cognition over and against other ways of learning and perceiving the world fail to recognize the constitutively affective and aesthetic work of his writing. Here Mayo cites Nita Freire's reflections on her husband's work and the impossibility of translating his unique aesthetic sensibility: "He used words of such beauty and plasticity, organized in phrases and these in turn in the context of the totality of the text, with such aesthetic and political force that, I repeat, they cannot be transposed so easily into other languages because a language cannot be translated literally" (2004, 9). As with Freire's depiction of pedagogy cited above, once again the interwoven and mutually reinforcing dimensions of aesthetic beauty, philosophical inquiry, and political force are emphasized. Thus what many authors have missed is how Freire's writing style is in many ways a model for the internally productive role of aesthetics in the pedagogy of the oppressed as such. The poetics of Freire's educational theory reveal a certain performativity of language—a performance of what Rancière refers to as mute speech which resists easy translation. In this sense, the key to understanding Freire's insistence on the need for constant reinvention of his methods lies in the poetry of his words which themselves remain in surplus of any particular translation.

In what follows I will explore this hypothesis further in relation to Rancière's work on aesthetics. In the end I will return to Freire and suggest that what is most valuable and most problematic in his dialogic pedagogy is not his theory of dialogue at all, but rather the aesthetic event that creates the visual and verbal stage wherein dialogue may take place. It is this event as the sudden, dissensual break with the status quo of banking education that is the political force of Freire's practice.

Jacques Rancière and the Aesthetics of Politics

For Rancière there are two aspects of the general field of the political, the first of which is the police. Expanding the notion of the police beyond the state, Rancière explains "The police is, essentially, the law, generally implicit, that defines a party's share or lack of it. But to define this, you first must define the configuration of the perceptible in which one or the other is inscribed. The police is thus first an order of bodies that defines the allocation of ways of doing, ways of being, and ways of saying, and sees that those bodies are assigned by name to a particular place and task; it is an order of the visible and the sayable that sees that a particular activity is visible and another is not, that this speech is understood as discourse and another as noise" (1999, 29). Deeper than Foucault's theory of disciplinary power, the police order does not really act to discipline, train, and monitor individuals. Rather, the police governs the very appearance of bodies and subjects in the first place through the ordering principle of visibility and sayability upon which circuits of disciplinary power are drawn, bodies controlled, borders demarked, and so on. But, as Rancière is quick to point out, every police order, every hierarchical distribution of what can be seen, heard, and organized according to common sense, is at its base predicated on a dis-organizing appearance of equality. In *The Philosopher and His Poor* (2004c), Rancière demonstrates that every police order (hierarchically distributed regime) is supported by an equality that is nevertheless suppressed.

In opposition to the consensus of the police order, Rancière poses the antagonistic principle of political disagreement which verifies this suppressed equality. If the police-mechanism maintains the distribution of bodies, parts, groups, and parties within a certain sensible distribution, then politics proper is "whatever breaks with the tangible configuration whereby parties and parts or lack of them are defined by a presupposition that, by definition, has no place in that configuration—that of the part that has no part" (1999, 29–30). Politics "undoes the perceptible divisions of the police order by implementing a basically heterogeneous assumption, that of a part of those who have no part, an assumption that, at the end of the day, itself demonstrates the sheer contingency of the order" (Rancière 1999, 30). As explored in the introduction to this book, politics emerges with a rupture in divisions that constitute social spaces and social identities—a "breach" of the sensible ordering of thoughts, sights, and sounds. By fundamentally rupturing divisions between the audible and inaudible, the visible and the invisible, etc., politics opens up a radical space where those that have been uncounted by the police become visible and audible—"a counting of the uncounted" (Rancière 1999, 38). The uncounted proclaim a wrong and demand the affirmation of social equality by creating a disagreement concerning who has a part in the established order. In other words, politics is an operation in which equality is confirmed, forcing a revolutionary transformation or reconfiguration of the field of social interaction. As a count of those who are uncounted, politics proper is a breaking in of those who refuse to enact their predetermined social role.

Aesthetics and politics are intimately linked because aesthetics "means first freeing up the norms of representation, and second, constituting a

kind of community of sense experience that works on the world of assumptions, of the *as if* that includes those who are not included by revealing a
mode of existence of sense experience that has eluded the allocation of
parties and lots" (Rancière 2006c, 38). If the police codifies and organizes
the distribution of the sensible, then an aesthetic politics "intervene[s]
in the general distribution of ways of doing and making as well as in the
relationships they maintain to modes of being and forms of visibility"
(Rancière 2006c, 13). Aesthetic disruption blurs boundaries between what
can and cannot be said, can and cannot be seen, thus expanding, recon-
figuring, and mixing notions of what is common to a community. Within
political statements there exists an aesthetic kernel that creates "uncertain
communities that contribute to the formation of enunciative collectives
that call into question the distribution of roles, territories, and languages"
(Rancière 2006c, 40). The aesthetic dimension is a "heterology" (Rancière
2006c, 63) in which the meaningful world of the police is ruptured by a
sensorial revolt that allows for a new political action or a new enunciation
to take place. The essence of political equality for Rancière is thus not
unity of the community but the "two of division" (Rancière 2007c, 32) that
undoes the false harmony of the collective space and allows a wrong to be
heard.

Perhaps it would not be too extreme to suggest that if the police
order configures the distribution of the sensible through administration,
calculation, and categorization, then the mixing, rerouting, and cross-
contamination of divisions found within the aesthetic suggests a liberatory
rethinking of synesthesia as a political capacity rather than simply a
neurological disorder (for an overview of synesthesia see Dunn 1998).
As Daniel Heller-Roazen reminds us, the original meaning of synesthesia
is a "perceiving-with" (2009, 84) or a perception of joining two or more
sensations together which do not coincide. Synesthesia mixes sensory
compartmentalization opening up spaces for aesthetic redistribution of
what can be perceived that, for Rancière, would hold political value. As
stated above, the ability to transgress boundaries and thus articulate what
"has eluded the allocation of parties and lots" is a moment of synesthetic
invention. In fact, Rancière himself argues that the paradox of aesthetics
is best understood as a form of synesthesia. In his critique of discourses
that emphasize the "purity" of "modernist" art, Rancière writes, "You
cannot understand people like Malevich, Mondrian or Schoenberg if you
don't remember that their 'pure' art is inscribed in the midst of questions
regarding synaesthesia, the construction of an individual or collective
setting for life, utopias of community, new forms of spirituality, etc."

(Rancière 2003b, 206). In other words, artists working within the aesthetic regime constantly undermine any idea of a pure art, mixing media, mixing sensory experiences, and challenging any strict divisions between art and life or the relation between image and affect. In a slightly different formulation, Rancière argues that democracy itself is a "work of fiction, which consists not in telling stories but in establishing new relations between words and visible forms, speech and writing, a here and an elsewhere, a then and a now" (2009c, 102). This complex relation between visibility and signification points to a radical rethinking of synesthesia as a particularly democratic machine able to produce new metaphors by contaminating senses and signification. If synesthesia is an aesthetic perception of motley contamination, then it is the act of translation that puts these synesthetic deformations into circulation.

Freire's Aesthetic Pedagogy

Freire clearly understands the role of the teacher as fundamentally aesthetic. In his interviews with Shor, Freire agrees that teaching is an "artistic process, uncovering key themes and access points to consciousness, and then recomposing them into an unsettling critical investigation, orchestrating a prolonged study" (1987, 115). This artistic process involves more than simply challenging conscious beliefs but more importantly, recomposing the sights and sounds of the classroom. In fact Shor argues that the teacher has to understand the classroom as a place that has "visual and auditory dimensions" which must be altered in order to "stimulate unfamiliar critical attention in students" (Shor and Freire 1987, 116). Thus Shor enters the classroom intentionally modifying the tone of his voice from "didactic, lecturing tones" to "conversational rhythms" creating a small intervention into the "verbal domination" (Shor and Freire 1987, 117) of a classroom by the traditional stultifying expert. In the same dialogue, Freire agrees with Shor's analysis emphatically proclaiming "I agree absolutely with you about this question of the teacher as an artist" (Shor and Freire 1987, 118). Using Rancière's terminology, we can argue that Freirian dialogue is an event that offers up a new partitioning of the sensible—an inaugural redistribution of what is seen and heard in a classroom. In relation to teaching, the "artistic event" that Freire describes is precisely this fundamental rupture within the student/ teacher dichotomy. Education against "banking" (Freire 2001b) begins in the aesthetic realm of the senses which enables dis-identification of one's identity (as passive student or as active teacher). The result of this rupture is the enunciation of an impossible and largely inaudible utterance (a synesthetic moment of mixing and confusion of divisions) in which all participants in dialogue are "simultaneously teachers *and* students" (Freire 2001b, 72). The precise name for this new relationship seems to lie beyond the language of the police, a nameless relation that must nevertheless articulate itself in the very language of the police to be heard. This is Rancière's uncertain community that creates new relations between speaking, seeing, and acting. It is within student/teacher dis-identification that the rupture of democracy as an aesthetic event within pedagogy alters the police order, creating a new configuration that attempts to verify the appearance of a new dialogic relation between teacher and student.

While it is natural to speak of the audible and the inaudible within Freire's pedagogy, it seems less intuitive to speak of the visible and the invisible. Freire himself argues that "... from the moment we come into the classroom, at the moment you say, Hello! How are you?, to the students, you necessarily start an aesthetic relationship" (Shor and Freire 1987, 118). Thus we cannot forget that "from the moment we come into the classroom" our perception of the room and the students in the room already constitutes a pre-linguistic field of perceptions and affects in which dialogue is always already immersed. Equally important in all acts of teaching is the possibility for destabilizing the realm of what can and cannot be *seen* through a visual redistribution. In the realm of the visible, the aesthetic of sight opens up or closes down a field in which students are perceived as active participants in education. In banking education, the pedagogical field of vision is organized by a particular gaze: the disciplining gaze. This gaze is predicated on regulation, normalization, and homogenization rather than a practice of freedom. The gaze defines hierarchies of inclusion and exclusion, and maintains these hierarchies through the structure of the teacher/student division. Even in the "progressive" or critical classroom, this gaze may work covertly to situate the student within discourses of deficits, abnormalities, and behavioral problems. In sum, the gaze is a visual practice of mastery and control (Lewis 2006). Pedagogical aesthetics of vision have to be reworked so as to resist the reproduction of the stultifying gaze that imposes ignorance onto some subjects and not others.

Perhaps a model could be found in what Mieke Bal (1996)—appropriating the concept from Norman Bryson—refers to as the glance. For her, the glance is a temporally bound, self-aware, and always already partial form of looking and perceiving. Furthermore, the glance is receptive to the agency of the other. Rather than see the other as simply a passive object to be consumed, dominated, or subjected to social exclusion in the form of a no-count, the glance destabilizes the recognizability of the other as an object with a corresponding set of predicates. The glance is a form of visualization that opens up a space outside of normalization, criminalization, and pathologization inherent in the gaze. Rather than a position of mastery, as with the gaze, the glance is always an *ignorant* form of seeing and perceiving and thus curious as to what it will find when it opens itself up to the other. The resolution of the teacher/student dialectic demands a new aesthetics of visualization that will allow the teacher to see in the student a speaking subject capable of entering into a problem-posing dialogue—a subject capable of interruption. The exchange of glances scrambles codes and divisions structuring the banking classroom and as such is a synesthetic moment wherein all teaching becomes learning and all learning becomes teaching. For instance, in the moment of synesthetic rupture, one *sees* a teacher (as the one supposed to know) and yet one *hears* in the voice of the teacher that of the student (as the one who asks questions, searches for answers). And vice versa, one *sees* the student (as the passive object) and suddenly *hears* in the voice of the student that of the teacher (as the one who knows). In sum, Freire's pedagogy has to be supported by an aesthetic rupture of the visible/audible, transforming the detached, omniscient, authoritarian gaze of banking education into the ruptural gesture of the glance.

Hence Freire's dis-identification of the teacher as explicator and subjectivation of the teacher as witness. The witness is a deactivation of the gaze of the explicator/banking educator through the pedagogical technology of the glance. Rather than one who imposes from outside and above, the teacher in Freire's account becomes a "humble and courageous witness" that emerges from "cooperation in a shared effort—the liberation of women and men" (2001b, 176). The witness is in Freire's hands dialectically fused with the teacher, becoming simultaneously one who records the experiences of others as well as one who actively intervenes into the very processes which silence, marginalize, and exploit the oppressed through an aesthetic reconstruction of what can be heard, seen, and experienced. And it is the type of intervention that is crucial. If the role of the philosopher for Rancière is not to give voice to the silenced or to interpret these voices from a position of authority (a type of critical enterprise) but to hear these voices and make them circulate, then the pedagogical equivalent is surely Freire's description of the teacher as a witness. Making the connection explicit, Michael Dillon argues that the key role of the philosopher and the teacher for Rancière is ultimately "the work of witnessing that brings to presence an excess, or incalculability" (2005, 443) that is the verification of equality. Thus through education as an aesthetic event, both teacher and student undergo a dis-identificaiton that displaces the order of things within the classroom. The teacher becomes an equal actor in the struggle for liberation. As an actor, he or she exchanges glances with the other students in a moment of shared performance. Such glances do not determine who can and cannot speak or think (as with the gaze) but rather bear witness to the verification of equality.

The Beauty of Teaching: From Beautiful Solidarity to Sublime Uncertainty

In sum, it is not that Freire neglected to define a place for aesthetics or that aesthetics resides in the creative constructivism of dialogue or that aesthetics is a field for applying Freirian principles. Education becomes an artistic event at the precise moment it becomes political, i.e. at the moment when banking is ruptured through a repartitioning of the sensible. We can now clarify that for Freire this aesthetic is the reconfiguration of the student/teacher relationship—a dis-identification that results in a synesthetic utterance. Through this aesthetic reconfiguration, the teacher as stultifier undergoes a fundamental short-circuiting, opening up a stage wherein every teacher is a student and every student a teacher.

Yet we must complicate this picture somewhat. Throughout this chapter, I have utilized Rancière's theory of poetics to help elucidate Freire's pedagogy of the oppressed as an artistic event. Yet this exploration of Freire's event also reveals a certain limit to Freire's conception of politics. In other words, the poetics of Freire's pedagogical thought undermine his radical political project. Here we must remember that for Freire, problem-posing dialogue makes him "proud of the beauty" (1998, 95) of his teaching practice. Further, Freire argues, "... aesthetics is the very nature of educational practice, meaning we must not be alien to beauty" (1996, 117). In these quotations, Freire emphasizes the beautiful nature of education wherein teacher and student come to *recognize* one another as mutual actors in naming the world. As Davide Panagia argues (2006), Kant's concept of the beautiful replaces coercive rhetoric with the possibility for mutually recognizable representability. Through mimetic narration, the political community gains commonality with itself, and in turn achieves a type of full presence. If, for Kant, beauty is the aesthetic experience of harmony between the faculties and the senses, then the political equivalent would be a community accounting for all of its parts within a shared common sense. This valence of the beautiful reveals its political implications for Freire when teaching leads to "solidarity" (2001b, 49–50) with the oppressed. Solidarity is a form of class suicide wherein the teacher joins with the oppressed as a witness and as an activist against oppression. Symbolic and material suicide closes the gap between teacher and student so that "a class can be reborn as revolutionary workers, completely identified with the deepest aspirations of the people to which they belong" (Freire and Faundez 1989, 74). What is unique about the experience of the beautiful, in Kant's aesthetic philosophy, is precisely its disinterested quality. In other words, a subject makes an aesthetic judgment regardless of his or her personal interests or desires in the object. Class-suicide is a form of dis-identification with one's material interests in sustaining inequality and one's class-specific desires in order to make a political commitment to the *universal validity* of the struggle of the oppressed. Thus class-suicide is a political and pedagogical equivalent to aesthetic disinterestedness.

The corresponding identitarian solidarity results in a profound "trust" (Freire 2001b, 66) between student and teacher wherein the student trusts in the correct political orientation of the teacher and the teacher trusts in the ability of the oppressed to think critically. The unity of teacher and student in a moment of mutual recognition and intersubjective "speaking with" is based on a political certainty that enables the teacher to facilitate critical consciousness raising without the use of coercive rhetoric. As Freire argues, the teacher must possess "political clarity" (Horton and Freire 1990, 104) in order to have transparent and mutual recognition with the oppressed. Stated differently, the goal of this pedagogical and political solidarity is to close the gap between the educator's "here and now" and the educands' "there and then" (Freire 2004a, 47). Summarizing, Freire writes, "you never get *there* by starting from *there*, you get *there* by starting from *here*" (2004a, 47), meaning that consensus about the world cannot be imposed through lecture but must arise through a critical appraisal of the oppressed from where they are at that moment. Only then can *there* become *here* and solidarity be achieved through speaking with rather than at or to or for the oppressed—a sort of hermeneutical fusion of horizons where here and there become one in the same position.

As long as solidarity remains informed by an aesthetic commitment which is modeled on the beautiful as an intersubjective space of mutual recognition, mimetic identity, and narrative agreement, Freire's pedagogy is unable to face the relationship between democracy and dissensual aesthetics internal to educational relationships precisely because he erases the power dynamics that exist between two individual wills. Rather than recognizability and fully transparent narratives of struggle (stories that can be told in order to identify collective belonging to the universality of the oppressed), the classroom is more often than not rife with differences that exceed the particular staging of the event of dialogue in Freire's model. In short, if naming the world is situated in a mimetic reproduction of experience in order to combat the narration sickness of the oppressed (a culture of silence), then this narrative seems to reach a limit condition when faced with difference that cannot be accounted for within the count of narrative totalization. Freirian dialogue verifies that the student can speak and think but only in order to take up an existing identity (the oppressed) with a corresponding set of interests that are determined by their subject positions within the social relations of production. As opposed to identification, Gert Biesta highlights Rancière's emphasis on subjectivation which is the appearance of "a way of being that had no place and no part in the existing order of things" (2010, 547) thus acting as a supplement that divides the police order. Subjectivation is a form of speech that ruptures the distribution of the sensible and thus challenges any correspondence between ways of doing, seeing, speaking, and specific locations. Subjectivation troubles notions of solidarity based on shared class interests determined in advance by particular locations within a social totality. The initial subjectivation of the pedagogy of the oppressed which undermines the police logic of the teacher and the learner is, in the last instance, only politically progressive if it is a subjectivation *based on an identification* of the "proper" interests of the oppressed—an ontological vocation that is conditioned by their class position. Here the precise term "ontological vocation" which Freire repeatedly emphasizes becomes important. Vocation (as opposed to occupation) finds its roots in the Latin word *vocare* or to call. Thus vocation is a calling—an interpolation or hailing that, as Althusser would argue, *produces* a recognizable subject. Subjectivation on the other hand is not a calling or a hailing from a master/sovereign into a preexisting subject position but is rather the *production of something new*—a position that cannot be hailed because it does not yet have a proper name or proper location. In fact, subjectivation is precisely about occupying the "wrong names" and the "wrong locations" by acting "as if." The subject must assume a position to which they have not been called, for which they have no vocation. Subjectivation demands synesthetic translations across the senses without privileging preexisting narrative structures for imparting meaning on these translations.

Even in Freire's "postmodern turn" toward "oneness in difference" (2004a, 137), the articulation of differences remains within the logic of identity politics where one's class, race, and gender determine a specific standpoint and set of corresponding interests. While Freire agrees with Antonio Faundez's passing comment that "it is precisely the differences between us which enable us to engage in dialogue" (1989, 100), these differences remain *internal* to a politics of solidarity, trust, and mutual witnessing/affirming. Thus although Freire writes that identities are not "predetermined" (1998, 70), the notion of identity is what is problematic here. Identity for Freire is always defined as "doing things in a certain way, by thinking or speaking in a certain way ... by having certain likes and habits" that enable *recognition* of the self as "being similar" to others (1998, 71). The result is a notion of identity as a "categorization" (Freire 1998, 71) within a certain partitioning of the sensible. In these citations, we clearly see the logic of identification, which implies an established context or set of categories that predefine perceptual similarities or dissimilarities. Subjectivation, on the other hand, is based on the attention to the sudden appearance of new perceptions and sensations that elude identification of this or that "type" or this or that "categorization." As Davide Panagia argues, it is the political dimension of subjectivation that "invites a relinquishing and a reconfiguration of ourselves" (2009, 11) beyond the recognition of specific identity categories. The problem for both Biesta and Panagia (drawing on Rancière) is that Freire's theory of identity is—even in its postmodern moment—predicated on an inadequate political response to the appearance of new subjectivities, to the appearance of a supernumerary surplus or remainder that seems to have no place within his narrative. As Panagia argues, one of the central problems with political theory today—and I would add pedagogical theories, both liberal and conservative—is that they fail to recognize that "difference is not a property assignable to individuals or groups but is, instead, the associational power that allows for politics to occur, a kind of energistic asymmetry that resides in things in an undersigned world" (2006, 8). This is the realm of what Panagia refers to as the "revolutionary sublime" (2006, 84) or a realm of excess, contamination, synesthetic blurring, and rude interruption.

For Rancière, the social totality is always divided against itself, every count is a miscount, producing a sublime remnant at the heart of all political counting that escapes measure. "The political wrong [that divides a community] does not get righted. It is addressed as something irreconcilable within a community that is always unstable and heterogeneous" (Rancière 2007c, 103). In other words, unlike Freire's beautiful vision of education, Rancière argues that the miscounted introduces a condition of excess into all educational practices. Here the naming of the world is never complete but always includes a surplus, a supernumerary remainder that haunts the count and forces a disagreement, an excess of words that cannot be recognized as belonging to any predefined subject. This supernumerary remainder is what Biesta refers to as the "incalculable" or "what cannot be known to be excluded in terms of the existing order" (2007, 9). In other words, if the beautiful heals the rupture between student and teacher through solidarity (creating a collective space of mutual recognition, consensus, shared identification, and action), then the sublime heightens the sense of rupture by creating a stage and a time for witnessing continual disagreement (not in terms of the unrepresentable as such or in terms of mere argumentation but in terms of the aesthetic staging of words before they are assigned meanings, proper locations, and proper functions within a discourse). Katharine Wolfe aptly summarizes the politics of the sublime as a "sense without recognition" (2006, n.p.). Without recognizing the political efficacy of a sublime miscount, Freire's redistribution of subject positions in problem-posing education merely solidifies/calcifies into a new police order (a new set of identities where proper names correspond to ontological vocations) that closes down on the possibilities which his poetics open up (a new partitioning of subjectivations).

Of course this new division of the sensible might in fact be a better police order than that of banking education but at the same time, it is a pedagogy that misses the "continuous event" (Freire 1985a, 89) of "cultural revolution" (Freire 1985a, 54) that Freire demands. The sublime suggests that the unity of learning and teaching in the mutual recognition of every student and teacher as active participants in the construction of shared, intersubjective knowledge is far from a clear and present solidarity, but is fraught with division and divisiveness that cannot be remedied by a beautiful pedagogy wherein everyone's vocations can be clarified and a common will can be forged through stories. In short, if Freire's model of the teacher as artist is political through his or her identification with the universal vocation of the oppressed (solidarity through class-suicide) then for Rancière, the situation is precisely the reverse. In his preface to the book *La Politique des Poètes: Pourquoi des Poètes en Temps de Détresse?* (Rancière and Badiou 1992), Rancière argues that often poets speak in the name of the oppressed, but in the end speak beyond the partition of oppressed/ oppressor, opening up a space of democratic dissensus in surplus of the ordering of the police. If the artist belongs, he or she belongs only as far as he/she is a stranger, speaking in the name not of the oppressors or the oppressed but in the name of freedom and of equality with excessively rude and dissonant words that remain disorderly and illegitimate. Likewise the teacher as artist stages democracy not through belonging to or identifying with this or that set of particular interests but through the act of dis-identification that is the atopic space of the stranger (the position of the miscounted). Here the teacher does not know the form that the play will take, cannot help the student correlate appearance with ontological reality, cannot certify the proper names for the world. The resulting community is an *uncertain* community of equals—equally ignorant, equally caught up in the moment of disagreement over what roles to play, how to play them, and so on.

Thus the issue here is that Freire's pedagogical act is informed by the political aesthetics of the beautiful rather than the sublime. This in the end transforms the democratic moment of his pedagogical rupture into a verification of preexisting interests (the interests of the oppressed versus the interests of the oppressors) that can be recognized through the act of witnessing and mimetic narration. Yet Freire's emphasis on beautiful, intersubjective relationality misses the existence of the part for which there is no part, and thus the profoundly democratic possibilities of the glance. In fact, it is the glance that offers a key shift from a beautiful to a sublime aesthetic. If the gaze is a disinterested optic through which the beautiful can be contemplated without contamination of the teacher's class interest (i.e. class suicide) then the glance is incapable of such distance and is fully caught within the matrix of contingent relations that make up the theatrical stage of education. Far from limiting the political efficacy of Freire's work, such an observation opens up education to a politics that remains in process without the guarantee of recognition as this or that type of subject with this or that corresponding vocation. Sublime equality is an equality without recognition and, as such, maintains a space of dissensus within education. I would argue that we can rehabilitate Freire's beautiful aesthetic from within the beautiful itself by demonstrating that the sublime already exists in latent form within the beautiful and all that is needed is a formal reversal for the implicit to become explicit in problem-posing dialogue.

Certainly the beautiful is important for maintaining the possibility of a shared sensory world, but without the supplement of the sublime (of the incalculable), this community loses the possibility of disagreement. Simply telling or sharing stories replaces the *agonizing* and *passionate* process of rupture that resists proportional measure within a given *sensus communis*. It is the nature of the sublime to engender the feeling of dissensus, of inoperative communication necessary for an uncertain community to remain open to the possibility of politics. This is not an identity-defined community so much as a community organized around dissensus. If Rancière has attacked Lyotard's theory of the sublime on several occasions, he has also made a similar observation, arguing that his theory of aesthetic community is to be located in the sublime nature of the beautiful itself. For Rancière, the beautiful always already contains "the double bind of attraction and repulsion" (2009a, 97). Because dissensus lies at the very core of the aesthetic experience of the beautiful, all attempts to define community in terms of consensual harmony also contain the element of "dissensual common sense" (Rancière 2009a, 98). In particular, the aesthetic experience of the beautiful, according to Rancière's reading of Kant, is dissensual in two ways, rupturing the hierarchical relationship between perception and understanding and separating sensation from desire. In short, the beautiful suspends the law of conceptual determination as well as consumable desire. And it is here that the aesthetic of the sublime contains its political valence, for this revolution in sensory distribution is fundamentally a "neutralization of the very forms by which power is exercised" (Rancière 2009a, 99). Resistance of the beautiful sublime is thus resistance to any strict law of measure that partitions the sensible according to hierarchies of value, desire, and utility. In education, the sublime appears when students proclaim their ability to think and speak at precisely those moments when the script (a) denies them such capacities (as in the pedagogy of the oppressors) or (b) prescribes certain capacities and vocations (as in the pedagogy of the oppressed). Thus, in the end, we have to read Freire and Rancière together as forming a beautifully sublime and thus perpetually agonistic relation that can never be reduced to a community of One.

Intermission:

Equality, Freedom, and Emancipation: A Case for Pedagogical Dramaturgy

In his introduction to the work of Jacques Rancière, Joseph Tanke (2011) makes a rather surprising and insightful observation. According to Tanke, there is a crucial displacement in Rancière's aesthetic theory of the problematic of freedom. Although drawing heavily from Kant, Schiller, Hegel and others, Rancière does not comment on their shared interest in aesthetic experience and the quest for freedom. Instead, Rancière focuses exclusively on equality. As I have argued, Rancière is interested in the expressivity of the aesthetic arts that overturns the hierarchical ordering of literary styles in the representative regime. In short, all subject matter becomes equally aestheticized. Likewise, with the aesthetic arts, there is no longer any definitive description of or mastery over this super-saturated world of signs and meanings. If all objects speak, this speech is silent, recalcitrant to the authority or power of any one individual artist. Objects speak, but they also refuse to confess their true natures. By refusing full disclosure, objects remain open to endless artistic articulations without closure, always leaving room for the possibility of new possibilities, new aesthetic articulations. Furthermore, Rancière focuses on the equality of the senses in the aesthetic moment. *Pathos* and *logos* are no longer held in strict hierarchical order, and there is "free play" of the faculties, which becomes a kind of allegory for social free play or democratic equality amongst individuals, bridging the gap between aesthetics and politics. Yet in all of Rancière's reflections on the connections between the aesthetic-arts, equality, and democracy, there is little or no mention of the relation between equality and freedom. In fact, freedom seems to recede from the equation entirely.

In this brief intermission, I wish to explore Tanke's thesis in relation to education. What does it mean if universal teaching remains silent on the question of freedom? Here I will argue that the model of universal teaching is predicated on an (unconscious) debt to Kant's metaphysics of morals and his formulation of the categorical imperative. While Kant's ethical philosophy emphasizes equality of all human beings under the law (it is categorical), this law is also a command (hence its form as an imperative). This empty commandment results in a rather odd notion of individual freedom: freedom is found only in one's duty to the law. Freedom of will is free only in so far as this will conforms to the categorical imperative. A similar aporia is discovered in the command of universal teaching: the equality of intelligence is predicated on a dutiful sacrifice to the imperative to think and speak. What is at stake here is defining a more robust notion of emancipation, one that includes *both* the concept of equality and freedom. If traditionally equality and freedom are thought of as conflicting—equality always limits individual freedom and vice versa—then this paradox cannot be solved simply by ignoring or repressing its insistence. In conclusion, I suggest that if Rancière enables us to fully grasp the centrality of rethinking equality, then perhaps we can turn to Freire to enable us to rethink freedom, and in turn, holding them together as awkward educational neighbors will produce a new notion of educational community and in turn a richer (and much more complex) notion of educational emancipation. If Rancière betrays the aesthetics of education through his turn to Kantian ethics, then Freire betrays his agonistic politics of freedom by reinstating authority as critical expertise. These betrayals can only be overcome by once again turning to the question of theatre—a turn that will in the end reunite the question of will with acting (rather than obedience) and freedom with improvisation (rather than the expertise of the authority).

Kant's Theory of Freedom as Voluntary Servitude

In *Groundwork of the Metaphysics of Morals* (2006 [1785]), Kant outlines his general critique of practical reason and sets forth his own theory of the categorical imperative as the "*supreme principle of morality*" (4:391). For my purposes here, I want to draw upon several key features of this theory in order to make an argument concerning equality and freedom in relation to education. Thus, I will not provide a full analysis of his argument and will focus only on the key claims underlying Kant's critique: the good will and its relation to a formal, anti-foundational command. First and foremost what must be noticed is that Kant clearly links ethics with a *good will*. The will is an absolute foundation for Kant because the good will is incorruptible, determined solely by the ethical law. What Kant discovers through his analysis of the good will is that the only maxims upon which a subject should act are those that he/she wills as a rational, self-legislator. Thus the categorical imperative is anti-foundational in that it lacks a ground outside of itself in either nature or God. There is, in other words, no final evidence that can "prove" the existence of the ethical law beyond its own self-legislation, its own rhetorical powers of persuasion. It is an uncaused cause.

This self-legislator is morally superior to those motivated by desire (sympathy) because he/she is not conditioned by any individual likes or dislikes but only by pure reason. Even if the act of the sympathetic person is a socially positive one, the act, according to Kant, lacks *ethical* content. He writes, "An action from duty has its moral work *not in its purpose* to be attained by it but in the maxim in accordance with which it is decided upon, and therefore does not depend upon the realization of the object of the action but merely upon the *principle of volition* in accordance with which the action is done without regard for any object of the faculty of desire" (4:400). An ethical person's will is independent of results and of purposes (inclinations and desires). The only factor that tells us if the act is an ethical one is the type of will that animates it. If the will is good and recognizes its fundamental duty in obedience to a rational and universal law, then the outcome of the action is beside the point. Kant is only interested in intentions here, not extrinsic results, which may be subjected to contingent forces beyond the control of the ethical subject. An ethical act is guided by reason because reason is not specific or particular to any one individual (it is universally valid rather than contingently situated). The universality of the law is therefore predicated on the belief in the universality of reason, and in the ability of any reasonable person to understand our actions *as long as* they conform to a maxim which is not contaminated by particular desires.

Duty to a categorical imperative is expressed in the form of an imperative. Because we are humans, we are rational but also have passions, desires, and perversions that are particular rather than universal. These passions continually interfere with our duty to the law, tempting us to act against pure reason. Thus we have to think of our duty as an imperative telling us what we ought to do even if this goes against our immediate inclinations. Imperatives *constrain* us to act in certain ways rather than others. In short, imperatives are *rules a subject adopts that command him or her how he or she should act in order to achieve the ethical good.*

The categorical imperative is a formal maxim which lacks any specific content. The two formulations of the imperative which Kant offers in *Groundwork* are as follows:

I ought never to act except in such a way that I could also will that my maxim should become a universal law (4:402).

Now I say that the human being and in general every rational being exists as an end in itself, not merely as a means to be used by this or that will at its discretion; instead he must in all his actions, whether directed to himself or also to other rational beings, always be regarded at the same time as an end (4:428).

The first formulation (a) is simply an abstract command directed at the will by pure reason. The second (b) emphasizes the *social* dimension of (a), grounding the categorical imperative in an intersubjective world of *equals* who are to be treated as ends in themselves rather than simply as means for our self-centered plans. Read together, the two versions suggest that respect for the law (a) is also respect for individuals (b) and vice versa. Kant summarizes, "Any respect for a person is properly only respect for the law (of integrity and so forth) of which he [sic] gives us an example" (4:401). To make someone else into a means is to disregard his or her rationality and thus subject him or her to externally imposed goals which may transform the other into a mere object rather than a reasoning subject. Therefore, in Kant's view, every person is equal to every other person in terms of the rights and duties they have, and the categorical imperative unconditionally applies to all people. In other words, the categorical imperative has a leveling effect on all social hierarchies and divisions of labor separating individuals in a society in terms of social roles, wealth, power, or privilege. All reasonable beings equally stand before the imperative to act out of a deep respect for the universal law.

If one is only free when one acts according to ethical duty, this Kantian notion of freedom is not without its paradoxes. Freedom is, as Kant writes, "consciousness of the *subordination* of my will to a law without the mediation of other influences on my sense" (4:401). Freedom is self-subjugation to a universal law that "we impose upon *ourselves* as yet as necessary in itself" (4:401). Because the ethical subject acts "*only to laws given by himself* [sic] *but still universal*" (4:432), then Kant can argue that the subject is only conforming to his or her own will and thus perfectly free. In sum, Kant states, "a free will and a will under moral laws are one and the same" (4:447). In this sense, the ethical subject is autonomous and "*sovereign*" (4:433) as long as it is subordinate and obedient to the universal laws that it gives itself. Yet this formulation of freedom under a universal law is difficult to fully accept. As Terry Eagleton (2009) argues, the law becomes "mysteriously coercive" (310), and the subject becomes nothing more than an "obedient function of the law" (310), emptied of all its contingencies, its sensations, and its sentiments which are reduced to nothing more than incidental perversions. Freedom to act in accordance to duty and duty alone is a rather otherworldly, detached, and seemingly disembodied notion of freedom. Hannah Arendt makes a similar observation concerning the paradoxical nature of the Kantian categorical imperative. Because the will can say no to reason, Kant felt the need to introduce an obligation into this ethical philosophy. Yet, for Arendt, the obligation "is by no means self-evident" (2003, 77). In other words, the justification for the obligation cannot rest in reason alone. Behind every imperative there lies a disavowed dependency on the power of God or the implicit rules of a community to enforce a particular rule. Instead of categorical propositions, which cannot command but only persuade, Kant's categorical imperative, as it were, "brought back the concept of obedience, through a back door" (Arendt 2003, 72). The individual is both subject and subjected in the same philosophical move.

With this brief overview, we can now summarize some key features of Kant's argument that have influenced Rancière's theory of universal teaching, thus revealing a latent neo-Kantianism at work within his educational writings. First, there is the emphasis on the good will as the key ethical faculty. In this way, Kant strips bare the complex constellation of virtues inherited from Aristotle in order to expose ethical being in all its nakedness to the contingencies of embedded and embodied living within real communities. Second, the universal law is anti-foundational (an uncaused cause), formal (without content of its own), and universal (it is directed at everyone equally). In this sense, the universality of the law *insures* a certain level of democratic equality to all regardless of their nationality, social status, or privilege. Third, the law is an imperative, a command directed at the will by pure reason. The resulting notion of freedom is paradoxical—a peculiar kind of *willed* servitude to a law that is both inside of us and also radically transcendent of us. Because the categorical imperative is empty and purely formal, we can never fully verify if we are in fact acting in strict accordance with our duty to the universal law—we can only act "as if" we are free or that natural ends *may* correspond to the free acts of the good will. If the equality of the law solves the question of the stranger (everyone is, after all, subjected to the exact same categorical imperative without exception), it does not seem to solve the problem of freedom, leaving us with a vague notion of voluntary servitude or freedom through obedience.

Rancière's Neo-Kantian Categorical Imperative

For Rancière, universal teaching bears a striking resemblance to Kant's formulation of the categorical imperative. To begin with, universal teaching is always a will directed at another will. In fact, universal teaching is nothing other than a "pure relationship of will to will" (1991, 13) between master and student. Separating will from the question of intelligence is absolutely essential for universal teaching. Will is a universal, *equalizing* capacity for Rancière whereas intelligence—not unlike sentiment in Kant's argument—is particular, contingent, and privative. "It is useless," argues Rancière, "to discuss whether their 'lesser' intelligence is an effect of nature or an effect of society: they develop the intelligence that the needs and circumstances of their existence demand of them" (1991, 51). As such, intelligence is contextually specific, conditioned by historical forces and external causes that are not its own. Stripping away the contingencies of intelligence, privilege, skill, and so on, the ignorant schoolmaster directs his or her will directly to the will of the student.

The relation between wills is one of command. In fact, in its strongest formulation, the hypothesis of the equality of intelligences takes the form of the "egalitarian maxim" (Rancière 2010b, 168). Here I would like to emphasize the importance of this shift from the hypothesis (as discussed in previous chapters) to the maxim. If one is an opinion to be tested, the other is a *universal principle to be respected and obeyed*. The maxim of universal teaching "knows no compromises" and "absolutely commands" (Rancière 1991, 38). In such moments, the latent Kantian strain of Rancière's thought becomes apparent. The emphatic emphasis on equality causes a shift from the question of freedom (to test out a hypothesis) to that of duty (toward a universal and necessary principle of action). As such there is a certain sacrifice that accompanies the legal discourse of the maxim that Rancière never directly faces and that bears a certain burden which will only become fully recognizable through Rancière's description of universal teaching.

The ignorant schoolmaster's function is to enunciate a categorical imperative to which the student's will must conform. It is categorical in that it applies to everyone equally, and it is an imperative because it is a command to express one's will despite one's belief in unequal intelligences, despite certain obstacles, and despite the apparent powerlessness of one's ignorance. Thus the ignorant schoolmaster orders the student to "say *what he* [sic] *sees, what he thinks about it, what he makes of it*" (Rancière 1991, 20). Simply put, the categorical imperative of universal teaching is

"Follow *your* path" (Rancière 1991, 57). This command has no content in itself—it does not teach any *specific* lesson. The ignorant schoolmaster is, after all, *ignorant* of the content that is to be taught. The command is purely formal, and the ignorant schoolmaster is nothing more than a sovereign order to obey the egalitarian maxim by exercising the will. Because it is an empty command, the role of the ignorant schoolmaster is radically empty as well. Thus anyone can occupy this vacant position, including fathers and mothers who are not "qualified" to teach what they do not know. In this sense, the categorical imperative of universal teaching emphasizes the equality of intelligences between expert and novice, qualified and unqualified, knowledgeable and ignorant—all of whom are unconditionally held by an indiscriminate command.

It is also anti-foundational. For Rancière, we can never prove the equality of intelligences (which are always contingent and thus never measurable outside of their contextually specific manifestations). The equality of intelligences remains an opinion to be tested, a perpetual hypothesis. The ignorant schoolmaster must "act as if ..." the intelligences of his or her students are all equal in order to facilitate universal teaching. "We can never say: take two equal minds and place them in such and such a condition. We know intelligence by its effects. But we cannot isolate it, measure it. We are reduced to multiplying the experiments inspired by that opinion. Be we can never say: all intelligence is equal" (Rancière 1991, 46). And in the end, *this is not the point* of universal teaching. The point is "seeing what can be done under that supposition [equality of intelligences]" and therefore "it's enough for us that the opinion be possible" (Rancière 1991, 46). As with Kant's theory of ethical freedom, the equality of intelligences can never be proven empirically, nor is it derived from empirical existence. We must presuppose that such an equality is *possible*, and we have every reason to hope that it is verifiable even if in particular, empirical settings it is difficult to demonstrate with any certainty. For instance, Rancière argues that universal teaching is not interested in every child becoming a great artist. Rather, emancipation occurs at the exact moment the student proclaims "Me too, I'm a painter" (1991, 65) and thus acts "as if" he or she is an artist.

If Kant's categorical imperative resulted in a paradoxical notion of freedom as voluntary servitude, the same paradox is replicated in Rancière's reflections on universal teaching. Describing the relationship between the ignorant schoolmaster and the student, Rancière writes, "A pure relationship of will to will had been established between master and student: a relationship wherein the master's domination resulted in an entirely liberated relationship between the intelligence of the student and that of the book—the intelligence of the book that was also the thing in common, the egalitarian intellectual link between master and student" (1991, 13). It is this domination of the master over the student that must give us pause. Equality of intelligence might be verified in such a relationship but at what expense? What role does freedom play in this relationship? Is freedom nothing more than obedience to the categorical imperative of universal teaching?

These questions become more pronounced when we turn to another passage from *The Ignorant Schoolmaster* in which Rancière describes the subjection of the will of the student to the will of the master. "A person—and a child in particular—may need a master when his own will is not strong enough to set him on track and keep him there. But that subjection is purely one of will over will. It becomes stultification when it links an intelligence to another intelligence. In the act of teaching and learning there are two wills and two intelligences. We will call their coincidence stultification" (1991, 13). If equality of intelligences overcomes enforced stultification, the result is an *enforced equality* that does not seem to leave space for freedom of individual choice. Of course, the categorical imperative of universal teaching is, as stated above, nothing more than the simple command "Follow *your* path" (Rancière 1991, 57). As with Kant, the imperative uttered from above is, in the last instance, nothing more than our *own* path, our *own* maxim directed at ourselves. Thus to resist such a command would be tantamount to rejecting one's own path. In fact, genius for Rancière is only possible through the direction and actualization of the will according to this path. "'I can't,'" is for Rancière, "a sentence of self-forgetfulness, a sentence from which the reasonable individual has withdrawn" (1991, 57). In sum, the student has *no choice not to will, not to follow his or her path.*

Rancière's "emancipatory" teaching sounds uncannily like Kant's own educational philosophy. In his discussion of ethical education, Kant stresses the teaching of maxims rather than discipline. Whereas discipline lacks universality (and thus is an arbitrary imposition), maxims are recognized by the students as inherently good because of their appeal to pure reason. To form the foundations of an ethical character, students should be taught to act in accordance to maxims. As such the first lesson of ethical education is obedience. This obedience, according to Kant (2003 [1899]), has two features, "including absolute obedience to his [sic] master's commands, and obedience to what he feels to be a good and reasonable will" (86). These two forms of obedience—absolute and voluntary—are necessarily connected as they are in Rancière's writings: the commands of the teacher are categorical and imperative, a relation of will to will, and thus embody the very principle of the universal law. The absolute embodies the voluntary, and the voluntary is made concrete through the command of the teacher.

Certainly, Rancière's work on equality has had a major impact in education which cannot be underestimated. As Gert Biesta argues (2008), Rancière has enabled theorists to rethink what emancipation means in education. For Biesta, the contradictions in educational emancipation are threefold. First, more often than not emancipatory education constitutes unequal dependencies in the act of emancipating. In this sense, equality seems perpetually deferred. Second, the starting point for all emancipatory education is the presupposition of inequality. Yet, as Rancière insists, the moment inequality is presupposed, the educator and student are trapped within its deadly circle, unable to escape from the eternal return of hierarchical distributions of roles. Finally, although emancipation is done in the "best interests" of those involved, it is done with a suspicion or distrust concerning the beliefs, knowledges, and experiences of those being emancipated. If Biesta emphasizes emancipation and equality, then I would argue that emancipation is a much more complex concept, one that equally includes the question of freedom.

It is only by returning to the question of the dramaturgy of education that we can clarify the role of freedom in Rancière's depiction of universal teaching. While Rancière at times wavers too far into the terrain of Kant's second critique and its paradoxical notion of freedom in relation to the universal maxim, the theatrical nature of emancipation takes a startlingly different path. If the form of the maxim appears in universal teaching, we must read this appearance as a *parody* of the law, as a comedy that appropriates the law in order to suspend the law. In this sense, there is something anarchistic in universal teaching precisely at the moment when it most approximates the form of a maxim. The theatrical "as if ..." is performed *as not* the categorical "as if ..." of the law. These formulations neighbor one another in a kind of profanation where the two are simultaneously distinct and inseparable, where the law is suspended at precisely the moment it is parodied. While Rancière seems to privilege the latter over the former, I would argue that it is the near distance of the pair that best captures the politics of theatre and the theatre of education. Parody turns obedience into comedic performance, mastery into ignorance, duty into a profane, anarchic stage and the good will into the theatrical will to perform roles without the guarantee of a legislator. Thus the theatricality of education redeems freedom at the precise moment when it seems lost in Rancière's glissade into Kant's critique of practical reason. It is only through the aesthetics of education that we are able to stay true to the politics of education as such, and in turn offer a radical new practice of universal teaching that exists despite all laws.

Freire on Freedom and Authority

If it is striking how absent any discussion of freedom is in Rancière's political, aesthetic, and educational work, then it is equally striking how prevalent it is in Freire's. The strongest emphasis on freedom is found, not surprisingly, in one of his final works titled *Pedagogy of Freedom* (2001a)—a book that is a decisive polemic against neoliberal impositions on teachers and educators. But with the emphasis on freedom at the exclusion of equality, an equally thin notion of emancipation ultimately emerges, one that reinstitutes the authority of the teacher over the student. As I will argue, this return to the problem of expert authority is actually unnecessary for Freire, who provides two alternative arguments for democratic freedom without the need for reliance on such a hierarchy. Yet, because Freire never fully tackles the problem of the relation between equality and freedom, the problematic nature of his formulation of authority is never fully addressed. The result is a reaffirmation of an authority that is largely unnecessary according to the internal logic of his own argument for freedom. I will end with a turn to theatre as a possible solution to this problem. If Freire accepts a certain notion of education as a beautiful aesthetic form, it is only in the sublime dimension of theatre as an impro-visational and spontaneous rupture with the beautiful that equality can be maintained alongside Freire's emphatic plea for freedom.

In his work, Freire makes it abundantly clear that pedagogy for emancipation is always a "pedagogy of autonomy" that "should be centered on experiences that stimulate decision making and responsibility" (2001a, 98). Freedom is fundamental to Freire as long as it is accompanied by the realization that every act of freedom implies an ethical responsibility for that act. In this way, Freire is not endorsing some sort of abstract or limitless freedom. Freedom is constrained by the burden of responsi-bility. Thus Freire writes, "... it is essential to the learning experience of decision making that the consequences of any decision be assumed by the decision maker" (2001a, 97). The first constraint on freedom is *internal* to freedom itself in that the consequences for any action will produce further actions that may or may not be intended and for which the subject must take responsibility. Students should be allowed to take risks because risks demonstrate how actions produce unforeseen consequences that we ultimately have to take responsibility for. As opposed to Kantian non-consequentialism, here it is the result which matters most, not the intention. In fact, it is the *aesthetic* effects of actions that concern Freire the most. We must bear responsibility for any harm done to the *beauty* of the world, the sentiments that bind community together, and the recognition of shared interests.

But apparently this first constraint on limitless freedom is not strong enough for Freire, who quickly offers a second. Freedom reaches a certain limit when it enters into the sphere of exchange with other freedoms. Here Freire argues "freedom becomes mature in confrontation with other freedoms" (2001a, 97). In this passage, Freire suggests that in an intersubjective world of actors, two freedoms interacting with one another will place certain limits on possible actions. The confrontation thus described is one of mutual *confrontation* and thus is an agonistic form of politics. The equality of freedoms, where each person's individual freedoms necessitate interrelations with other freedoms, creates the possibility for a shared world but also for political struggles between competing claims to freedom. These claims in turn are enunciated as competing rights and struggles for institutional recognition.

Thus far, the two arguments for constraining limitless freedom are internal to freedom itself. In particular, the latter argument suggests that the *equality* of freedoms circulating in society will result in a kind of dialectical sublation through agonistic confrontation. Yet because Freire separates the question of freedom from that of equality, he quickly misses his own insight and turns to another limitation of absolute freedom: the expertise of authority. From the equality of freedoms—an anarchic notion for sure—to the call for a necessary inequality in the form of the judicious use of authority, Freire slides into an argument for hierarchical dependencies outside of the contestation of freedom by and through freedom. It is this move that reestablishes the authority of the teacher over and above the freedom of the student. The question of freedom then becomes a question of *justifying* the inequality inherent in the claim to authority and the *nature* of this authority. And with this displacement, the agonistic politics of disagreement internal to the clash of competing freedoms becomes the administration of risks by an informed, competent educator.

It might appear to be strange to argue that Freire's pedagogy of the oppressed lacks a concept of equality. Freire is, after all, famous for stating

"The teacher is no longer merely the-one-who-teaches, but one who is himself taught in dialogue with the students, who in turn while being taught also teach. ... In the process, arguments based on 'authority' are no longer valid" (2001b, 80). As if to stop any misunderstandings, Freire insistently argues for fidelity not only to freedom but also to authority *on the side of* freedom. Freedom can only be safeguarded by the judicious use of authority. The pedagogy of autonomy is also a pedagogy of inequality. Freire summarizes as follows: "What I have sought always is to live the tension, the contradiction, between authority and freedom so as to maintain respect for both. To separate them is to provoke the infraction of one or the other" (2001a, 99). The proper use of authority safeguards the freedom of the student while also directing it, "advising" its development. Freire refers to such authority as "democratic authority" (2001a, 86) because it (a) respects the freedom of students and their right to take risks, (b) is informed by professional competence, (c) remains humble and generous with students, (d) has self-confidence/self-respect, and (e) is never afraid to expose itself to critique. In this formulation, democratic authority might be on the side of freedom, but still remains antagonistic to it. Thus democracy is seen as an agonistic struggle, and freedom and authority (even an authority that exists only in an advisory capacity) remains combative.

Yet this emphasis on the politics of freedom as a struggle against authority is once again eclipsed in Freire's work by a turn to the notion of the beautiful. Rather than a confrontation of necessary opposites, Freire also proposes that the pedagogy of the oppressed is a "harmony between authority and freedom" that resists the "tyranny of freedom and the tyranny of exacerbated authority" (2001a, 83). If there was a productive tension between freedom and authority, it is now, in the last instance, replaced by "harmony," erasing any residual contradiction. This beautiful harmony between authority and freedom is no longer the agonism of freedom confronting freedom, nor is it the agonism of freedom confronting authority. The inequality between teacher and student is not an infringement on the freedoms of the student precisely because of this harmony—the teacher's solidarity with the student erases the power differential between wills in a moment of beautiful symmetry. If universal teaching is a command without expert authority, then here Freire offers us *expert authority without command.* No command is needed when there is already a harmony between freedom and authority guaranteed by the self-critical yet competent knowledge of the teacher and his or her political solidarity with the oppressed to overcome their limit situations. This description sounds strikingly similar to any number of liberal pleas for an enlightened form of representative democracy. In both cases, the freedom of the masses must be granted but only through a certain inequality predicated on expertise or specialized knowledge that determines which risks are acceptable for students to take, what counts as professional competence, what virtues determine ethical and political purity, and which forms of knowledge count as critical.

Commentators, especially those from within the field of critical pedagogy, are quick to point out that Freire's project does not simply abandon the question of authority but rehabilitates it for struggling teachers. Although Henry Giroux complicates conservative notions of authority and universalist notions of certainty, he ardently speaks to the need for critical educators to "fashion an alternative and emancipatory view of authority" that "legitimates schools as democratic, public spheres and teachers as transformative intellectuals who work towards a realization of their views of community, social justice, empowerment, and social reform" (2005, 72–3). In sum, Giroux's emancipatory authority "suggests that teachers are bearers of critical knowledge, rules, and values through which they consciously articulate and problematize their relationship to each other, to students, to subject matter, and to the wider community" (2005, 90). Giroux is attempting to rehabilitate the notion of authority as critical expertise through a different theory of authorial activation in the name of democracy and freedom. In this sense, Giroux follows Freire's clarification of the relationship between freedom and authority in relation to the current struggles of teachers in the United States against the bureaucratization of their intellectual work. While this clarification might be empowering to teachers who struggle against the instrumentalization of their profession, it once again creates an inequality not only between teacher and student but between the professional and novice. In other words, if professional teachers need to see themselves as empowered intellectual cultural workers, this project simultaneously dismisses the radical possibility of universal teaching which can be done anywhere by anyone regardless of expertise or training. Once again, inequality becomes a necessary tool for the critical pedagogue to safeguard the freedom not only of students but also of teachers.

If Rancière's emphasis on equality represses the question of freedom, then in Freire's work we see a perfectly symmetrical operation whereby equality is repressed in the name of freedom. And as with Rancière, the problem with Freire's argument is that he does not hold true to his own intonations of the dramaturgy of pedagogy. In Rancière's case, the main problem was with the glissade from performance to duty/obedience, from hypothesis to maxim. Thus we see a betrayal of the performativity of subjectivation. In Freire's case, the main problem becomes a misunderstanding of the script of universal teaching. As discussed previously the script is improvisational, and thus no expert knowledge is reserved for the ignorant schoolmaster. The radical equality of the script is written by all the performers simultaneously with the performance. All actors have the freedom to play multiple roles and take multiple risks. The only constraint on these risks is the aleatory clashing of atoms, the confrontation of freedoms that appear between actors. In this way, the freedom of this script is not limitless but rather has certain parameters created by the multiple voices that form on the stage. In such a script, there is always room for interruption by the no-count, by those who have no place on stage, who have no authorial expertise to play the role of teacher or student. Thus the stage is itself a ground for dispute. If the teacher has a special role it is to invite dispute over what can be seen or heard through gestures of placing and pointing that interrupt any partitioning of the sensible into "harmonious" parts. This is a sublime staging of agonisms rather than a harmony of authority and freedom. It is only by returning to the theatrical model of performance, staging, and scripting that Freire's insight into the *internal* and *autonomous* limits on freedom can be fully appreciated and redeemed for educational practice.

The Educational and Political Importance of the Theatrical Turn

In conclusion, we can use Rancière and Freire to test the aesthetics of pedagogical dramatization. While both authors provide important insights into equality and freedom, when these two problematics are separated and divided, the result is an impoverished notion of emancipation. Emancipation recedes from its political horizon when freedom is sacrificed for equality or equality is sacrificed for freedom. The result, for Rancière, is a notion of acting "as if ..." that comes dangerously close to being captured by the abstract law of reason, and, for Freire, a notion of freedom that temporarily forgets its power to challenge authority in the name of its own dynamic autonomy. To think emancipation as a kind of theatrical improvisation is to think the tension of freedom and equality as a constant struggle, where the equilibrium that is achieved within a political community is also ripe with the possibilities for its own contingent undoing in the moment of dissensus.

Yet questions remain. Why does the student obey the ignorant schoolmaster if the command is nothing more than a parody of the law rather than the law itself? While scholars such as Jason E. Smith (2011) have argued that Rancière decouples mastery from the question of intelligence while maintaining the form of command and obedience, I would suggest that such an argument precisely misses the parodic quality of the ignorant schoolmaster. This parodic performance of mastery reserved for the "expert" introduces a gap between wills while at the same time offering a disruption to the fetishization of mastery found in Althusser's public pedagogy. But when this gap is introduced through parody, the question of motivation is only heightened. Certainly for Kant, the subject acts out of respect for the law. But the question of motivation is not so clear for Rancière and his description of universal teaching. Once the law becomes a parody, it would seem that "respect" to the "dignity" of the command of the ignorant schoolmaster is also thrown out the window. In the next chapter, I will argue that the gap between command and obedience that is opened by the parodic turn necessitates an aesthetic solution. The missing motivational mechanism here is curiosity—not simply as an aesthetic response but also as an educational opening to willful pursuit. Curiosity is not simply a passive, sensual affliction or simply a personal interest but is an aesthetic force which poses a certain challenge to the will. Thus the challenge to the will comes not from a command external to the student but from the affective passion of curiosity which redistributes what can and cannot be sensed. Consequently, the will takes up the challenge of curiosity by performing the "as if ..." (engendering a chain of equivalences between intelligences). In this manner, universal teaching helps students recognize the dynamic movement between curiosity and theatrical will as the space and time of freedom *and* equality.

Chapter Four:

The Aesthetics of Curiosity

We cannot, therefore, cooperate with people who openly state that the workers are too uneducated to emancipate themselves and must first be freed from above by philanthropic big bourgeois and petty bourgeois.
— *Karl Marx*, Selected Works, *Vol. 3, 94*

Curiouser and curiouser!
— *Lewis Carroll*, Alice's Adventures in Wonderland

Often when I am teaching philosophy of education, my students begin the process of inquiry by prefacing their questions with something along the lines of "I'm just curious, but ..." Why do we feel compelled as teachers and as students to express our curiosity as *just* curiosity? Perhaps there is a slight embarrassment in proclaiming our curiosity, which, in its strongest formulation, appears to be too assertive, too aggressive, or too inappropriate to speak in public in front of others. In this sense, curiosity is itself problematic, something to be slightly ashamed of. Or are we afraid that our teachers and our classmates will think that our questions are motivated by something more than mere curiosity, or less than, like stupidity? The assumption here is the exact reverse of the former argument. Here it is curiosity that is innocent, naïve, and pure while all other possible motivations for asking questions are somehow perverse or tainted by questionable assumptions or ulterior ends. In fact, we can position this second explanation within a larger historical framework. In *Wonders and the Order of Nature* (2001), Lorraine Daston and Katharine Park chart an important historical shift from an emphasis on pre-modern wonder to the curiosity of the natural sciences. With this fundamental paradigm shift, wonder becomes increasingly disreputable as a popular, amateurish, and childish passion as opposed to the rational, credible, and educated characteristics of modern, enlightened curiosity. The passion, revulsion, and wonderment of inquiry into strange, seemingly unexplainable facts are thus replaced by disinterested, Cartesian doubt and curiosity in the regularities of nature. The phrase "just curious" indicates a "tamed," "safe," "reasonable," or "gentrified" form of wonder that emphasizes its distance from the passions and thus from any notion of sensorial contamination.

While the problem of confronting "just curiosity" is of general concern, it forms the central epistemological question driving Paulo Freire's *Pedagogy of the Oppressed*. If there is a philosophy of mind in Freire's work, it must begin from a careful analysis of curiosity as the central cognitive process that either enables or disables critical consciousness raising. To begin to understand Freire's work and how he posses his project against *just* curiosity, we can follow two lines of investigation. Recently, the work of Daniel Cho (2005b) has problematized the ontological dimension of Freire's analysis of curiosity. For Freire, we are all born with "spontaneous curiosity" (2001a, 83) that is then either transformed into "epistemological curiosity" through critical pedagogy or "anesthetized" (1997, 100) by banking pedagogy. Importantly this notion of naïve or spontaneous curiosity is inherently linked to our ontological unfinishedness. "This [ontological] incompleteness implies for us a permanent movement of search" (Freire 2001a, 57) that is directed through our curiosity toward the world. If dialogic/problem-posing education raises this innately curious disposition to the level of epistemological reflection on the relation between self and world, then banking education puts such curiosity to sleep (an ideological slumber for sure) through the cognitive and affective "bureaucratizing of the mind" (Freire 2001a, 111). For Cho, Freire's mistake lies in his recourse to ontological arguments concerning curiosity. Cho proposes a provocative counter-model that founds curiosity in a traumatic event rather than human nature—thus shifting Freire's materialism from ontological considerations of the human to language and signification.

However, my project takes aim at another key assumption in Freire's argument: his connection between curiosity and epistemology. In what follows, I will argue that curiosity is better located on the register of aesthetics. The implications for this shift will be examined through the work of Rancière, whose reflections on the politics of aesthetics provide us with a counter-measure to Freire's interpretation of curiosity. Stated simply, for Freire, intelligence is essentially the critical capacity for unmasking, whereas for Rancière, it is a poetic capacity for translation. In the end, I propose that curiosity in any form is always implicated in politics, and that the politics of curiosity concern the distribution of the visible and the invisible, the audible and the inaudible. It is by rethinking the relationship between curiosity and politics through both Freire and Rancière that we can begin to understand how a critical intervention into the world is not simply the unveiling of social reality through critical consciousness raising but rather a redistribution of the sensual through perceptual alternation.

In a previous chapter, I utilized Rancière's theory to problematize the aesthetic form of Freire's pedagogical event. I will now turn to Freire's theory of learning with particular attention paid to the question of curiosity, epistemology, and aesthetics. The goal is to recapture the emancipatory spirit of Freire's project through a rehabilitation and reworking of certain elements in his theory that move us from critique to poetics, from unveiling to invention, and from epistemology to aesthetics. In turn, emphasis on curiosity as an *educational issue* connects two disconnected concepts in Rancière's work: his reflec-tions on curiosity in the aesthetic experience and the role of will in education.

Sensing Curiosity

As stated above, Freire's critical consciousness raising project unfolds through the development and evolution of spontaneous curiosity into epistemological curiosity. In this section of the chapter, I examine and unfold this logic more carefully in order to explicate the internal relationship between Freire's theory of curiosity, his epistemological claims, and his project of consciousness raising. Because human beings are ontologically incomplete, they have a curious disposition toward the world. This fundamental disposition is equally apparent for Freire in peasants as well as in scientists, both of whom discover and experiment with their environments. But it is through the process of a dialogic and democratic pedagogy that this ingenious or spontaneously occurring form of curiosity "becomes capable of self-criticism" (Freire 2001a, 37). Through dialogue, our collectively spontaneous and thus naturally occurring curious dispo-sitions become intensified and refined, bolstering native processes with "methodological exactitude" (2001a, 37). Indeed, Freire argues that naïve curiosity is transformed into epistemological reflection on the self and the world, and that this transformation is "one of the primordial tasks of progressive education" (2004b, 91). Summarizing this primordial task, Freire writes:

Curiosity, intrinsic to the vital experience, deepens and improves in the world of human existence. Disquieted by the world outside of the self, startled by the unknown, by mystery, driven by a desire to know, to unveil what is hidden, to seek an explanation for the facts, to verify, to investigate in order to apprehend—curiosity is the engine for the process of knowing. Directed or intended toward an object, curiosity makes it possible to apprehend the constitutive notes of that object and to produce an understanding of it ... (2004b, 87)

In other words, curiosity a) unveils what is hidden by everyday appearances, b) seeks explanations for certain phenomena, and c) leads to an understanding of these phenomena through a process of knowing. In other words, Freire has a rather traditional theory of knowledge. Through the agreement of knowledge with its object, we can come to know external reality. Epistemological curiosity is the faculty that enables us to come in contact with this reality, with the manifold, and thus build an understanding based on a methodologically rigorous investigation. On this view, curiosity is "directed" by and through a conscious intention to apprehend the world. Although the move from curiosity to investigation to knowledge is a rather abstract or generic model, in most of Freire's work this process is cast in decisively critical and political terms. Thus the process of unveiling becomes that of ideological critique, the explanation for phenomena becomes the explanation of oppression and exploitation, and finally the knowledge that emerges is a revolutionary and critical knowledge.

While it is not uncommon for Freirian scholars to make the claim that there are in fact two Freires—an earlier more Marxist Freire and a later much more postmodern Freire—the retention of an emphasis on the unveiling of objects behind appearances remains attached—either directly or indirectly—to Freire's earlier claim that dialogic pedagogy promotes the examination of "scientific bases" (1996, 86) for supporting political actions and ethical interventions. Thus, when Freire writes, "Theories considering liberation as a given fact of history, or basing it exclusively on scientific knowledge, never excited me very much" (1997, 87), he is arguing against positivist science as the objective interpretation of "facts" without comprehension of these facts within the context of history and of social struggle. This approach to science is to be contrasted with the "methodological rigor that takes knowledge from the level of *common sense* to that of scientific knowledge ... allow[ing] for a greater or lesser *precision* in the knowledge produced or found through our epistemological quest" (Freire 1997, 97). Freire's second notion of science is an endorsement of *critical* science mediated through an understanding of history and an ethico-political appreciation for the struggles of the oppressed. Freire also refers to this science as a "dialectical" science that moves "beyond the common-sense understanding of how the society works" (Horton and Freire 1990, 101). As Freire writes, epistemological curiosity and its scientific rigor enable us to "seek the reason for being of facts" (1997, 94) through the "unveiling of hidden truths" (97) within the complexity of our historical location. This truth must be unveiled because it has been "hidden" by ideological distortions and colonialist cultural invasion. Such distortions are internalized and rendered natural or transparent by the oppressed who are then led to believe in the fatalism of the present over the potentiality of the future.

Schooling has played a crucial role in this mystification process. Banking education works to "conceal certain facts which explain the way human beings exist in the world" (Freire 2001a, 83). Once hidden, the world recedes from our apprehension, and curiosity is decisively put to sleep. In this scenario, curiosity becomes *just* curious, not in terms of innocence but rather in terms of complicity with the order of things. *Just* curious is a form of anaesthetized curiosity that resigns itself to the status quo. The "just" in "just curious" indicates a compliance with a dominant reality principle thereby concealing a deeper, more critically attuned truth which is bolstered and guaranteed by the facts of our ontological condition. The (unconscious) sensation of transgressing this social order remains latent in the promise of curiosity itself. Thus in the phrase "just curious," we hear the simultaneous disavow of curiosity (it is *just* curiosity after all) and the unavoidable guilt in the confession that curiosity remains even if in an anaesthetized state.

The world is thus conceived of as ideologically mired in illusion and mystification only to be uncovered by the methodological rigor that defines epistemological curiosity. Dialogical and problem-posing education is an attempt to reawaken curiosity, which "requires that the world be unveiled" (2001b, 169). In fact, in a moment that sounds surprisingly similar to Georg Lukacs' theory of the vanguard party (see Lewis 2007), Freire argues, "... leftist parties must become truly pedagogical instruments ... authenticat[ing] themselves through the effort of unveiling truths" (1997, 52–3). Whether the party or the teacher, an external supplement is necessary in order to reconnect curiosity to the critical science of unveiling and apprehending the world. Summarizing, Freire argues, "Studying is, above all, thinking about experience, and thinking about experience is the best way to think accurately" (1985a, 3). Thinking accurately about one's experience is to rediscover the "class knowledge" (Freire 2004a, 18) specific to the location of the oppressed within the social relations of oppression—a knowledge linked to the laborer's "syntax and rhythm" (19) within the system of oppression. He writes, "Educands' concrete localization is the point of departure for the knowledge they create of the world" (2004a, 72). It is this knowledge that Freire privileges as necessary to the "political struggle for the transformation of the concrete conditions in which oppression prevails" (1997, 23). Set defiantly against the mythologization of the world, conscientization as the critical appraisal of experience is the ability to think accurately and precisely from one's location in the relations of production. The accuracy and precision of critical consciousness raising involve the theorization of class knowledge as the primary starting point for comprehending the world as agonistic.

For Freire, the educator must undertake extensive research within the community in order to pull from the general, everyday language, generative words that are phonically rich, psychologically meaningful, and capable of encapsulating the social reality of the oppressed. The generative words will, in turn, act as a platform for problem-posing dialogue and the literacy process. Thus curiosity is awakened through a set of words, drawn from the linguistic practices of the oppressed, that embody their interests in social transformation, and that produce new narratives beyond the fatalism instilled through banking education. These words *reflect* their class knowledge, their class interests, and their class mission to overcome limit situations in the name of humanization and emancipation. Through these generative words, Freire glimpses the world of the oppressed (both in its present needs and its future, revolutionary potential), organizes this world into a clear set of themes and codifications, and in turn initiates a process of consciousness-raising.

From this brief overview we can draw a series of conclusions that are central to Freire's philosophy of mind. First, the world is distorted through ideological mystification that puts curiosity to sleep—in other words, renders all curiosity into *just* curiosity as a domesticated curiosity consigned to the fatalism of the perpetual, ahistorical present and to scientific positivism that equates actuality with rationality. In this state, curiosity is reduced to the confines of gossip, fashion, technological fetishism, and other mundane aspects of existence that deflect our focus from pressing political, economic, and social struggles to realize freedom from oppression. Second, it is the goal of problem-posing dialogue and critical literacy to help us shift from anaesthetized curiosity to epistemological curiosity which methodologically unveils the world so as to "think accurately" and "precisely" about experience from the standpoint of class knowledge. Third, this new scientific basis for thinking enables a new formulation of theory in practice and practice in theory that has the potential to transform the social relations that have created the preconditions for ideological mystification. The expulsion of imposed cultural myths enables the decodification of the world through generative words and attending themes and in the process returns curiosity to its rightful place as *the* revolutionary cognitive faculty.

While Freire is no stranger to the sensuality of knowing and learning, it is important to read him to the letter and understand problem-posing education as "above all" learning to cognize the world and the word "accurately" according to class knowledge. As such, we must pose the question of the relation between science, aesthetics and curiosity. To move from fatalism to hope and, in turn, acquiescence to activism, an aesthetic supplement is needed. Freire argues that anaesthetized curiosity creates a "narration sickness" (2001a, 71) in the oppressed as a form of imaginary fatalism. A new narrative must be produced that anchors the creative powers of the oppressed within a utopian horizon. Freire ultimately frames his own theoretical project in terms of an aesthetic refusal of fatalism "and its inflexible negation of the right to dream differently, to dream utopia" (2001a, 22). In fact, Freire argues, "... the necessary process from ingenuous to critical curiosity should also be accompanied by a rigorous ethical formation side by side with an aesthetic appreciation" (2001a, 38). What is interesting in this quote is that development of epistemological curiosity must be accompanied by aesthetic appreciation or an appreciation for the aesthetic dimension of liberatory existence. In other words, while appearing to be of equal importance, epistemological curiosity and aesthetics, unveiling and narrativizing, are separate functions or separate dimensions of educational experience. Epistemological curiosity does not "refuse to consider the aesthetic" but rather "avails itself of it" (Freire 1997, 96) in order to enrich the pleasurability of consciousness-raising and of our appreciation for human potentiality. In other words, curiosity has an epistemological function of clarifying the world as it really is and which takes advantage of a supplementary aesthetic pleasure. Availing is not only a separate process but also proceeds *after* the scientific unveiling of the world. Freire summarizes, "Through methodological curiosity, the reading of the world can lead to moving beyond *conjecture* per se to a *vision for the world*" (2004b, 18). Here we move from unveiling to narrativizing, from conjecture (aesthetic illusion) to utopia (epistemologically rigorous and scientifically precise understanding of the potentiality of reality for transformation). Summarizing this relationship, Freire writes, "World transformation requires dreaming, but the indispensable authenticity of that dream depends on the faithfulness of those who dream to their historic and material circumstances and to the levels of technological scientific development of their context" (2004b, 32). Class consciousness needs a dream to animate action, and this dream only becomes "authentic" when it is related to a critical comprehension of the limits and possibilities of particular historical contexts. The aesthetic event of vision is the *imaginative* supplement to scientific unveiling.

Vision's own aesthetic possibilities enable us to "add to it [i.e., the world] something of our own making" (2001a, 38). Science without this supplement lacks a motivational dimension—it is simply critique. Hope demands the narrative pleasure of that which is possible yet absent in the present. Thus the aesthetic supplement to science adds not simply a vision for the world but also a motivation to achieve this new vision: hope in the promise of pleasure/happiness. Here beauty of a possible future liberation produces the affective lure—hope—needed for activism. It is only in this revolutionary future that appearance can be reconciled with ontology. In short, Freire seems to argue that (a) aesthetics and science are distinct yet connected and (b) that aesthetic narrativization follows the unveiling of reality in order to (c) add an imaginative vision of future possibilities to critique. Epistemological curiosity enables us to examine with precision while in turn the imagination allows us to narrate these scientific findings into a political vision of action.

If critique without aesthetic narrative misses the mark, then so too does aesthetic narrative without the scientific accuracy and precision of class knowledge. For Freire, aesthetic narrative uninformed by a critical and scientific apprehension of the world results in ideological distortion or mystification. For instance, banking education for Freire is an indoctrination into a regime of images that mask reality by universalizing the class interests of the oppressors. Freire writes, "banking education … attempts, by mythicizing reality, to conceal certain facts which explain the way human beings exist in the world" (2001b, 83). A mythologized consciousness is in fact the internalization of the "image of the oppressor" (Freire 2001b, 47) to such a point that "the oppressed want at any cost to resemble the oppressors, to imitate them, to follow them" (2001b, 62). Imitation leads the oppressed to become "prisoners of artifice" (Freire 1998, 113), which leads to "narration sickness" (Freire 2001b, 71) or the *inability to accurately think* through the conditions of oppression. Ideology is, in other words, a set of images detached from the truth of social relations, leading to misidentifications of the oppressed with the oppressor (imitation).

Yet, when Freire separates science from aesthetics, epistemology from affect, and sets them in a linear (if not causal) relation, there are paradoxical results that enable stultification to return through the backdoor. Here are two short examples of the educational and political ramification of this philosophical distinction. In a telling example, Freire recalls a study of peasant families in and around Recife. Surprisingly, Freire discovered that families along the Pontas de Pedra coast told "legends of individual freedom" (2004a, 12). The "fishers' fantastic stories" were informed by an active "imagination" that contradicted how "unfree they really were" (Freire 2004a, 13). Here Freire reduces the belief in freedom to mere delusion concealing the "truth" of their unfreedom. He cannot accept that their belief is anything more than a delusion of false appearances informed by mythological legends and fantastic imagination that does not correspond to the truth of their implicit class knowledge. Thus under the exclamation of a freedom which the oppressed are not supposed to have, Freire symptomatically detects the signs of a more objective oppression that waits for the dialogue with the educator to be fully awakened. Ironically, the first obstacle to revolutionary critical consciousness raising is not so much narrative sickness or internalization of the ideologies of the oppressors but rather the spontaneous ideology of the fishers themselves—an ideology that *imitates* the freedoms that are supposed to occur *only after* a teleological struggle for liberation. In other words, the fishers, like the poets in Plato's *Republic*, do not think what they should think, and it is this confusion between their historical location and their actions that threatens to undermine the dialectical contradiction that critical consciousness is supposed to reveal. Dialogue is necessary to reorient curiosity in order to pinpoint the gap in the fishers' epistemological knowledge by piercing the veil of illusion that binds the oppressed to naïve imaginings. What is problematic here is the dismissal of the legends as mere distortions denying "the truth" rather than as claims that could be used to verify the freedom of the fishers within yet against the most oppressive of systems. Read differently, the fishers could embody what Charles Bingham and Gert Biesta (2010) refer to as an "agnostic relationship" to epistemological truth that embraces the poetic possibility of democracy as a staging, a performance that verifies equality *in spite of* "objective truths." Yet it is this agnostic and heretic relation to truth that Freire misses.

Second, an educator once recalled a story to Freire wherein a peasant proclaimed: "We have something very important to tell you, new friend. If you're here to teach us that we're exploited, don't bother. We know that already" (2004a, 58). It is interesting to note that Freire seems to miss the point of this exchange. Rather than hear a proclamation of equal understanding of the structures of oppression, he focuses on the "wealth" of the peasant's "symbolism" and a respect for the lyricism of their language. Reducing this statement of equal understanding and epistemological clarity to aesthetic appreciation both (a) recognizes the politics of aesthetic form while simultaneously (b) de-politicizing the actual content of the statement. Freire's tribute to the poetic language of the oppressed is thus a paradoxical instantiation of what Rancière refers to as "exclusion by homage" (Rancière 2004c, xxvi) wherein respect coincides with a paternalistic approach to education. In other words, the gap between the educator and the educand is sustained through the gesture that separates epistemology and aesthetics (i.e., renders the latter external and inferior to the former). Stated differently, the very emphasis on the wealth and symbolism of the aesthetics of the oppressed is predicated on Rancière's description of the "axiom of inequality" whose logic assumes that there is a distinction between two types of intelligence: "for children and common minds there are stories, for rational beings there are reasons" (Bingham, Biesta, and Rancière 2010, 4). Certainly Freire would want to support Rancière's fundamental "hypothesis of confidence" (Rancière 2010b, 173) in the capacity for equal intelligence, but at the same time, the division between science and aesthetics subtly yet importantly replays itself in the classroom between two types of knowing that are placed in decisively *hierarchical* relation to one another.

In other words, the division between science and aesthetics all too easily allows Freire to dismiss the stories of freedom told by the fishers as mere illusions lacking a scientific basis in class knowledge. And, shockingly, the same division enables Freire to dismiss claims of scientific knowledge as merely aesthetic statements conveying the beauty of the language of the oppressed. When aesthetics and epistemology are split and set in a causal relation (where narrativization must follow from proper naming or else delusion is sure to set in), so too are social divisions reconstituted in the very gesture of respect that was meant to level such divisions in the first place.

It is my contention that Freire's fleeting comments on the relation between curiosity and aesthetics are provocative challenges that have the potential to radically alter our understanding of the function of curiosity in critical pedagogy and thus have the potential to move beyond this aporia. Rather than an add-on to the process of epistemological clarity and its methodological rigor, a rethinking of aesthetics as *internal* to curiosity *as such* enables us to shift gears from "unveiling" to "creative invention" in a much more convincing manner than Freire's original conceptual frame allows. This shift enables us to overcome the symptomological analysis of the speech of the educand which reduced what the fishers said to mere aesthetic illusion. But in order to explore the implications of curiosity—as creative and generative rather than clarifying—we have to once again return to Rancière, whose theory of the aesthetics of politics will demonstrate the need for the critical pedagogue to understand the central role played by aesthetic experience in the disturbance of the partitioning of the sensible relations between teachers and students—a disturbance that opens up the possibility of new narratives and new, unexpected subjectivations.

The Aesthetics of Curiosity

In his most recent work, Rancière offers a radically different understanding of curiosity than found in Freire's model. For Rancière, curiosity does not concern the critique of appearance but rather the redistribution of appearance under the sign of equality. In other words, curiosity does not unveil a deeper, hidden meaning to the order of things but rather interrupts the distribution of things themselves. Second, whereas Freire posits science and narrative as necessary yet separate dimensions, Rancière problematizes any a priori division between science and narrative. And, third, overcoming this division reorients education from a utopian horizon to the active aesthetic performance of the theatrical will in the here and now. Yet, what is most peculiar in Rancière's work is that curiosity remains a strictly aesthetic sensitivity or affliction and thus lacks a connection to his educational theory. The repercussions of this conceptual gap in Rancière's educational reflections are felt in the margins. For instance, Rancière writes, "Jacotot's 'ignorant schoolmaster' sets in motion a scholar's logic, one that pursues the world of knowledge on the basis of a small number of fundamental data, those of a human mind that is identical in each speaking subject" (2011d, 42). Although Rancière's writings on education detail the function of the will in enabling one to *pursue* the world of knowledge through attentiveness, he has little to say concerning the more fundamental moment of *setting in motion* the scholar's logic. My central claim is that curiosity is the *enlivening* of attention while the will *sustains* this attention through the difficulties of the pursuit. Although curiosity only appears in Rancière's writings on aesthetics and the emancipated spectator, and will only appear in his writings on the emancipated student, it is my contention that Rancière's fundamental thesis of the ignorant schoolmaster as a kind of artist opens up the possibility for articulating the two. When the teacher places the book in front of the student to translate, this gesture is more than a simple command to be obeyed and the book is more than simply a pedagogical device. The scene that is enacted is an artistic staging of a scene of emancipation. As such, the book becomes an art object, eliciting the curiosity of the student who is both actor and learner. When viewed from this perspective, the work of the will (the effort needed to attend to one's studies) is dependent upon yet distinct from the work of curiosity (as an aesthetic opening to new perceptions). It is the complexity of this relation between capacities that I wish to tease out in the rest of this chapter, and in the process demonstrate how curiosity is a concern and a problem for the ignorant schoolmaster. Thus Freire's insight into the educational centrality of curiosity is critical for rethinking Rancière's project and vice versa.

For Rancière, curiosity is first and foremost aesthetic, "blur[ring] the false obviousness of strategic schemata" (2009c, 104). In other words, curiosity is a peculiar capacity that indicates a faltering in our understanding, a location where the eye "does not know in advance what it sees and thought does not know what it should make of it" (Rancière 2009c, 105). In this sense, curiosity is both the passive, sensual *affliction* of an anomalous detail that resists identification (and thus classification as this type of object, subject, or action) and an active capacity for searching out such details in the first place. The curious gaze does not penetrate below illusion to an obscure reality; rather it is more akin to a glance that reorients the field of the perceptible itself. The "labor of attention" that the curious glance produces is not about unveiling, as in Freire's model, so much as "encircling" (Rancière 2003c, 123) an appearance from another vantage point. Curiosity is the "action of a gaze that turns around and pulls its body along with it toward the place where its truth is in question" (Rancière 2003c, 116). In other words, curiosity is a turning away from the intentionally directed gaze toward a glance that simultaneously pulls us into the void and is pulled by the void. It is a capacity to move beyond the police order and its hierarchical partitioning of the sensible into an atopic space. If the gaze attempts to master from a location of superior knowledge, skill, or methodological rigor, the glance remains ignorant, and thus perpetually curious, perpetually encircling and turning on the lip of the void.

Rancière's vivid description of Irene's psychological state in Roberto Rossellini's film *Europa '51* (1952) clearly maps onto his later theorization of curiosity:

The moment arrives when the call of the void has an effect but no longer makes sense. The time to connect, explain, and heal has passed. Now something else is at stake: to repeat the event, go look somewhere else, see for oneself. This is how one falls into the unrepresentable, into a universe that is no longer the society sociologist and politicians talk about. For there are a finite number of possible statements, of credible ways of putting together a discourse or a set of images about society. And the moment arrives when the border is crossed and one enters into what makes there be sense, which for that very reason does not itself make sense, so that one must continue to walk under the sign of interruption, at the risk of losing the way. (2003c, 117)

Curiosity is a moment when we fall into that which we do not understand and thus glance at the void that exists in surplus of the categories, narratives, and principles of experts and professionals. The void here is not a lack but rather a gap or fissure between sense and sense opened by a strange call—not a call that interpellates us (as in Althusser's (2001) model of subjectivation) but rather a call that "makes no sense" and "interrupts" the smooth, seamless integration of the self into a recognizable social position. The subsequent fall is beyond the time to explain (to make sense), and instead is the exploratory time of going to "see for oneself" what can be done in the absence of grounds, names, and representational content. The fall of curiosity is always a rupture of sense by the anomalous detail—in Irene's case, the question revolving her son's last testimonial before his death—which offers something new and unexpected, a new path or space which is not reducible to the given order of things. The re-presentation of the movement of the curious subject (a fall) is precisely what makes Rossellini's films educational—it is not their political content or their social critique which is important but rather their visual examination of the work of the curious glance as it constantly gets lost (stumbles around) in the enigma of the void. For Irene, the work of curiosity pulls her away from easy answers to her son's suicide. She must leave the professional interpretations of the doctor and the socialist convictions of her cousin, Andrea, in order to follow a curiosity that she both identifies with (it is *her* curiosity) but also exceeds her conscious intentions. It is this strange capacity which is both subjective and pre-subjective, active and passive, responding and eliciting that sets Irene in motion, moving her beyond the frame of medical science or social critique into the atopic world of grace/madness which she finally discovers on her own. As Rancière argues, no longer is Irene invited to gaze "behind things" (to discover a hidden truth beyond appearance) but rather to look "to the side" (2003c, 121) and thus experience a shift in the distribution of the sensible, an aleatory encounter between clashing appearances. If, for Althusser, interpellation is a gesture of turning around, then the gesture of turning to the side is radically different. While the former is an act of identification (comporting the body to a pre-defined subject position), the latter is an act of dis-identification (comporting the body to a void that lacks a proper name).

Rancière describes his own scholarly activity in similar terms. In his attempts to unsettle taken-for-granted Marxist interpretations of working-class culture, he suddenly "stumbled across the famous passage in Book II of *The Republic* where Plato speaks of the workers who have no time to do anything but work, and the passage in Book VI where he criticizes the 'little bald tinker' and those with 'disfigured bodies' and 'battered and mutilated souls' who 'betake themselves to philosophy'" (Rancière 1997, 30). As with Irene, Rancière stumbles across an anomalous detail that pulls him in a new direction, one that enables a new connection to be built between Marxist assumptions and a repressed Platonic inheritance. To stumble or trip over the detail means that such discoveries are unintentional, largely beyond our conscious control. The scholar, like Irene, is an accidental witness to a disruption or disordering of the perceptual world of appearances. Stumbling is a kind of failed gesture, a moment that breaks a line of thought, an intended purpose, or an immediate communication. Yet, as Andrew Hewitt describes in a different context, "Stumbling needs not to be thought of as a loss of footing but rather as a finding of one's feet: it is the act in which the body rights itself by a retraction and the mind becomes aware of the operation of measure and balance—'a secret force'—operating in and through the body" (2005, 89). Rather than a fall, the stumble is a recuperation through a slight movement to the side, an adjustment of the gestures of the body to the appearance of an interruption. As a specific kind of fall, the stumble falls short of itself, enabling the curious subject "to repeat the event" (Rancière 2003c, 117), to circle or retrace it from the side. Simply put, stumbling is the activity of the curious subject—a kind of *spontaneous improvisation* of a script that is written precisely at the moment of its interruption.

The secret ability of the body to recalibrate itself after an interruption/stumble is the first sign of intelligence. Rancière summarizes, "Intelligence's act is to see and to compare what has been seen. It sees first by chance" (1991, 55). The chance collision of atoms, the aleatory event, the sudden loss of one's feet: these are the contingencies or chance happenings that jump-start intelligence. Importantly, intelligence here is not formulated in terms of an explanation or argument, epistemological clarity or exacting apprehension, a set of skills or dispositions. Rather intelligence is recuperation, a shifting of the glance to the side of common sense in order to compare. To be intelligent is to experience the unsettling effects of curiosity on and in our bodily capacities. Rancière's disagreement with Freire becomes clear: the latter emphasizes the consciously directed and deliberate work of education to awaken curiosity and connect it with proper objects and proper goals while the former emphasizes the contingencies of an embodied curiosity to pull and be pulled in unforeseen directions that escape the conscious intentionality of the subject.

In short, *thinking accurately changes to sensing differently, and the educational goal shifts from consciousness-raising to perceptual alternation.* Indeed, curiosity resists both identification of the subject with the image of the oppressor (as in ideological internalization) or with a specific set of interests determined by one's location within the relations of production (as in scientific critique). In both cases, identification attempts to fix, classify, and partition the sensible according to interests defined in advance by the oppressors (who desire nothing less than conformity to the exploitative status quo) or the leftist party (whose class suicide enables it to have the proper political orientation). If for Freire, the oppressed become curious through reflection and discussion of generative words that embody or encapsulate their social, political, and economic reality, then for Rancière, curiosity is turned toward precisely what we do not recognize, to the words that are *not* our own. It always takes us away from our presumed class knowledge, our "objective" class interests, or our familiar ways of talking, behaving, and thinking. Curiosity is in other words a deviation from the revolutionary path prescribed by the Freirian researcher who collects generative words in order to raise consciousness out of ignorance and fatalism toward accurate knowledge and hope. The sensation of curiosity is a "disarticulation" or "disfiguration" of any given order, providing an "experience of unrepresentability" (Panagia 2009, 2) outside of a con*sensual* agreement concerning the proper and improper (who should be doing/believing/saying/feeling what). Curiosity perpetually stumbles into the void at the heart of the order of things and thus suspends our ability to name/identify such and such according to prescribed criteria—it effectively disconnects objects and beliefs by tripping over the detail, remnant, no count.

Returning to the example above we can say that Freire's own curiosity about the "oppressed" remains oddly superficial—merely confirming his existing beliefs and missing the anomalous detail which his own text reveals: that they know how to think about their experience without the help of his pedagogical intervention. In this example, Freire's pedagogical curiosity seems to miss precisely what is political in being curious. For Rancière, all sensory mixing introduces a "democratic excess" into the order of things—an excess that reveals "governors are like the governed, the young like the old, slaves like their masters, pupils like teachers, animals like their masters" (2006c, 38). In other words, democracy thrives on the contamination and heretical mixing that in-distinguishes who can and cannot speak, who can and cannot be seen, as well as the competencies that organize roles in society. Curiosity is precisely the affective perception of the *mark* or *detail* of such in-distinguishing. *To be democratic is to remain curious without the guarantee of a ground or proper knowledge base or generative words.*

Extending Rancière's analysis, I would argue that education is not "thinking accurately" about experience according to class knowledge and class interests, but rather the act of translating senses unleashed through a question posed by an initial curiosity ("What caused me to stumble? How can I retrace (circle back) and understand what happened?"). Curiosity in this sense is not an opening to the critique of appearance in order to gaze upon the truth but rather an opening to what Rancière would call the "poetic labour of translation" (2006c, 10). All translation is the re-partitioning of our perceptions with other perceptions across distances that cannot be sheared up through a pedagogical practice of beautiful collaboration where interests are transparently "witnessed" by the teacher as artist. For Rancière, "emancipation takes place by the establishment of translatability" (2011d, 9). Translation is essential to Rancière because it operates under the principal axiom of the equality of intelligences. Every act of translation indicates the ability to hear, think, and then speak about the subject undergoing trans- lation. The three attending paradigms of translation—and thus the three modalities through which the equality of intelligence is verified—include learning the mother tongue, the freedom of the written word to circulate, and the ability of objects to create an equal playing field between subjects. In all three cases, there is a movement between words, written letters, and things without the mediation of a schoolmaster's explications. In other words, this is not an educational exercise in piercing the veil of images to extract the hidden facts of social reality as in Freire's epistemological model but rather an exercise in forging a "new cartography of the perceptible, the thinkable and the feasible" (Rancière 2009c, 72), opened in the curious moment when we recognize our capacity to translate. Rancière summarizes, "The point is not to counter-pose reality to its appearances," but rather to "construct different realities, different forms of common sense—that is to say, different spatiotemporal systems, different communities of words and things, forms and meanings" (1999, 88). The construction of a different reality—a material fiction composed of the theatrical stage, the time of the now, and the performance of a democratic script composed of new relations between the visible and the auditory—is not escapism or simply a flight of fancy; it is the presentation of new coordinates for perceiving-with. In this sense, curiosity ignites our will to theatre—our will to play roles that are not those assigned to us and, in turn, explore the possibilities for new subjectivations derived from the appearance of the anomalous detail. This is not the capacity of the oppressed to recognize their pre-defined "objective" interests but rather their ability to claim that which is not their own, to be improper, to travel where they are not supposed to go and to be who they are not supposed to be.

In short, for Freire, dialogic pedagogy *raises* consciousness above ideological distortion or mystification to reveal the greater truth of social complexity, to reconnect objects to their specific reasons *behind* the back of appearances. Epistemological reflection becomes the democratic weapon par excellence in that it clarifies and provides methodological rigor for the development of action. There is thus a separation of the faculties, which are subsequently set in a hierarchical relation. Reason is not only prior to imagination, but it is also, in some ways, privileged as the bulwark against ideological distortion. For Rancière, however, the critical move is not so much to posit a distorted reality that must be overcome through a vertical raising of consciousness. This move only creates a hierarchical separation of the senses from their synesthetic co-belonging, and consequently institutes a political distinction between those who think correctly and those who do not. In Rancière's conception, consciousness undergoes a *horizontal* movement of redistribution of sensation that results in a new collage of the sensible whose synesthetic mixing and contamination cannot be measured within any existing order. There is no linear connection binding epistemological clarity and scientific bases to practice. Rather there are only aesthetic lines of connection and disconnection which challenge how we look, speak, and feel with others. In short, when we are curious, intelligence suddenly is embodied in a new sensorium.

At this point, we come to Freire's second major hypothesis: that science and narrative can in fact be separated into two interrelated yet ultimately distinct practices. As with Rancière's critique of social scientists, Marxist historiographers, and the *Annalistes*, in Freire we see a "historical science released from the indeterminacy of the words and phrases of stories, thus capable of transforming into real cognition what was still only the 'novel of human life'" (1994, 5). The critical scientist examines the world in order to expose layers of illusion and mystification in order to bring to life the ontological reality that rests beneath the surface of social life, thus providing a grounding for the utopian imagination. What Freire seems to miss is that this critical apprehension of the world is always already an aesthetic narrative, that scientific knowledge is always already infused with and informed by certain metaphors, narrative structures, and plot devices.

For Rancière, narrative does not arrive as a supplement to thinking accurately but is at the very core of what it means to engage in the democratic possibilities of knowledge production. Stated differently, if Freire wants to narrativize the "scientific bases" of his thought (thus trans-forming what he refers to as *"doxa,"* or appearance, into *"logos"* [2007, 12] in order to achieve *praxis*), then Rancière demonstrates that science is itself already a narrative to begin with. In other words, the *fact* of inequality is not simply material but also involves a level of perception. In relation to Plato's *Republic*, Rancière argues that the inequality of the utopian society is predicated on both a material division of labor (workers simply do not have the time or energy to contemplate the questions that occupy the philosopher kings) and an aesthetic perception that these inequalities are real and natural (according to the myth of metals). Thus, for inequality to legitimate itself, workers must "sense it" as if it were true that they cannot think and speak along with the philosophers (Rancière 2009f). In other words, facts and perceptions are interwoven *all the way down*. Likewise, the history of counter-revolution and revolt is a discourse-narrative or a *"mythos* that is a *logos"* (Rancière 1994, 56) lacking an exterior ontological referent outside of aesthetic contamination. Any material redistribution of the means of production must be accompanied by a redistribution of the sensible or an aesthetic emancipation that reframes time and space. Indeed, the "democratic man" is someone who is "capable of embracing a distance between words and things that is not deception, not trickery, but humanity" (2007c, 51). For Freire, the political arrives with the proper assumption of one's class knowledge while for Rancière, politics arrive in the very denial of a proper location or correspondence between thinking, acting, and speaking under the sign of equality. As Rancière argues "The first worker-militants began by taking themselves for poets or knights, priests or dandies" (2004c, 200) creating a heterodoxia of theatrical thinking, speaking, perceiving, and acting.

In this sense it is interesting to compare Rancière's treatment of workers in *The Nights of Labor* (1989) with Freire's treatment of the fishers outlined above. For Rancière, the role of the philosopher is not to reduce the discourses of workers to symptoms, ideological illusions according to a critical science of the world, or mere aesthetic rhythms that can be appreciated by the intellectual. If workers are supposed to be "mute" (and thus capable of nothing more than manual labor), then, according to Rancière, Freire's dialogical pedagogy would not so much refute this muteness as constitute yet another form of muteness: mute speech ... speech incapable of knowing itself, speech reduced to illusion and thus in need of the speech of the other (the educator or the leftist party) to *make it speak the truth.* Opposed to this method, Rancière does not attempt to decipher the hidden symptoms of oppression in the speech of the worker but rather to create a stage of translation wherein we bring to sense the tension that arises between the specific discourses that the worker is supposed to have (according to his or her implicit class knowledge) and the discourses of the worker who encounters the words of others. For Freire, there must be a firm connection between names and referents, between narratives and class knowledge—a correspondence that closes the dangerous gap between words and things, performance and ontology, subjectivity and social location in the act of unveiling, naming, and narrativizing. Emancipation occurs not through improper mixing and performances but rather when the oppressed recognize their *proper interests* as subject-objects of history with a particular vocation. Proper interests, proper vocations, and proper ideological orientations identified through epistemological curiosity are necessary to ensure the overcoming of narration sickness. Yet, Rancière testifies to the theatrical experiments of those who encounter words from elsewhere and engage in acts of translation beyond the divide between science and narrative.

These theatrical experiments take place in the here and now rather than in some deferred utopian future. In other words, the problem with the division between aesthetics and science in the pedagogy of the oppressed is that it stages education in terms of an infinitely deferred process of archeological retrieval of "really real reality" in the promise of a utopian future to come. Yet this excavation remains captivated by a temporal infinitude that recedes the more we chip away at appearances. As Freire writes, humanization as an ontological vocation is "always a process, and always a becoming" that "requires, indisputably, the adoption of a utopia" (2004a, 84). The aesthetic event of vision orients us towards the future. In other words, the process of becoming is an imaginative projection into a world that is otherwise than the present world. Yet this orientation seems to miss that new communities of sense appear around us *all the time* that cannot be reduced to mere ideological illusions or distortions. For Rancière, these theatrical experiments should be seen as dissensual ruptures that refuse any ordering of who can and cannot proclaim/perform freedom and live in defiance of the postponement of utopia for a distant horizon. In other words there is no delay or lag-time between appearance and ontology or aesthetics and science because the aesthetics of politics and the politics of aesthetics are constitutive of our primordial apprehension of the world (our pre-conscious, pre-rational sensible familiarity) and the most basic aspects of being a political animal (our *philia*). Curiosity does not ignite a future-oriented hope in overcoming the divide between being and imagining. Rather it concentrates attention on the appearance of the anomalous within atopic spaces necessary for new performances and new subjectivations beyond the gulf compartmentalizing reason and sensation.

I would argue that, according to Rancière's own logic, *curiosity poses a sensual challenge to the will to translate the aporia of the beautiful sublime into new narratives, new performances/stages, and new ways of speaking that embody the hypothesis of equality.* Thus understanding the aesthetic form of education enables us to synthesize both curiosity and will in Rancière's work and move toward a richer understanding of the complexities of teaching and learning. In *The Ignorant Schoolmaster: Five Lessons in Intellectual Emancipation,* Rancière clearly connects aesthetics not only to politics but also to "universal teaching." Throughout the book, Rancière posits the artist as the true embodiment of universal teaching (the ability of anyone to teach anything) over and above the stultifying power of the professor (which is based on a hierarchy of intelligences). Racine is cited as a model teacher precisely because his genius lies in "having not believed himself superior to those he was speaking to" (1991, 70) thus encouraging the verification of his work through the active translation and counter-translation of the audience. In fact, to understand the lesson of education for emancipation, Rancière turns his back on grammarians and orators (who only want to command) and instead looks toward the poet/playwright for the true lesson of universal teaching: "equality and intelligence are equal terms" (1991, 73). But his lesson is not learned from the verification of the will alone. The teacher as artist must compose the stage of learning in relation to curiosity just as much as to the will. In *The Ignorant Schoolmaster,* this stage was exemplified by a bilingual edition of the book *Télémaque.* Although Rancière describes the use of the book solely in relation to its effect on the will of the students, I would argue that he misses a more determinate moment in the learning process—the moment of curiosity which challenges the will to sustain attention to the text and subsequently translate it through performance. Only by connecting curiosity with will can the will itself be reconceptualized as a *will to theatre*—a will that enacts the "as if . . ." of democratic dissensus by playing an illegitimate role in the scandalous and illicit drama of equality.

But if curiosity is a type of stumble or chance encounter, is this not beyond the scope of universal teaching and thus the "authority" of the ignorant schoolmaster? Neither Irene nor the scholar had teachers in any traditional sense of the term beyond their own short voyages to the lands of the people. Before answering these questions, we must first address two fundamental social and political techniques that sustain intellectual stultification: shock and interpretation. Once again drawing on the films of Rossellini, Rancière argues that the prototypical experience of shock is the factory, which is "in the first place an uninterrupted movement that hurts the eyes, that gives you a headache" through "a constant and unceasing procession of sensory shocks, in which, along with the ability to look, the possibility of thoughtfulness and respect is lost" (2003c, 125). In sum, the factory produces conditions of unending shocks that assault the senses, preventing curiosity from an intimate encounter with the void, surplus, remnant (which both draws out and is drawn out by curiosity and its glance). If the factory bombards the senses and overloads the mind (producing intolerable headaches), then the Rorschach blot represents the other social assault on curiosity: interpretation. The Rorschach blot and the attending explanatory systems make the subject reliant upon expert opinion, explication, and leads to dependency upon a whole matrix of discipline and power which stimulates curiosity only to stultify it. The void, as a perceptual glitch in the order of things, has no right to exist according to the expert, who must interrogate the subject, in order to make him or her speak the truth. The mastery of interpretation (as opposed to translation) always presupposes that there is something hidden beneath the surface, something that must be unveiled. Behind ignorance lies a truth which only the knowledge of the professional can uncover. In this sense, Rancière desires to liberate the curious glance from either the violence of shock or the stultification of interpretation/explication, thus connecting the glance to the surplus that remains incalculable according to the order of things. Shock petrifies the glance, makes it turn away, and premature interpretation closes off the event of interruption. Curiosity is therefore too fragile for shock, and too impressionable for interpretation. The turning and encircling of curiosity demands a certain space and time that falls outside of either the linear production of the factory or the panoptic treatment of the clinic/asylum.

This lesson in curiosity is absolutely essential for educators, especially critical pedagogues who all too often rely on the shock of exploitation followed by an explication of global capitalism in order to provoke critical consciousness raising. From Walter Benjamin's analysis of Baudelaire's "shock factor" (1968, 163) to Fredric Jameson's characterization of the "shock of demystification" (1971, 381), shock has been the affective tool of Marxist pedagogies from the very beginning of critical theory. Yet the form of traumatic shock followed by interpretation merely repeats the social and political logic of economic production (the factory) and therapy (the Rorschach blot) now joined together at the hip, the former necessitating the latter in a mutually self-sustaining and unending circle of co-dependency. Thus critique reveals its parasitic dependency on the internal aesthetic logics of shock and interpretation that maintain the status quo. In both cases, the opportunity to stimulate curiosity might very well be lost. In fact, it is the very metaphor of consciousness-raising that necessitates the pedagogy of shock—a violent "waking up" of sleeping, anaesthetized curiosity. Yet if the sleeping consciousness is rejected as a viable model for conceptualizing curiosity in the first place, shock becomes excessive and unnecessary. In other words, it is not a matter of waking curiosity from a deep slumber by the proverbial slap in the face of critical pedagogy but of simply shifting the parameters of a curiosity that is always already there in the form of the "just curious."

The slightest of provocations might shift the glance, orienting vision toward a detail which, when given the attention of the glance, throws the entire field into a new focus. When the ignorant schoolmaster points to ("Isn't that strange ...") or places before ("Did you look at this?"), he or she causes an aesthetic redistribution of the sensible. This fundamental inter-ruption in the partitioning of what can be seen or heard is an opening to the void that exists when hierarchies between aesthetic and scientific intel-ligences are suspended. Curiosity circles the void from the side, constantly stumbling around along its edge. Here, in this atopic zone, the student must go and see for him or herself—thus the time of expert explanation is supplanted by experimental exploration in sensing differently. The process of verifying the will is thus dependent upon an aesthetic interruption in the field of perception, which splits sense from sense, exposing the subject to an excess that has not been accounted for. In this way, the ignorant school-master as artist does not simply place an object on the table but rather places a void in an object by pointing to a (dis)location that needs further investigation and perhaps even disput. In this initial gesture, the relation between student and teacher is therefore neither one of command nor a form of beautiful and harmonious solidarity. The teacher remains ahead of the student in the moment of pointing to the void, offering an invitation to look, hear, or sense differently. The teacher is ahead in terms of his or her ignorance, opening and sustaining a gap between sense and sense! If the subsequent verification of willful pursuit takes the form of a command, it is a command that is nevertheless parodic, circling around the void from which it is born.

This sequence should not be thought of as a method to be memorized and reproduced as if it were a predefined script. In fact, in Jocotot's practice, "the method was purely the student's" (Rancière 1991, 14). If there is a method (for students or teachers), it should be thought of in terms of the Greek terms *methodos* whose root is *hodos* meaning journey or motion. The "method" of the ignorant schoolmaster is not a pre-determined protocol, and thus resists the transformation into an "-ology" or abstracted procedure. Interruption is not a method that can be taught and reproduced. It is a contingent collision of atoms in the moment of pointing. Interruption and verification, like Freire's pedagogy of the oppressed, are anti-methodological. Yet, it is instructive to compare the two anti-methods in terms of their purported starting points and end points. Freire's educational sequence begins with an anaesthetized curiosity (it has fallen asleep) in order to wake it out of aesthetic illusion. Thus, passivity and activity are distinct states of being represented by dichotomous pairs such as sleep versus action, fatalism versus hope, aesthetic illusion versus scientific apprehension. And in the process of dialectical negation, the very real democratic politics of perceptual alternation are subjected to an imaginative teleological unfolding that transforms equality from a starting point into an end point, from a hypothesis to be verified *now* to an ontology that is "not-yet" completed. The peculiar result: heresy is put to sleep when ingenious curiosity is "awakened."

Curiosity and the Imagination

As Joseph Tanke rightly points out (2011), Rancière lacks a theory of imagination. Although turning to theorists such as Kant and Schiller, Rancière seems to ignore the role of imagination in their writings on aesthetics. Unlike Freire, who privileges the relation between education, politics, and the imagination, Rancière's aesthetic experience, for Tanke, seems oddly detached from the faculty of imagination, which in turn, impoverishes his politics. Stated differently, without anchoring in the creative potential of the imagination, dissensus remains overly abstract. "To say that they [the operations of dissensus] open worlds does not provide a fully embodied sense of what it is like to invent art and politics, nor do these concepts themselves prompt action" (Tanke 2011, 162). Because of this oversight, Tanke feels compelled to supplement Rancière's theory with his own account of the imagination as a social capacity for activating new sensory worlds through relations of equality with others. The trans-subjective imagination needs others in order to be fully activated, thus presupposing an equality of intelligences while at the same time transforming dissensus into a creative process for producing the world as it could exist otherwise.

While Tanke is correct in that the secondary literature on Rancière has largely neglected the connection between faculties/capacities and the aesthetics of politics, the turn to imagination is problematic. First, Tanke fails to take into account the role of curiosity in Rancière's aesthetic reflections, and thus fails to see how his own analysis of Rancière's "abstractness" is itself abstract. Second, an emphasis on imagination stands in sharp contrast to Davide Panagia's reading of Rancière. As Panagia aptly summarizes (2009), for Rancière, politics lies below or before the act of imaginative narration which harmonizes the correspondence between perception and signification. Although Panagia does not cite Rancière's reflections on curiosity in his analysis, it is not difficult to see connections between attention to the disorganizing field of sensual rupture and my own description of curiosity outlined above. Both are forms of what Panagia calls "somacognition" (2009, 10) or a pre-conscious, pre-reflective, pre-imaginative sensorial openness to disturbances that exist prior to any type of imaginative organization. Curiosity as somacognition—an embodied and embedded intelligence that cannot be abstracted from the eye, ear, and so on—privileges the event of appearance that, for Panagia is "a disjunctive event that disarticulates the regimes of perception which allow us to establish the identity of an appearance" (2009, 11). Imagination has the problem of reifying the sensorial opening to difference that curiosity exposes us to. The result is a deferral of equality from the present moment of the event of appearance to a future point wherein appearance (image) and reality (ontology) can once again be reunited.

As opposed to this model of deferral, curiosity is the *capacity to sense things otherwise now, in the moment of perceptual rupture.* In other words, curiosity places a decisive emphasis on what we are experiencing in the fluctuating perceptual field, and it is this opening/void in the partitioning of sense that is the aesthetic principle of emancipatory education. The theatrical will sustains our relation to the questioning process that emerges from our curiosity and thus is the effort needed to remain in the space of ignorance (an atopia without a name) without turning to the explicator for help or without prematurely closing off our sensorial experiment. In sum, we can draw from Panagia in order to make two claims: first, that the politics of curiosity can exist autonomously from the figuration and narrativization of the imagination, and second, curiosity precedes imaginative presentation. If imagination is to realize its political potential (as Tanke so emphatically desires), it is only in relation to curiosity that it sustains an essential relation to the event of democratic disjunction, producing narratives that resist narratocracy (the organization of perception into a readable, recognizable, and interpretable whole) by always remaining *curious* to the void out of which the imagination draws its powers.

In this way, it is the lost world of curiosity that should be privileged in education. If Tanke argues that intersubjective imagining—its social dimension—is what prevents narratocratic closure, I am suggesting that the attentive nature of curiosity itself undermines any narratocracy. It is only in relation to the curiously unexpected void, surplus, supernumerary remainder that imagination resists toppling over into a reified narrative. To be curious is to remain in touch—literally—with the sublime, disruptive surplus of sensation—the muteness within every expressive gesture, object, or event. Without a *touch of curiosity*, the dangers that haunt Freire's model will return to once again undermine the *political* importance of the aesthetics of education.

Conclusion

In Rancière's description of the educator as artist, we can see an emergent problematization of Freire's model of emancipatory education that derives from Freire's fundamental split between aesthetics and epistemology, sensation and reason, science and narrative. Most importantly, Rancière's notion of the ignorant schoolmaster as an artist suggests that curiosity is not awakened through the process of epistemological rigor or proper thinking but rather is turned or swerved through disruption of perceptual fixity and identity. The goal is no longer ideological critique of mystified reality and imaginative reconstruction so much as the configuring of situations, of doing and saying what you are not supposed to be able to do or say according to the hypothesis of equality. This configuring or re-partitioning does not defer freedom to a utopian future but rather finds its resources within the aesthetics of atopian theatrical performance in the present.

It is not that Freire dismisses the aesthetic dimension of teaching or the role of the teacher as artist. Rather, the problem lies with his description of the learning process as an artistic happening which has been overdetermined by his scientific model of unveiling and proper study—a model that compromises his understanding of the theatrical form of his problem-posing pedagogy. For Rancière, the ignorant schoolmaster as artist does not "form" the student—a concept that comes dangerously close to dialectically inverting itself into a banking model of education, transforming teaching into a representational art and the student into a reflection of a preexisting ideal—but rather creates a staging (a contingent and improvisational interruption, verification, and performance). It is the teacher's role not simply to verify the will of the student but to be attentive to curiosity as the crucial affective opening for the theatrics of the will to emerge. The aesthetic event of education is not an unveiling of an object but rather a certain momentum of translation (philosophical) and performance (social), both of which are jumpstarted by the affective *irritant* of curiosity—an exposure to an object or idea that is stumbled upon/over. Thus the aesthetic event is no longer a narrative or utopian add-on to critical consciousness raising, but a constituting principle. In other words, curiosity is not epistemological (concerned with how we know really real reality) but aesthetic (how we create new sensory experience to open up spaces for new performances of equality). Resisting the temptation to fold curiosity back into the model of ideological critique based on scientific foundations, Rancière enables us to liberate the aesthetic turn in Freire's work and thus realize its full potential to overcome the aporia of emancipation in critical pedagogy (Biesta 2008).

Returning to my opening remarks: curiosity is never *just* curiosity. Curiosity is never simply Heidegger's idle distraction (2008), nor is it simply the product of Enlightenment suspicion against the suspicious passions of wonderment. It is an affective anchoring point for the sudden appearance of rupture that disturbs the recognition and common sense of the police order. It is a creatively synesthetic moment where what can be sensed is sensed differently, in new permutations that lack specific names. Rather than be ashamed or embarrassed by curiosity—what is "just curious" if not some sort of preemptive apology that inadvertently displays our guilt at having sensed differently—universal teaching must enable students to embrace it openly and study those moments of sensorial appearance that reconfigure the divide between cognition and sensation, reason and feeling. Experimental classrooms are classrooms of artists whose translations of curious encounters across distances speak to the ever-present possibility for sensing the world differently. Such educational communities cannot be easily dismissed as mere mirages that distract from the real work of ideological critique, but must be seen as an insistence on the centrality of sensual displacement and rupture. "I am just curious" is therefore a faint inscription in the police order of a greater promise: a promise not of enlightened or proper thinking but rather of aesthetic perturbations that float along the contours of our everyday classroom relations. Let us *assert* curiosity, in our curiosity remain attentive to the theatre we as teachers and learners produce.

Chapter Five:

The Knowledge of Ignorance

Ignorance is not a lack of knowledge.
—*Rancière,* "The Aesthetic Heterotopia"

For Paulo Freire, competency is an important educational issue. He writes, "How can one teach literacy without the necessary knowledge about language acquisition, about language and ideology, about techniques and methods for teaching reading and writing … As an educator, I need to constantly 'read,' better and better …." (2004b, 63). A teacher must be well versed in reading the world and the word in order to facilitate this process and keep it on track for others, and this means constantly updating one's knowledge base through research. Although Freire is clear that this knowledge is never complete and thus in a constant dialectic with ignorance, he nevertheless is emphatic: "I cannot teach what I do not know" (2001a, 89). In fact, attempting to teach what one does not know is immoral for Freire, who considers it a kind of academic "license" (1998, 17) and an abuse of authority. Yet for Rancière, "competency" in terms of content knowledge or pedagogical skills seems less an issue. In fact, the major lesson of Joseph Jacotot is precisely that "one can teach what one doesn't know" (Rancière 1991, 15).

The position that Rancière holds seems paradoxical, and at first blush, many of us would side with Freire for pedagogical as well as political reasons. For instance, Jodi Dean (2009) argues that Rancière's emphasis on ignorance and its relationship to emancipation is particularly dangerous given the present historical moment. While such a turn might have been a politically democratic gesture at the time of Joseph Jacotot's writing (1800s), in the present postmodern moment it would seem that nothing is more valued than sustained ignorance. Dean writes, "Over the last decade, the United States has witnessed the supplanting of expert knowledge by gut instinct, by religious faith, by capacities to know simply by seeing or feeling, and by the rejection of detail and complexity as elitist, unnecessary, and unwarranted" (2009, 24). In this quote, Dean explicitly links praise of ignorance with dangerous right-wing fundamentalism. After all, it is a type of willed ignorance that enables white privilege in the United States to perpetuate itself (Sullivan and Tuana 2007). Seeming to agree with Dean, Peter Hallward criticizes Rancière's theatrocracy for overemphasizing improvisation and ignorance over and above informed knowledge/organization. "Does political action," challenges Hallward, "no longer need to be informed by a detailed understanding of how the contemporary world works, how exploitation operates, how transnational corporations go about their business?" (2006, 127). And finally, in defense of the knowledge generated by critical sociology, Alberto Toscano reiterates this basic argument: "To think that explanation, strategy and knowledge, and indeed sociology itself, are not intrinsic components of politics is not only debilitating, it dispossesses—potentially in a more severe way than Bourdieu's sociology—those forced into positions of 'minority' of the very tools of emancipation" (2011, 232). In other words, Freire, Dean, Hallward, and Toscano all argue for a certain kind of competence, knowledge, and strategy *necessary* for political emancipation. Within the practice of education, the implication is that teachers cannot emancipate students without this vital knowledge, and in turn, students will be held captive by the oppressive forces which remain invisible to them.

If the opening quotation seems to suggest an indifference to knowledge (a certain ambivalence as to its emancipatory value), at other times, Rancière seems to agree with his ardent critics. He warns that ignorance is *preferred* by educational and philosophical stultifiers precisely because it maintains a strict division of labor. In relation to Plato's ideal city-state in *The Republic*, Rancière argues, "Idleness and incompetence are the dispositions best suited to ensuring what is singularly important, that the artisan does only one thing, the thing that marks him off and serves to put him in his place" (2004c, 22). In other words, ignorance is a necessary condition for stabilizing Plato's social hierarchy. Here, Rancière is, like Freire and others, skeptical of any claim that ignorance is "liberatory." In fact, it is the competence of the sophists in multiple domains that seem to most distress Plato and disorganize his political architectonic. Furthermore, in his strident polemic against Althusser (2011b), Rancière repeatedly emphasizes the relationship between ignorance and intellectual hierarchization which justifies the work of the philosopher who must correct the flawed thinking of the workers. How then are we to reconcile these two depictions of ignorance found in Rancière's work?

In this chapter, I claim that Freire and Rancière are both right and wrong. The ignorant schoolmaster does not have either content or procedural knowledge, but does have knowledge of something. It is the ambiguous status of this something that concerns me here. In order to avoid either stultified ignorance or stultifying learning, I suggest that we must utilize Rancière to theorize the paradoxical knowledge that constitutes what I will refer to as democratic ignorance. Here I will connect the theme of ignorance with that of curiosity outlined in Chapter Four. Instead of the curiosity of the student, I will loop back to the curiosity of the teacher in order to argue that the aesthetics of curiosity are precisely what safeguard democratic ignorance from toppling over into the stultified ignorance that Dean criticizes and that Rancière highlights as the condition of perpetual hierarchical dependence. As such, I will polemically defend Rancière with certain qualifications. While these qualifications of ignorance might not satisfy his critics, they nevertheless enable us to move into a position that avoids easy caricatures of ignorance.

Rancière on Ignorance: Minimal and Maximal Claims

In the book *The Ignorant Schoolmaster: Five Lessons in Intellectual Emancipation*, Rancière writes, "The act of learning could be produced according to four variously combined determinations: by an emancipatory master or by a stultifying one, by a learned master or by an ignorant one" (1991, 14). Here Rancière demonstrates a certain ambivalence toward knowledge. Learning can be inaugurated by those with or without knowledge. But here we must read Rancière to the letter. *Learning* is what is being emphasized here, *not* emancipation. Certainly a learned teacher can teach his or her knowledge. And certainly a student can learn this knowledge. But, there is no necessary connection between learning and emancipation for Rancière. In fact, it is the knowledge of the learned teacher that continually gets in the way of emancipation. First, if one "knows something" then there is always the temptation to explain. While explanation in and of itself does not necessarily lead to stultification (as in the simple act of sharing information between recognized equals), there is a distinct tendency toward stultification when the other is not already emancipated. Citing Jacotot, Rancière writes, "Opposed to the word of the explainer is the entry into a universe of language provided by the lesson of generalized things, where one appropriates the art of orators of all views, and where a learned schoolmaster himself may be used, but only on the condition of being precisely treated as a thing: 'A learned teacher is a fact full of instruction: listen, look, watch closely, dissect; *faciatis exerimentum in professore*. Learn him, check him, imitate him, translate him; he has done scientific work, do your own'" (2011d, 42). In other words, the student must *already* be emancipated in order to resist the stultification of the explanations offered by the learned schoolmaster. The onus is on the student to realize that if explanations are given, they hold no more authority than any other object to be appropriated and translated. In this sense, the content and procedural knowledges of the learned teacher become *obstacles* for the student—obstacles that can only be overcome if the student understands the power of the axiom of equality of intelligences ahead of time.

While acquiring the right knowledge is the major problem for Freire's pedagogy, it is the exact opposite for Rancière: how to remain ignorant. In other words, part of the emancipation of the schoolmaster is the recognition that he or she does not need the competencies that are emphasized by Freire and others in order to teach. Jacotot's own experience is exemplary of this point:

> Since it had at least shown that it wasn't the master's knowledge that instructed the student, then nothing prevented the master from teaching something other than his science, something he didn't know. Joseph Jacotot applied himself to varying the experiment, to repeating on purpose what chance had once produced. He began to teach two subjects at which he was notably incompetent: painting and the piano. (Rancière 1991, 15).

Jacotot's ignorance was not at all limiting, rather, his ability to teach what he did not know became, for Rancière, a foundational experiment in democracy itself.

But immediately we run into an important question. Is it not true that Jacotot was competent in something? If so, what is the nature of this "competence" and of the "something" to which it corresponds? According to Jacotot's testimony and Rancière's performance of the story, it is certainly not some sort of content knowledge—knowledge of a certain subject matter for instance. Nor can it be some sort of procedural knowledge—knowledge of proper pedagogical techniques and methods. If we understand method as (a) a rule-bound, prescriptive procedure that (b) is guided by a pre-defined representation of success conditions, then universal teaching and the process of verification cannot be considered a "method" in any traditional sense of the term. Yet despite this, Jacotot is a

master—a parodic master of his own ignorance. This paradoxical competency, which distinguishes the emancipatory educator from the stultifying
explicator, is Jacotot's ignorance. The ignorant schoolmaster is, as Rancière
describes, truly ignorant of "the inequality of intelligence" (2009c, 11), but
what I want to argue is that this ignorance is not simply *negative* but also has
positive content as well.

If the minimal claim argues that ignorance is not limiting (it does not
prohibit teaching), the maximal claim argues that ignorance is actually
enabling and thus *necessary* for universal teaching. In this stronger sense,
the educator must ask him or herself the provocative question: How can I
become a "master" of my own ignorance? What is the positive content of
this ignorance?

In Rancière's work, we can discover several keys to answering these
questions. For Rancière, the democratic subject has certain constitutive
features that include: the virtue of trust, the hypothesis of equality, and
the poetic sensitivity to embrace the "unreality of representation" (2007c,
51–2). In other words, ignorant schoolmasters, as democratic subjects,
must have a certain ethical virtue, a certain social hypothesis, and finally a
poetic being. These are the unthematic, tacit dimensions of ignorance that
form the positive background of universal teaching.

Let us examine each of these features in turn. First, ethical virtue.
Rancière is clear that the democratic subject should begin from a location
of trust rather than distrust. "Behind things is where their reasons lie"
(Rancière 2003c, 122) is the fundamental logic of distrust, and this logic
reproduces hierarchies between those who see and those who are blind
to the "truth," those who know "how the world really works" and those
who are slaves to illusion. In fact, "anyone who starts out from distrust,
who assumes inequality and proposes to reduce it, can only succeed in
setting up a hierarchy of inequalities, a hierarchy of priorities, a hierarchy
of intelligences—and will reproduce inequality ad infinitum" (2007c, 52).
To distrust is to embrace the "syllogism of suspicion" (2007c, 53) that
presupposes (a) a deep truth concealed from everyday intelligence and
(b) a corresponding hierarchy of intelligences. Such syllogisms abound in
critical theory, critical pedagogy, and critical sociology. In *The Philosopher
and His Poor* (2004c), Rancière argues that leftist educational sociologists
such as Pierre Bourdieu simply reinforce the traditional division of labor
through a syllogism of suspicion. Sociology assumes that schools reproduce
social inequality. But this thesis is problematic on two levels: (a) the strict
divisions as described by Bourdieu miss those very real moments of mixing
that introduce confusion into social stratification (as when excluded

students suddenly reveal themselves capable of excelling in the very disciplines which schooling implicitly excludes them from), and (b) Bourdieu remains an elitist, for only the critical sociologist can read and correctly interpret how schools reproduce inequality. In other words, it is assumed that without the sociologist, teachers and students would never be able to understand the ways in which the school system excludes or oppresses them. Thus philosophy and sociology have consistently denied the ability of everyone to think and to speak. These disciplines *fundamentally distrust* the assumed "naïve consciousness" of those subjected to oppressive systems. The result of this distrust is a syllogism of suspicion that reinforces the stultifying practices they are arguing against.

In his rejection of the hermeneutic of suspicion, Rancière stands in stark contrast to his fellow Parisian critical theorists, philosophers, and critical sociologists. As Terry Eagleton (2009) insightfully points out, the French avant-garde has traditionally held a "deep-seated skepticism of common speech" (279) and the politics of everyday life, resulting in an "ethical elitism" (281) that only finds truth and virtue in extreme cataclysm, revolutionary upheavals, and apocalyptic confrontations with the Real. The result is that the "close-at-hand is always impoverished" (Eagleton 2009, 281) as a mere delusion. Yet with Rancière we see an alternative that rejects both the tragic heroism of the avant-garde and the complacency of the liberal or the conservative. If the former embraces the transcendent miracle as the only test for truth while the latter rejects the possibility of the impossible in the first place, then Rancière's ethic of trust suggests that *the impossible happens here and now* through the everyday verification of equality. In other words, Rancière finds confirmation of equality in the struggles of common men and women, in their aesthetic pleasures, in their curious glances, and in their collective practices of disagreement.

As an alternative to the syllogism of suspicion, Rancière theorizes a syllogism of trust that "completely reject[s] any notion of hidden truth and its demystification" (2007c, 45). For Rancière, "Trust affirms that no one can see for those who do not see and turn others' ignorance into knowledge" (2003c, 123). In other words, there are no experts or philosopher kings to guide us to truth or pass judgment on our actions, nor is there a strict division of labor between those who can speak and think and those who are meant to labor. Here it is important to remember Freire's notion of trust introduced in Chapter Three. While Freire's instinct might be correct on this matter, his notion of trust is, as I argued, identitarian. In other words, it is a trust in those who share a correct political orientation and similar class interests. Such trust is radically different from the trust espoused by Rancière. Rather than trust only those who are like us, who stand in clear solidarity with our causes, the trusting syllogism trusts in the *demos* (in its anonymity, strangeness, and multiplicity) to verify equality for itself, by its actions without the need for experts or critical pedagogues. As opposed to practices that continually set out to find inequalities, syllogisms of trust continually set out to verify the hypothesis of equality. As an illustration of this alternative logic, Rancière turns to the texts of French strike movements following the revolution of 1830. Here is a summary of the syllogistic logic of the strike:

> The major premise of this syllogism is simple: the Charter promulgated in 1830 says in its preamble that all French people are equal before the law, and this equality constitutes the syllogism's major premise. The minor premise is derived rather from direct experience. For example, in 1833, workers in the Paris tailoring trade went on strike because the master tailors refused to respond to their demands relating to rates of pay, working hours, and working conditions. Here, then, the minor premises would run something like this: now Monsieur Schwartz, head of the master tailors' association, refuses to listen to our case. What we are putting to him is a case for revised rates of pay. He can verify this case but he refuses to do so. He is therefore not treating us as equals. And he is therefore contradicting the equality inscribed in the charter. (2007c, 45–6)

The major premise consists of the inscription of equality in the law and the minor premise consists in the historical actions done elsewhere. The ethic of distrust would read the ensuing contradiction as proof of the existence of inequality whereas the ethic of trust would read the inscription of equality as an opening for staging a dispute by the *demos*. In other words, the charter is not simply an ideological illusion, but rather the "grounds for a claim" (Rancière 2007c, 47) that forces the police order to recognize its failure to embody equality. Thus critique (a demand for recognition/compensation for a wrong) is supplanted by demonstration (an action that embodies directly the rights of those who have no rights). Taking up the words of the charter, "what had to be demonstrated was, precisely, equality" (Rancière 2007c, 47). Here it is important to note that the logical demonstration of the proof transforms into the political demonstration or strike of the workers (philosophical reflection is exchanged for direct, political engagement). If, as Rancière writes, "The strike takes on the form of a logical proof" (2007c, 47) then so too does the logical proof take on the dramatic staging of a political strike. Rather than a critique of inequality, what is produced is a figure of political and aesthetic dissensus. This event is thoroughly historical and contextual. Thus the abstract "method" of the syllogism becomes an embodied and embedded practice of politics, contextually specific to the power relations operative within a historical situation. Logical revolts are lived syllogisms—a logic that profanes any pre-determined script which the people are supposed to perform. What then is the use of the syllogism if it does not judge or prescribe actions? As the formulation of the event of politics in terms of a logical proof, the trusting syllogism proclaims to others that they need to pay attention to a certain interruption in the order of things, that something new has appeared that does not fit into what counts within a police order. Stated differently, the logic of the demonstration demonstrates, to use Rancière's words, that "revolt is also the scene of speech and reasons: neither the eruption (often celebrated in those years) of a popular unruliness irreducible to the disciplines of power, nor the expression of a historical necessity and legitimacy" (2011d, 10). The syllogism is a sort of theoretical stage in both logical *and* dramatic senses, an index pointing at the reason and speech in those denied these capacities. In fact, Rancière himself argues that political performers have the "peculiar role of inventing *arguments* and *demonstra-tions*—in the double, logical and aesthetic, senses of the terms" (1999, 89). Rather than simply dismiss the egalitarian inscription of the law as ideologi-cally mystifying, democratic subjects invent a syllogistic demonstration that simultaneously performs both the principle of equality and its absence in the same dramatic and philosophical gesture.

This logical formulation is coterminous with political demonstration, overcoming the temporal lag time that separates the syllogism from action. In fact, it is the temporal dimension of the syllogism that most acutely separates its two ethical modalities: distrust and trust. For instance, the distrusting syllogism of political philosophy is always temporally displaced from action. It either forecasts the "proper" action that should be taken according to specific historical laws or retrospectively gazes back upon the past in order to pass judgment over political movements (both projective and retrospective teleologies deny the fundamental muteness of things). The distrusting syllogism of political philosophy always "comes too late" (Rancière 1999, 62), or, I would add, too early. And this in spite of the fact that "the *demos* is already there" (Rancière 1999, 62) embodying the simul-taneous demonstration of its political/economic needs and its logical revolt. In short, the temporality of trusting and distrusting syllogisms is the ultimate distinction between two types of intellectual operations:

in the first, a political staging within and by the actions of the people themselves, and in the second, a judgment enacted over and against the actions (past and future) of a people from the position of intellectual superiority and detachment. It is not so much what we must do in order to achieve communism in the future that concerns Rancière but rather *what we have done* and *are doing in the present* to verify equality which is always already operative in spite of oppressive systems. This is the temporality of trust.

At this point, it is important to remind ourselves of a fundamental difference between Socrates and the ignorant schoolmaster—a difference that turns on the use of the syllogism, or at least the use of philosophy as the organization or elucidation of reasons. First, like the ignorant schoolmaster, Socrates proclaims himself to be "ignorant." As Gregory Vlastos argues (1991), Socrates's claim to ignorance is an ironic claim. In the "Apology," Socrates makes two surprising statements. First, when he is told that the oracle at Delphi has declared he is the wisest man in Athens, Socrates begins questioning everyone he can that professes wisdom. His goal is to test the Oracle's statement. He finds that on being examined, those who say they have wisdom, have none. What separates them from Socrates? Socrates says "he [who alleges wisdom] thinks he knows something when he does not, whereas when I do not know, neither do I think I know" (21d). Thus what makes Socrates wise is his realization that he is ignorant, that he does not have wisdom. Second, during his trial, Meletus accuses Socrates of corrupting the sons of Athens, yet Socrates says he cannot be blamed for corrupting youth because he has never been anyone's teacher. "I have never been anyone's teacher. If anyone, young or old, desires to listen to me when I am talking and dealing with my own concerns, I have never begrudged this to anyone, but I do not converse when I receive a fee and not when I do not. I am equally ready to question the rich and the poor if anyone is willing to answer my questions and listen to what I say" (33a).

So if Socrates knows nothing except that he does not know anything and if he does not teach anyone anything, why does Rancière draw a decisive line between Socrates and the ignorant schoolmaster? These are, for Vlastos, expressions of Socratic irony: "what is said both is and is not what is meant" (1991, 31). In other words, Socrates's claim to ignorance is complex. On the one hand, he *is* ignorant of positive, substantive knowledge (or as we would say today, content area knowledge). On the other hand, he does teach a particular form of reasoning: he teaches procedural knowledge or a method of inquiry. And this method will allow students to discover for themselves the truth. Socrates teaches a certain way of thinking and organizing reasons, of evaluating arguments, of concept clarification, and principles for practical judgments. The ethic here is one of distrust: students do not know how to think properly and thus must be given the proper tools to help orient them toward the truth. Without these tools they will simply remain prisoners of the cave of ignorance into which they were born.

The structure of complex irony also allows the philosopher to rule through the noble lie. The noble lie—as an ironic pedagogical tool—both is and is not true. It reveals as it conceals and conceals as it reveals. As Rancière rightly points out, "playing, lying, and appearance" (2004c, 17) are exclusively reserved for philosophers in Plato's utopia. Philosophers need to be ironic pedagogues because their fundamental assumption concerns the inequality of intelligences. Only some will be able to access the Truth while others must remain dependent on noble lies to help guide them. There are, in this sense, two manifestations of the distrusting syllogism in Rancière's work. The first, outlined above, is critical sociology, which argues that equality is an ideological illusion concealing the seemingly inevitable reproduction of class distinctions. The lesson is clear: each of us is pre-determined to play the role assigned to us in the relations of production and thus exhibit our class-specific mode of cultural capital. Such a position denies the possibility of the politics of demonstration. And while Leftists might attempt to employ irony for liberatory ends—Brecht's epic theatre (see Bogad 2005) and Althusser's pedagogical practice (see Rancière 2011b, 146) are both exemplary in this respect—the result is always a stultifying hierarchy between those who possess true knowledge and those who are ignorant (and subsequently must be shocked awake and taught to think critically about their ideological illusions). The second, which we find in Platonic dialogues, is the noble lie. Here the "whole Truth" must be reserved for those with certain capacities (gold souls) and the rest of us must be told the dangers of imitation through imitation. In both cases, the distrusting syllogism is ironic: critical sociology produces that which it is describing and Socratic pedagogy teaches Truth through the play of appearance.

As opposed to either of these options, the democratic subject is a subject *without irony.* His or her claim to ignorance is genuine—there is no hidden knowledge (either content or procedural) behind his or her opinions (see below). Unlike critical sociology or the noble lie (which presuppose differences in capacities), the trusting syllogism never begins from an assumed location of superiority. There are no buried or hidden meanings behind appearances that remain inaccessible to the oppressed. Furthermore, guiding the syllogism is not a philosophical analysis (where abstract methods of analysis are superimposed on actions in the world from the top down) so much as a virtue of trust that the actions of the poor must have a logical structure in and for themselves. Rather than irony, the democratic subject is directed by *parody*—an improper imitation of that which one is not supposed to do or be. Parody is not an ironic concealment (a hiding behind the mask) but rather an appropriation (of masks)—a redistribution of roles and actions. It is the enacting of the "as if ..." of the democratic subject which is never simply a repetition or iteration but rather an appropriation that invents a new, unnamed subject position. In fact, it is the work of parodic performance that suspends distinctions between sacred and profane, actors and audience, reality and fiction, opening up a democratically dissensual stage.

The second dimension of the democratic subject is the hypothesis of equality, which follows from the ethic of trust. Without the supplement of equality, ethics—even a trusting ethic—can become aligned with consensus politics. For Rancière, current society all too easily replaces political dissensus with the ideal of the "ethical community" that "gathers together a single people in which everyone is supposed to be counted" (2010c, 189). The ethic of trust thus becomes a way of fostering the development of extended social bonds without the remainder of political dissent. In the social sphere, the result of this ethical community is consensus politics or, in the educational sphere, the result is policy such as "No Child Left Behind" or "Race to the Top." While it might appear that the ethical community would eradicate violence, this is in fact not the case. Hence the extended "humanitarian war" against terror, or the escalating suspension and expulsion rates in schools for poor minority students—both measures are deemed to be "ethical responses" to crises within a community. To revitalize democracy and thus call into question the consensus underlying the ethical community, the virtue of trust must be supplemented with the polemical hypothesis of equality. Summarizing the intimate interconnection of trust and equality in relation to teaching children to draw, Rancière writes: "We will thus trust in the child's will to imitate. But we are going to *verify* that will" (1991, 65). If one trusts in the ability of all to think, speak, act, or imitate without the need for explication, then the democratic potentiality of this ethical virtue is grounded in or through the hypothesis of equality. It is important to note that the hypothesis of equality is a *hypothesis* that must be verified. A hypothesis is not a form of knowledge offering grounds for an objective (and ultimately predictive) theory of x, y, or z phenomena. For Rancière, a hypothesis is much more akin to an opinion than to theoretical knowledge. As opposed to explicators (like Socrates) who have us believe that opinion is "a feeling we form about facts we have superficially observed" that grow in "weak and common minds" (Rancirère 1991, 45), opinion for Rancière opens up to the inherently democratic possibilities of dissensus. As long as we do not mistake opinion for knowledge (or as a type of pre-knowledge), then opinion becomes a groundless ground for testing and acting. It becomes the location for experimentation. As Rancière summarizes: "Our problem isn't proving that all intelligence is equal. It's seeing what can be done under that supposition" (1991, 46). In short, democratic subjects do not have knowledge (content or procedural) nor do they merely have uninformed opinions which they cling to as knowledge (i.e., white supremacist ideology). Rather *they have opinions that become hypotheses in need of verification.* The democratic subject first and foremost starts "from the point of view of equality, asserting equality, assuming equality as a given, working out from equality, trying to see how productive it can be and thus maximizing all possible liberty and equality" (Rancière 2007c, 51–2). Opinion becomes a moving force pressing into an experiment that is a "working out" of this opinion in particular situations and contexts in order to see what can be achieved according to the hypothesis. If the demonstration exhibits, then the experiment creates.

These experiments do not have to have prescribed protocols. Rather they are radically open-ended and thus genuinely experimental. Here, Jan Masschelein's work on philosophy of education as a type of experiment is important. According to Masschelein, the experiment is not critique—where critique rests on a certain distance from the object, concept, or reality under scrutiny. Drawing on both Foucault and Arendt, Masschelein proposes a theory of experiment that is embodied and embedded in a particular art of living without the reassuring distance of critical thinking to safeguard its truth. Quoting Masschelein, "thinking is an activity immediately related to an existential question of how to live in the present" (in press, 4). This thinking is not oriented toward knowledge so much as toward opening possibilities for living differently, for testing new hypotheses. Importantly, it is not that such experimentation lacks methodological rigor. The point is that such methodologies are not *outside* the experiment itself but are rather generated through the experiment as an event of creation—the creation of new ways of interacting, perceiving, living. This creation does not "prove" the accuracy of any one opinion, but rather attempts to demonstrate what can be translated, staged, and thus performed as a result of the hypothesis of equality. Such performances might not satisfy social scientists or empiricists that intelligence is equal, but they do create the open possibility for democracy to suddenly appear in the most unexpected of locations. As Todd May argues (2011), it is not the end result that concerns Rancière's notion of the democratic experiment (equality is, after all, not a state to be achieved so much as a state waiting to be verified) but rather the process itself. Thus the goal of emancipatory education is not to realize a missing equality but rather to re-create the efficacy of acting "as if ..." in the present moment. In this sense, experimentation is much more akin to aesthetic practice than scientific discovery or philosophical speculation (as it is traditionally understood within the discipline).

It is important to recognize the democratic politics of the hypothesis of equality by comparing it with its conservative and neoliberal counterparts. We must not conflate Rancière's emphasis on equality of intelligences as synonymous with conservative calls in education for poor minority students to "pick-themselves-up-by-their-bootstraps" (Noguera 2009). The bootstrap theory denies unequal access to educational resources, arguing that education is meritocratic. If students fail in school it is because of their own individual deficits. Thus blame for "failure" can be placed on students for personal lack of initiative. The corresponding social roles (low-paying jobs or prison) are, in essence, reflections of their internal capacities transformed into a social reality. If conservative narratives are grounded in the certainty of a self-fulfilling prophesy (these students will fail because of certain deficits in intelligence and will), Rancière's aesthetic redistribution of who can and cannot be heard or seen disrupts this prophesy and its narrative telos, opening up a contingently atopic space where those who were consigned to failure suddenly verify their capacities for thinking and speaking against the stereotypes projected onto them. This moment of sensorial disorganization of regimes and practices of silencing and invisibility (the gaze of power over and against students) is precisely the moment of educational equality. Rancière's argument does not deny educational inequalities, rather he chooses to focus on moments when the logic of inequality is subverted by those who have been discounted or are of no account and therefore write their own scripts and perform their own roles rather than those assigned to them within a system of self-fulfilling prophesies.

Second, the hypothesis of equality must be radically differentiated from the neoliberal "equality of the market." In the afterword to *The Politics of Aesthetics*, Slavoj Žižek critiques Rancière for marginalizing the key issue of radical politics: a critique of capitalism. Yet, I would argue that critique is not the issue. What is at stake in the hypothesis of equality is an experiment that creates new subject positions through the verification of equality beyond the logic of capitalist exploitation. If the equality of the market erases differences through the abstraction of exchange-value (an economic form of consensus where *a* can always be exchanged for *b*), then the former exceeds such measure/capture and thus remains sublime (supernumerary), open to dissensus, open to democratic disagreement. Stated differently, the hypothesis of equality cannot be captured or reified into a value to be exchanged for other commodities. It is a surplus that cannot be subsumed within the surplus-value generated by and through capitalist production. In this sense, the hypothesis of equality is not only radically different from the hypothesis of exchange but also fundamentally opposed. In education, this would mean that the purported "equality" of standardized, technocratic curricular reforms always misses its political mark precisely because it misrecognizes exchange (an abstraction and reification for continual circulation) as equality (a political interruption through a particular verification). The very same logic of exchange has transformed *students* (as bearers of equal intelligences who struggle to study) into *customers* (buying a product/diploma) or *products* (to be exchanged in a "free market").

This last observation leads us naturally to the remaining feature of the democratic subject: a poetic way of perceiving the world. Without this poetic way of perceiving, the places, sounds, subjects, and sensory coordinates of the community would never be challenged, and in turn dissensus would be reduced to mere negotiations for political, aesthetic, or educational recognition within a given police order. The democratic subject must have a poetic sensitivity and thus recognize "a distance between words and things which is not deception" (Rancière 2007c, 51) but an opening to a repartitioning of the sensible beyond common sense. The distance between words and things/actions creates a supplemental space of appearance—not of a deeper reality hidden behind illusion but of an appearance of that which has no count (and is thus of no account within the police order). From within this space of the surplus or the supernumerary remainder, the event of sensorial redistribution ruptures the field of perceptibility in order to hear, see, smell, touch differently. Through a repartitioning of the sensible, *the ignorant subject becomes a curious subject.* It is the distance perceived by the poetic subject that offers the creative space for curiosity to open up and seize hold of the anomalous detail or trace that disorganizes hierarchical relations, boundaries, and borders defining communities of consensus.

Thus far, I have provided an overview of the mutually constitutive dimensions of ignorance on the general or formal level of the democratic subject as such. Yet syllogisms of trust, the testing of hypotheses of equality, and poetic sensitivity manifest different qualities in relation to different forms of practice. At this point it is imperative to highlight key differences between the ignorant schoolmaster and Biesta's notion of the "ignorant citizen" (2011). Both are democratic subjects with a certain mastery of ignorance, but this mastery is specific to two different domains: politics (collective dissensus) and education (emancipation of individual intel-ligences). Of course, the boundaries between the two are mobile and permeable, but nevertheless, there are distinctions that must be drawn in order to recognize how ignorance partitions (in the sense of joining and separating) political disagreement and universal teaching.

For the ignorant citizen, a trusting virtue looks for the material inscription of equality within the commonwealth in order to make it into a dispute concerning a particular "we." The political inscription of "we, the people" is an interesting and important case in this respect. On the negative side, the ignorant citizen is ignorant of the specific content of "the people" (ignorant of any notion of the specific predicates separating the people from the rabble or the multitude, or what counts as citizenship according to a predefined set of criteria). Thus ignorance is enabling, allowing the citizen to call into dispute any particular limits placed on the meaning of the concept. And on the positive side, the ignorant citizen trusts that the body of the *demos* and the claim to equality are in fact one and the same, that there is a logic to revolt that does not rest on the judgment of experts or representative leadership. For the ignorant schoolmaster, a trusting virtue concerns the question of intelligence in relation to the will, and also shares negative and positive dimensions. The schoolmaster remains ignorant (or agnostic) of claims to separate and classify students according to learning ability, thus opening up a field for universal teaching. And universal teaching in turn trusts that the reason for different outcomes is not because of a fundamental difference between intelligences but rather because of a lack of opportunities to express the equality of wills.

Both figures—the citizen and the schoolmaster—once again converge and simultaneously diverge in relation to the hypothesis of equality. On the one hand, the ignorance of the ignorant citizen concerns opinions loosed from any relation to the Truth, creating the necessity for continual experimentation or disagreement concerning the nature of the count of the community. In other words, equality must be verified in relation to the fundamental question of the deictic "we" and its connection to "the people." The ignorant citizen produces a fictional people that exists precisely where it should not and acts in a name of the One that it is excluded from. This is the atopic space of the political "newcomer" as Biesta would argue—the subject that introduces something new into the order of things precisely because of the distance between the deictic "we" and the count of "the people" thus inaugurating a dispute. This experiment is tested on a social stage between classes of those who count and those who do not count, and is addressed to social, political, and economic laws that divide and maintain hierarchies.

On the other hand, the ignorant schoolmaster's hypothesis is tested between individual wills in order to verify the equality of intelligences. As Rancière argues, intellectual emancipation always starts with a "one-to-one relationship" (2011d, 46). This relationship takes the privileged form of the family. Here Rancière is clear that the "family" does not mean a retreat into a bourgeois, patriarchal, private sphere. Rather, the poor family is a stage of emancipation which redistributes roles and power according to the axiom of equality poised against institutional regulation, professionalization of education, and dependency on certified experts. Summarizing this radical reinterpretation of the family, Rancière writes, "The family deployed in this way does not withdraw into itself; it becomes the point of departure for a different sociability from that of collective fictions and institutional monopolies, the site where an individual is formed for whom being emancipated and emancipating are one and the same thing, experiencing in themselves the powers of reason and life and feeling these as principles of solidarity between individuals" (2011d, 24). If political disagreement is an agonistic relation between a collective "we" and the law (of the economy or the state), intellectual emancipation is an educational relation between two individuals tested in the family—or any location where the student and teacher meet in their mutual ignorance in order to verify the singular appearance of equality of intelligences. Certianly this relation is also agonistic, but the disagreement, again, rests between indivduals struggling to stage an equality of intelligences through the freedom and equality of curiosity and will.

Finally, there is the question of the differential relationship to aesthetics found in the ignorant citizen and the ignorant schoolmaster. The aesthetics of politics begins with a performance/demonstration that is also a dispute. The performance of "we" in "we, the people" produces a constitutive ambiguity that exceeds any particular manifestation of "the people." In other words, "we," as a *deictic* pronoun, becomes the sublime excess within the beautiful script of "the people"—the aesthetic surplus that provides a stage for a disagreement as the pronunciation of a wrong. The "we" is perpetually open to rearticulations and thus ongoing disputes over the content of the people. Summarizing his research of workers archives, the objects of his study were "neither the consciousness of an avant-garde instructed by science nor the systemization of ideas born out of the practice of the masses … not people who carried the word of the masses, but just people who carried the word; individuals separated from their supposed fellows by what they had grasped, caught up in the circuit of a speech that came from elsewhere …" (2011d, 28). In other words, the annunciation of a people is never based on the science of the intellectual or grounded in the standpoint of the masses but rather appears as a curious excess of opinion of those who "carried the word" separated from its proper location within the order of discourses.

In education, the performance is never of a people. Rather than a collective organization of a "we," the performance of ignorance is split into two equally important roles. On one hand, there is the ignorant schoolmaster who must enact a parodic command (a command that lacks any ground in content or procedural knowledge). On the other hand, there is the student who must perform a mastery which he/she is not sanctioned to have and thus remains ignorant of social divisions. Both have certain hazards which must be avoided: in the case of the former, parody must not become irony and, for the later, "as if…" cannot become a passionate attachment to mastery as expertise. Also, these roles are not always fixed. For instance, there are occasions when a student can act as an ignorant schoolmaster for another student. Rancière writes, "Each ignorant person could become for another ignorant person the master" (1991, 17). What is important here is that the performance of universal teaching is always a parody of the command of expertise—even in cases where fellow students point out or place before. This is decisively not the case in the political performance of a people (acting as ignorant citizens). Political performance excludes the role of the master (there is no vanguard of the *demos*). An example of an educational community where students act as ignorant schoolmasters for each other can be found in Rancière's retelling of the story of Gabriel Gauny, who, in 1893, described the "natural history collection of the poor" as follows:

> Without any funds to conduct our research, we threw ourselves into mineralogy, botany, numismatics, archaeology, and seized on the fossils we could glean from the quarries … starting from collections of pebbles; we sought the reasons for their colours and shapes, losing ourselves in wild conjecture in the attempt to discover these. (2011d, 39)

Here we see a clear illustration of the heretical knowledge of the emancipated poor that begins with a curiosity that "seizes them" and ignites a perpetual inquiry into the nature of minerals, and so on. This curiosity breaks with dependency on the schoolmaster as explicator and initiates an aesthetic redistribution of seeing and observing, "wild conjecture" and "scientific discourse." The amateur scientist has three important characteristics: a curiosity that exists despite his or her social and educational background, an emphatic will, and a surplus of "wild conjecture" or opinions that always have to be tested. Rather than the political subjectivation of a "we," Gauny and his associates present an educational subjectivation of wills directed toward a peculiar problem of scientific taxonomy. Through the assumption of roles, they enact an uncertain community that overturns any strict correlation between social location, thinking, experimenting, and presumed expertise. Gauny and fellow travelers undertake an *educational strike* against intellectual elitism in order to empower themselves to think and speak against all presumptions or expectations otherwise. In short, the curiosity of the amateur philosophers, musicians, and scientists disorganizes a perceptual field of inequalities, opening up an atopic space for the manifestation of their theatrical wills to be what they are not supposed to be and do what they are not supposed to be capable of doing.

In sum, the ignorant citizen and the ignorant schoolmaster share the same fundamental relation to democracy in that they both exhibit an ethic of trust, a hypothesis of equality, and a poetic sensitivity. Yet, these three dimensions of ignorance appear differently in each respective domain. Overlaps certainly exist, but so do tensions in terms of scale, staging, and performance. Without acknowledging these tensions, the fundamental scene of individual intellectual emancipation and the scene of collective political disagreement collapse into one another without recognizing the translation necessary to move between one and the other (Voelker 2011). If the above analysis focuses on distinctions, this is not to underestimate articulations. Rather, my goal has been to (a) emphasize the need to think the positive content of educational ignorance on its own terms without the importation of external political terminology (such as the ignorant citizen) and (b) provide a map which, precisely because it calls for distinctions, might be useful for highlighting the novelty and singularity of those important moments when domains and scales are ruptured, creating a new distribution of politics, aesthetics, and education. For instance, there are unique historical events wherein the uncertain community of curious students suddenly names itself and proclaims "we, the students" (the Chilean winter and the Occupy Student Debt Movements in 2011 speak to this phenomenon). This collective enunciation speaks beyond the trusting ethic of teacher/student relationships and directly addresses the *demos*. In other words, the community of curious experimenters makes a collective enunciation in the form of a dispute over a purported wrong. The hypothesis of equal intelligences becomes the hypothesis of the equality of all citizens to resist the instrumentalization of education within society conceptualized as a school obsessed with life-long learning and continual re-skilling to meet the needs of a fast-changing economy. And finally, the theatrical will to enact the mastery which one is not qualified to have translates into the will to enact the part of those who have no part yet take part. In sum, "we, the students" is a political subjectification of the student who "struggles to study" (Arsenjuk and Koerner 2009, 9) and perpetuates curiosity in the face of learning objectives, educational measurements, and the necessities of the market. The educational demand for the space and time of curiosity and willful experimentation becomes a political dissensus over the uses and abuses of time, space, and money in the learning society as such. In sum, ignorance—a positive having just as much as a lack— enables the translation across scales, scripts, and performances separating and conjoining educational emancipation and political disagreement, and thus acts as a truly democratic interface.

Conclusion

The challenge of Rancière's position can thus be formulated as follows: is it possible to think of a parodic master not simply as an "expert" who has detailed knowledge about this or that (content or process) and ignorance simply as praise for American fundamentalist populism? In the present conjunction could we not return to Freire and Rancière simultaneously in order to live within the space between ignorance and expertise, and in the process conceptualize the emancipatory schoolteacher as the one who is *a master in his or her ignorance*? This mastery is not knowledge per se (at least in the sense of critical consciousness raising, informed citizenship, or cognitive mapping) but rather composed of (a) an ethic of trust, (b) a hypothesis of equality, and (c) the aesthetics of equality. This is not a form of mastery *over* something (knowledge, students, political communities, etc.). Rather it is an *opening up* to something: one's capacity for democratic politics without the grounds or certainties of proper knowledge. Ignorance is not simply *not* a limitation on what one can do (the minimal claim) but also, and more importantly, an enabling condition (the maximal claim) that is necessary for not only universal teaching but democratic politics as well.

This formulation enables us to make a key distinction between two types of ignorance: the destructive, angry, violent, and discriminatory ignorance of the fundamentalist or white supremacist and the ignorance of the democratic subject. When we become masters in our own ignorance, we can transform a stultified ignorance into a democratic ignorance that does not reduce thinking to conformist ideology but rather retains the close connection with the dissensus of equality. Stated differently, could we not argue that stultified ignorance lacks what both Rancière and Freire, when read together, emphasize: a relation to ethics, equality, and aesthetics? Unlike stultified ignorance, Rancière's democratic ignorance does not close us off from the world (and thus produce enclaves of racist perception or white privilege) but rather opens us to the sublime beauty of the world through the work of curiosity on the aesthetics of our perception and the *philia* binding our communities together. My maximal reading of ignorance as positive and enabling thus meets the minimal criteria necessary to overcome the pure ideological closed-mindedness of the racist or the fanatic—both of whom mistake opinion for truth and stubbornness for curiosity. Rather than ignorance as an irrational response to the question of equality, Rancière enables us to recognize ignorance as a type of genius constitutive of the democratic subject.

At the same time, a rehabilitation of democratic ignorance addresses the problem of "public pedagogy" which its critics do not address but which Althusser fell victim to. As summarized previously, the problem with "public pedagogy" or "initiation pedagogy" is that implicit, progressive teleology—whereby the ignorant slowly become knowledgeable through the tutelage of the expert—never overcomes a certain dependency on explications. As Rancière argues, the persistent quest for "scientifically proven" methods of teaching which can be learned, enacted, and then generalized in the name of improvement only results in "the perfecting of *tethers*" (1991, 122) rather than in the support of equality and democracy. In other words, progressive pedagogical techniques, reforms, and so on are not political events so much as organizing principles of the police order that tether teachers and students to a regime of explications that must be deferred to in order to "improve" a system of dependencies. The result is that the progressive philosophy of the educator turns into a form of "enlightened despotism" (Rancière 2011b, 54) when put into practice. As Rancière argues, the matrix of all forms of explication and dependencies rests on four axes: good and evil, before and after (1991, 117). Using these terms we can formally represent the stultifying logics of both conservative and progressive public pedagogies as follows:

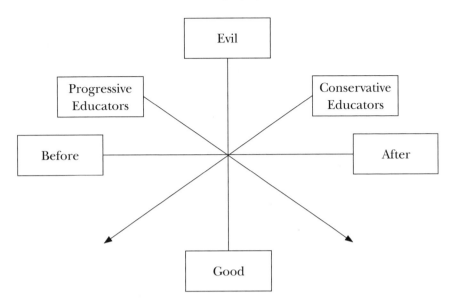

For both the conservatives and the progressives, public pedagogy is constructed along a temporal deferral where "good" is displaced into a romanticized past that we are constantly attempting to return to (conservatives) or a utopian future that we are struggling to realize (progressives). The projects of retrieving a lost essence (what it means to be a white, Christian nation) or safeguarding the democratic future (what it means to be an informed, multiculturally sensitive, and active citizen) both necessitate the competencies of the expert to guide, instruct, and keep the masses "on-track." Thus they cleave the political equality of the masses from the equality of intelligences, producing the very stultifying ignorance which they presuppose. If Freire argues that the oppressed have the capacity for knowledge and only lack the opportunity to express their wills, he nevertheless reconstitutes a kind of hierarchy between knowledges: the spontaneous ideology of lived experience (mired in ideology illusion) and dialectical science (which demystifies reality), which necessitates the intervention of the critical pedagogue who oversees the transition from aesthetic illusion (narrative sickness) to aesthetic utopianism (grounded in the critical science of historical materialism). This division in turn maintains a temporal deferral of emancipation where the ignorance of the oppressed can be overcome by correct knowledge, critical literacy, and new narratives. This position is perhaps best articulated through Freire's endorsement of Mao's famous proclamation: "You know I've proclaimed for a long time: we must teach the masses clearly what we have received

Freire and the Image: The Origins of the Problem

In the classic text *Education for Critical Consciousness* (1973), Freire argues for an education that is concerned with the "democratization of culture" (41) through the institutionalization of the "culture circle" (42). The culture circle, for Freire, is characterized by "debate either to clarify situations or to seek action arising from that clarification" (1973, 42). The existential goal of this program was to help students recognize their active role in the production and transformation of culture. As Freire summarizes, the program itself was not simply a preparation for democratic life but rather an attempt to "be an act of creation, capable of releasing other creative acts, one in which students would develop the impatience and vivacity which characterizes search and invention" (1973, 43). Drawing on the words of sculptor Abelardo da Hora, Freire argues "drawing the world, depicting things, using other languages, [is] not the exclusive privilege of a few. All people can make art ..." (1996, 117). Here Freire sounds remarkably similar to Rancière, who observes that one of the hypotheses of universal teaching is none other than "me too, I'm a painter" (1991, 67). In both cases, the focus of an emancipatory education is to redistribute the abilities of those who supposedly can and cannot create in order to verify that all students are reasonable beings capable of thinking, inventing, and speaking. This democratization of culture stands in solidarity with Rancière's emphasis on "common language" which presents a "struggle to cross the barrier between languages and worlds" by reappropriating a language that "had been appropriated by others" and in the process "affirm transgressively the assumption of equality" (2000a, 5).

To help students recognize themselves as *artistic* Subjects of history rather than Objects, Freire turns to the use of "codified" existential situations. Illustrated by Francisco Brenand, the ten codified images reproduced in *Education for Critical Consciousness* depict a movement from nature to culture, from "primitive" to "advanced" technology, and ultimately to self-conscious awareness of the culture circle itself and its significance in the literacy process. Thus each image was carefully designed to visually represent a particular stage of critical consciousness on its path toward self-recognition. As launching pads for dialogue in the culture circle, these images were to be "decoded" by the participants "with the help of the coordinator" (Freire 1973, 47). Thus for instance, the first image titled "Man in the World and With The World, Nature and Culture" depicts a man standing with book and hoe poised between a tree (nature) and a house and a well (culture). According to Freire, the image is supposed to represent the power of human beings to create and re-create the world or "the active role of men *in* and *with* their reality" (1973, 46). Reflecting on his own use of the image, Freire summarizes: "Through the discussion of this situation—man as a being of relationships—the participants arrive at the distinction between two worlds: that of nature and that of culture" (1973, 63). After the initial introduction to literacy and liberation illustrated in the Brenand sketches, subsequent codified images are projected along with a corresponding generative word "which graphically represents the oral expression of the object perceived" (Freire 1973, 52). Dialogue then continues until the decoding is "exhausted" (Freire 1973, 52).

In what follows, I will propose an alternative notion of the image that does not rely on this correspondence theory between intention, codification, decodification, and action. In this way, I will open up a space where Freire's original goal can be met: where students can be recognized as creative interpreters and translators. In order to better understand and ultimately move beyond Freire's limitations, we have to once again turn to Rancière. Through Rancière's work on the image, we can generate a new vocabulary which will help educators move from the discourse of codified images to pensive images, from passive to emancipated spectators.

The Pensive Image in Critical Pedagogy

At the outset, I do not want to argue that everything Freire said is wrong-headed and thus in need of complete philosophical revision. At the heart of his project are two fundamentally sound assumptions. First, that there is an aesthetic dimension to emancipation—where aesthetic refers to *aesthesis* or sensation/perception. And second, that there is a relationship between words and images, between the verbal and the visual that forms the crux of the politics of writing and literacy. Yet what is at stake here is the particular relationship between forms of visibility and manners of speaking. In what follows, I will argue that Freire falls prey to three fundamental fallacies of the "classical regime" of the arts: the intentional fallacy, the fallacy of artistic hierarchization, and the fallacy of spectatorship. While some have criticized the specific content of Brenand's images (Taylor 1993), my concern is first and foremost with the function of the images in relation to dialogue. It is the dialogue that transforms the images into scenes in a plot, thus silencing the images that thwart this progressive narrativization.

If Freire's stated goal is to use the images as tools to help create new knowledge, help students see themselves as active participants in their own worlds, and finally, to illustrate the democratization of culture ("me too, I'm a painter!"), we instantly see a contradiction between his goals and his description of the pedagogical implementation of Brenand's illustrations in classrooms—thus the initial correspondence between Freire and Rancière seems to be more of a surface coincidence than anything else. It is difficult to see how Freire can mediate his claim that, on the one hand, codification and de-codification can "be an act of creation, capable of releasing other creative acts" and, on the other hand, insist on the careful selection of codes to illustrate particular messages that will then correspond to particular stages of critical self-reflection culminating in a willingness to participate in the literacy program.

At the heart of this contradiction lies Freire's understanding of how images function. For him, the image transmits the message of the author/artist through a visual form. This message can then be de-coded in a rather transparent manner with the help of the teacher who guides the students to focus on specific aspects of the images in a specific order. Thus there is a clear correlation between the intention of the artist/author, the visual representation (the code), and the interpretation of the students (de-coding) which is then identified with a phonically rich generative word. Creation in this model is never the creation of the new, nor is agency the agency of invention, and the word appears as the result of an ideal causality that translates intentions to images to signs. In other words, there is no space in Freirian pedagogy of the oppressed for the oppressed to dis-identify themselves with their own pictorial representation. For instance, in the tenth illustrated situation entitled "A Culture Circle in Action—Synthesis of the Previous Discussions," the coordinator stands in front of a seated "audience" with pointer in hand, clearly indicating a connection between a specific verbal exchange and the attending image. Freire writes, "On seeing this situation, the Culture Circle participants easily identify themselves" (1973, 81). The active, creative, inventive participants thus are held captive to the image of themselves as a seated audience gazing upon the teacher who points, gestures, and guarantees the connection between intent and content, word and image. In this illustration, the image of the pointer and the pedagogical act of pointing visually represent the moment of dialogically guiding or "helping" shear the gap between image and reception, maintaining a seamless transmission of meaning and identification. In this sense, the pointer acts as a gaze orienting the glance of the student to the correct identification of themselves as an audience of this enunciation, of this image, of this political act. The image thus summarizes a certain contradiction at the heart of Freire's project: to empower students to see themselves as agents of cultural change they must first identify themselves as unequal partners in the pedagogical act of pointing and looking—an act that holds them in the very position of dependency which the pedagogy of the oppressed is attempting to counteract.

Here we can contrast Freire's description of pointing with that discussed in the last chapter. Rancière's schoolmaster points to an object of *shared* ignorance, some detail or object that is beyond the grasp of the teacher's knowledge. The results of the ignorant schoolmaster's gesture are thus unknown—the void into which the teacher and student enter remains enigmatic. Image and word, intent and content can never be fully sutured together to produce a linear path from aesthetic illusion to critical consciousness and from literacy to activism. The point of pointing is therefore radically different in both cases: for the critical pedagogue, pointing maintains the course toward critical consciousness raising and activism while for the ignorant schoolmaster, pointing interrupts such linear progression through perpetual stumbling. For Rancière, stumbling is never an obstacle so much as a contingently necessary condition for the verification of intelligences—no one intelligence knows what he or she points at or toward.

Although Freire clearly aligns himself with revolutionary political and social activism, it is the underlying logic of his use of images that locates him in a much more conservative classical understanding of the pedagogical function of images. Rancière describes the "pedagogical model" of art as follows: "what the viewer sees ... is a set of signs formed according to an artist's intention" (2010c, 135). Thus images within the pedagogical model embody the political intent of the artist to edify the audience as to social, political, or economic atrocities. This edification then corresponds to a particular action. "We may no longer believe that exhibiting virtues and vices on stage can improve human behavior, but we continue," writes Rancière, "to act as if reproducing a commercial idol in resin will engender resistance against the 'spectacle', and as if a series of photographs about the way colonizers represent the colonized will work to undermine the fallacies of mainstream representations of identities" (2010c, 136). Applying this definition to Freirian pedagogy, we can clearly see how his assumption is exactly the same: show images of people actively creating the world and the audience will identify with this subject position and consequently take action (i.e., take up the project of emancipation through literacy acquisition). The same acts in reverse: show images of atrocities and students will become outraged followed quickly by revolution. If Rancière argues against the naivety of this pedagogical model of art, I would also argue that the enemy is not the pedagogical model as such but rather this particular mode of pedagogy. Thus what is necessary here is not a decoupling of art and education but rather a reconfiguration of their relationship by rejecting the foundational logic of Freire's intentional fallacy.

The function of the work of art in relation to politics (or education for that matter) cannot be predicated on a direct cause and effect relationship between intention and political subjectivation, between the primacy of the word and representative function of the image. In the classical regime of art, there is, for Rancière, a "determined relation between the words and the visible" so that the "visible illustrated what the words said" (2000b, 22). This classical regime functioned according to a basic principle: "the belief that speech is what governs the forms of the visible" (Rancière 2000b, 22). In our present historical moment, the political equivalent of the classical regime of art is what Rancière refers to as the predominance of the "interpretation machine" (2010a, 131) over the proliferation of images. As opposed to others such as W. J. T. Mitchell (2006) who argues that we are witnessing a massive historical shift from the dominance of literature to the dominance of the image (the pictorial turn), Rancière suggests that what is unique in contemporary society is not so much the reign of the image but rather what I would call the "interpretive turn." According to Rancière, "the image does not constitute the heart of media power and its utilization by the authorities. The heart of the information machine is interpretation. No events, not even false ones, are needed because their interpretations are already there, because they pre-exist them and call them forth" (2010a, 130). In other words, events and their representation in images are reduced to mere symptoms of societal problems which are always already interpreted in advance according to an *a priori* logic. As with the classical regime of art, the interpretive regime of the media presents a determined relationship between word and image.

Freire's use of dialogue in his cultural circles seems to adopt a similar principle: the teacher uses the image to illustrate the word which is slowly unveiled through dialogic procession from one image to the next. If this is the case, then the student as "emancipated spectator" remains dependent on the word of the educator to point the way, demonstrate the correct path, provide guidance to the proper meaning of the image. Yet in the aesthetic regime of art, there is no presumed hierarchy between word and image. Summarizing this key difference, Rancière writes: "The aesthetic mode of art is the one where the arts are no longer distributed hierarchically according to their proximity with the power of words to make us see, where instead they are equivalent as languages" (2000b, 24). Instead of language interpreting the meaning of an image, it is *another mode of the sensible* that becomes visible, another relation between words and images that becomes possible. Rancière summarizes this position: "There is no straight path from the viewing of a spectacle to an understanding of the state of the world, and none from intellectual awareness to political action" (2010c, 143). In other words, images no longer passively illustrate existing intentions. Images can now speak back in their own language against the power of words, producing a "rupture in the relationship between sense and sense, between what is seen and what is thought, and between what is thought and what is felt" that "can never be calculated" (Rancière 2010c, 143). It is this measureless common between word and image that defies the intention of the teacher/coordinator, opening a space of dissensus or tension within the "sentence-image" (2007b) assemblage. Remaining within the classical regime of understanding word and image, Freire's use of illustrations as catalysts for emancipation remains problematic. The ten existential illustrations Freire employs in his literacy program are reduced to nothing more than preparation for democracy *after* literacy is established—after the image is conquered by and through the word. Rancière's axiom of equality (that equality must be seen as a point of departure rather than as a destination) is deferred until the student recognizes the message of liberation and identifies with this message through the work of critical literacy. In this sense, Freire's pedagogy of the oppressed reenacts the paradox of spectatorship found in avant-guard theatrical experiments that constitute the very distinction between passivity and activity they are attempting to overcome.

But emancipation, for Rancière, only begins when "we challenge the opposition between viewing and acting" (2009c, 13) by realizing that the spectator also acts through observing, selecting, and interpreting. Rather than decoding images (a transmission model of reception that grants creative agency to the artist), the spectator, for Rancière, translates images. The act of *translation* opens a space between intent and content, leading to dissensus rather than consensus over the image. It is here that democracy emerges as the possibility of disagreement over what is seen in the image. An emancipated community, in Rancière's view, is a community of translators rather than a community centered on the transmission of pre-existing interpretations. It is important to emphasize that translation for Rancière is not simply people disagreeing with each other about an interpretation of an action, statement, or meaning of a work of art (a game of "he said, she said" or of "counter-storytelling"). Rancière summarizes, "... dissensus [through translation] is not the opposition of interests or opinions" of subjects but is rather "the production, within a determined, sensible world, of a given that is heterogeneous to it" (2004c, 226). In other words dissensus is aesthetic "in that it makes visible what had been excluded from a perceptual field, and in that it makes audible what used to be inaudible" by "inscrib[ing] one perceptual world within another" (Rancière 2004c, 226). Thus whereas Freire attempts to orchestrate consensus through dialogue by sheering up the image (thus subordinating the image to the power of the word, of *aesthesis* to *noesis*, and thus denying any gap that would leave open room for dissensus), Rancière would argue that it is only in the moment of translational dissensus where the participants dis-identify themselves with the images that democracy becomes possible, revealing that spectatorship is an active form of engagement where the gap between sense and sense becomes constitutive of new subjectivities and new stages for dispute.

At this point, it is instructive to remember that for Freire, students move to the next image when dialogue has been "exhausted." Dialogue can only be exhausted if it is a means to reaching a predetermined, final destination determined by a pre-existing intention. The danger here is that dialogue might very well be reduced to nothing more than *dialogic interpretation*, where the image is forced into the subordinate position of mere illustration of a linear narrative of consciousness raising that terminates in an ontological vocation. Rancière argues that art under the aesthetic regime functions according to "silent speech" (1998). While the image might be a hieroglyph that begs for explanation and thus demands the speech of a spectator to unveil its hidden meaning, it also resists this speech, refusing explanation and thus remaining silent. Because of this constituting ambiguity of art, the image resists reduction to mere symptom which speech explains. To stay true to the ambiguity of the aesthetic regime of art, Rancière argues we must maintain the relation between the controlling inscription of speech and the silent discourse of the image which reminds the viewer of its lack of identity. It is here in the aporia of silent speech that a disruption between sense and sense becomes possible (a dissensus between our dialogical framework for interpretation and our sensual experience). Without dissensus, dialogue *silences the silence* of the image therefore missing the contingency of democratic politics that is unique to the visual arts of the aesthetic regime. Stated differently, Freire all too quickly reduces visual art to a speech act, removing its muteness. Yet the connection between art and politics is not a directly unilateral path from intention to codification to decodification to action. Rather, "artworks can produce effects of dissensus precisely because they neither give lessons nor have any destination" (Rancière 2010c, 140). In their silent speech, images "do not supply weapons for battles" but rather, "they help sketch new configurations of what can be seen, what can be said and what can be thought ... but they do so on condition that their meaning or effect is not anticipated" (Rancière 2009c, 103). What Freire has missed is the possibility that the image can effect a "dissensual re-configuration of the common experience of the sensible" (Rancière 2010c, 140) beyond the intention of the artist, beyond the pointing of the teacher, beyond the straight line between inscription, interpretation, and action—a dissensual re-configuration of our very abilities to see and to speak that results from the silent speech of the image.

What is necessary here is a new fundamental understanding of the image as "pensive." In describing what makes an image pensive, Rancière argues:

> It is not the aura or *punctum* of the unique apparition. But nor is it simply our ignorance of the author's thought or the resistance of the image to our interpretation. The pensiveness of the image is the result of this new status of the figure that conjoins two regimes of expression, without homogenizing them. (2009c, 122)

In this quotation, Rancière argues that pensiveness is not a resistance of the image to our interpretation, nor is it simply ignorance on the part of the viewer as to the author's "intentions." Rather it comes from our attention to the appearance of a seemingly anomalous combination of modes of representation juxtaposed next to one another in the same space. The juxtapositioning of elements in an image excites the senses by introducing a surplus in the field of the sensible. The pensiveness of the image can thus be defined as "this tangle between several forms of indeterminacy" (Rancière 2009c, 114). The resulting images are pensively "full of thoughts" (Rancière 2009c, 107) that cannot be contained within or by the agency of artist or teacher. Thus, we must question Freire's observation that participants in the culture circle "easily identify themselves" (1973, 81) with the tenth illustrated situation. Is this because the illustration interpellates the viewers through the immediacy of its visibility? Or is it that the dialogue—a tool for promoting democratic agency—becomes a wall between the students and the pensiveness (the silent speech) of the image at hand, and thus a tool of "narratocratic" power (Panagia 2009)? If this is indeed the case, what happens to the students' curiosity over the indeterminacy of the images, what happens to the fullness of thoughts that define the image? The question concerns how dialogue does or does not allow the pensiveness of the image to stimulate curiosity in the unaccounted-for detail. Here we can return to my initial analysis of the tenth illustrated situation entitled "A Culture Circle in Action—Synthesis of the Previous Discussions." If the represented gesture of the teacher works to identify students with the intention behind the image (an act of pointing out that bridges the "here" of the culture circle and the "there" of the illustration), then the gesture of the ignorant schoolmaster precisely functions in the opposite direction: it points to that which he or she is likewise ignorant of, to that which has no apparent intention lurking below the surface. What is at stake here are two functions of pedagogical "pointing to": the first attempts to coincide appearance and reality through beautiful symmetry/ mirror reflection while the second attempts to demonstrate a sublime excess or pensive detail that both draws in and is drawn out by curiosity.

In relation to the illustrations employed by Freire, there is a unique interweaving of different regimes of expression that open the images to a tangle of thoughts and questions which cannot be explained through a reliance on the intentions of the artist or teacher nor on the submissiveness of the image to the word. Unlike the classical regime of art with its assumption of pedagogical causality, art within the aesthetic regime disposes of hierarchies between artistic forms, objects, and modes of representation, disconnects style and subject matter, and finally creates an equality between "high" and "low" subjects (Rancière 2006c). As examples of the aesthetic regime, Brenand's illustrations are far more complex than Freire's analysis suggests. For instance, they are poised between journalistic realism, abstraction, and poetry. Throughout all ten images, the mimetic qualities of the images (rendering concrete the lives of men and women working in the countryside) are continually undermined by their modernist abstraction. Furthermore, the use of the images in a sequence supplemented with dialogue frames the illustrations as simultaneously independent pictures, staged theatrical sets, and cinematic frames. Thus the images are indeterminate in two senses: (a) within the images there is the juxtaposition of figuration and abstraction and (b) between images there is a constitutive tension between narrative sequentiality and visual interruption. In this indeterminacy between regimes of expression (inside and between images), the uniquely pensive quality of the images emerges. In terms of individual images, an equivalence is drawn between "high art" and journalistic "craft," symbolism and realism, figuration and abstraction that opens a gap between *poeisis* (production) and *aesthesis* (affect) that Freire's pedagogy quickly bypasses for a quick and easy identification between intention and reception, codification and decodification. As Freire guides the participants in the cultural circle from image to image (reading them as if they were a text, a play, or a film), there seems to be little room in his dialogue for the singular images and their details to break apart his rather Aristotelian dramaturgy. In Freire's own rush toward narrative closure, his pedagogical use of dialogue overrides the pensiveness of the images. Freire misses how art is political not simply because of its intended message (or the political commitment of the artist) but rather in its ability to produce new ways of seeing the world, new sensations, new sensorial disruptions through the pensive juxtapositioning of regimes of expression. The pensiveness works on the sensorial apparatus directly, altering what can be seen and what can be felt that exists in surplus of his causal assumption linking production and reception via dialogue as a guide.

But what exactly does this mixing or contaminating of regimes of expression enable us to see? If the form of the images speaks to a democratic leveling of hierarchical distributions of the visual (into high and low art or art and non-art) and the verbal (the language of art and the language of rural life), then this aesthetic pensiveness is restrained by Freire's own dialogical intervention which leads students away from the fundamental moment of pensive inquiry by the establishment of new hierarchies and dichotomies between nature and culture, literate and illiterate, human and animal. Thus, for instance, if the first situation is supposed to promote a clear understanding of the "distinction between two worlds: that of nature and that of culture" (Freire 1973, 63), the very system of values which Freire desires to convey are undermined by the form of the image itself—a form that exists in a state of creative exception between dichotomies. The image is in other words an embodiment of a redistribution of the partitioning of the sensibility which enables divisions to be constructed in the first place. In a surprising twist, it is not the man standing in the foreground of the image holding a book and a hoe that represents the democratic possibilities of the pensive image but rather the marginalized woman in the background who, like the form of the image itself, stands between worlds, between categories and thus refuses to identify with either nature or culture. The proper political gesture of the image is not of the man standing assuredly facing the audience with strength conveyed through physical power and emerging cultural mastery but rather of the woman *turning away from such identifications* and hierarchical distributions. Thus the only way to remain faithful to the democratic spirit of the image is to in fact dis-identify with Freire's intention and to remain true to the marginal, pensive detail: the woman with her back turned to the audience. If the man stands as an active protagonist against the passivity of nature, then the woman in the background cannot be clearly identified as either passive or active. The woman is actively leading the child, yet at the same time her abstracted form resembles the passive, mute bushes and trees more than the anthropomorphic figuration of the man. In other words, she stands between worlds as a kernel that resists definition or division between this or that, between active and passive, between silence and speech. She is the unstable element in the image that forces us to look differently at the world beyond hierarchical distributions to form new, unanticipated subject positions that remain uncounted within Freire's dialogical explication. She marks the unintended event of democratic disordering that is never reducible to intention or to mere mimetic representational content but rather emerges in and through the mixing of regimes of expression in the pensive image. Thus just as the image for Rancière marks "a condition that is indeterminately between the active and the passive ... between thought and non-thought ... [and] between art and non-art" (2009c, 107) so too the meek, seemingly trivial appearance of the woman throws Freire's project into confusion, disorganizing the field of the visual at the very moment that dialogue is attempting to colonize the fullness of its pensive presence. She is the "being-between: between several places and several identities, several modes of localization and identification" (Rancière 1994, 94). Even if a woman appears in the second illustration handing a book to a man (and thus emerging from her indeterminacy and marginality as an equal player in the acquisition of literacy), this gender equality does not absolve the first illustration of its ambiguity (thank heavens!). Rather the juxtaposition of the two images only heightens the fundamental question that suddenly ruptures Freire's teleological presentation which seamlessly leads from nature to culture, from visual to verbal, and from illiterate to literate. It is only through the opening up of this detail of the image—the woman who represents the "uncertainties of conjunction" (Rancière 1994, 94) rather than the subordination of explications—that there emerges the properly improper use of the visual in dialogue: the collective examination of the immeasurable excess of silent speech.

In discussing his book *The Ignorant Schoolmaster: Five Lessons in Emancipation*, Rancière argues:

> ... the mother doesn't intervene as a figure of fusion but rather in a very different form. She intervenes as a figure of equality. As long as the ideology of instruction opposes the teacher to the mother, she represents the equal capacity of anybody to be for anybody else a cause of learning. She carries the egalitarian power of the mother language, *la*

langue maternelle, which everybody learns without a schoolmaster … the
mother tongue is not a promise of fusion. It is rather an experience of
equality. There is a kind of learning that is involved in the acquisition
of the mother tongue … the idea that even the illiterate mother can
play for the child the role of the ignorant schoolmaster. In this case, the
mother is a figure of equality and not a figure of fusion. (2008a, 178)

In other words, as opposed to the hierarchical dependencies of stultifying
teaching, the mother stands for a fundamentally universal form of teaching
and learning open to everyone equally. The relation between mother and
child certainly conveys a continuity between life and learning as opposed
to the autonomous function of learning detached from life that comes to
form the backbone of schooling as an institution. Yet this continuity is not
some sort of primordial fusion, nor is it a romantic vision of the natural
dependency of the child on the mother. For Rancière, the mother in this
instance comes to represent a displacement of learning from the institutionalized expertise of the schoolmaster and a redistribution of who can
think and speak beyond the schoolhouse. If Freire once argued that the
pedagogy of the oppressed "does not give persons a license to teach what
they do not know" (1998, 17), then this figure ruptures the normative
criteria for determining who can and cannot teach, opening up a new
space for Rancière's theory of universal teaching to take shape. In relation
to Brenand's illustration, I would suggest that the woman/mother does
not represent the fusion of nature and culture so much as the promise of
equality—the promise that there need not be a specific relation between
teacher and student for learning to take place. In other words, the mother
in the image represents a teaching that is "mute" in the sense that, like
literature, it "goes hither and yon without knowing to whom it should or
should not speak" (Rancière 2000a, 8). In other words, in opposition to the
man, who stands for mastery of nature and of the word, the woman stands
for dissensus from this expert mastery, a turning away from the location
of mastery into the zone of indistinction where anybody can be a teacher,
even if they are ignorant of what they teach. Again, opening up the pensive
dimension of the image is not simply about creating a space in the dialogic
classroom for students to raise conflicting opinions about the ultimate
meaning of the image. Rather, focusing on the enigmatic detail of the
mother *shifts the stage of politics and education, shifts the very perceptual theatre*
of emancipation. In other words, attentive curiosity to the indeterminate
detail creates a new stage (the background becomes the foreground), a
new set of actors, and a new drama.

If the second illustration places man and woman side-by-side in the act of literacy, it also flattens the perceptual field, creating a one-dimensional foreground where action can only happen within a single, predetermined plane. The shifting ambiguity between foreground and background in the first image demonstrates the real connections between politics and the *mise-en-scène* of the image. The tension between these spaces—the foreground advance of masculine literacy and the background, subaltern gestures of the woman—demonstrates the indeterminacy of the phenomenal field of vision, providing a literal space for dis-identification. Yet the possibilities for political dissensus are snuffed out by the one-dimensional spatial uniformity of the second illustration wherein there is only *one, unanimous* gesture set upon a flattened, uniform stage.

Finally, there is the eighth situation entitled "Poetry." In this image, a book lies open—one page has a drawing of human forms intermingled with natural elements and on the other page the poem "A Bomba" is printed. The dialogue concerning the image emphasizes the distinction between nature and culture and how poetry is a distinct cultural artifact. Here we see in visual form a model distilling Freire's approach to literacy education in general which simultaneously links together words and images, poetry and language. Yet Freire ultimately retreats from the complexity of his own method, and the illustration, placed within the teleological framework of the images as they progress toward literacy, is reduced to nothing more than a mere prop, subservient to the arrival of the word as the final destination. What is missed is that the words themselves are images and the images are words, creating a state of open possibilities or dissensual arrest between literacy and illiteracy, between pre-political and political subjectivation. Thus the continuity between the image and the word is concealed even as its image forms the very core of Freire's literacy pedagogy. Freire argues that words are not to be memorized but rather are to be "visualized" (1973, 52) *as images* that can be broken down and recombined into new images. Stated differently, literacy begins by reinventing the image as word and word as image—a reconfiguration of the space of what can be considered visible and intelligible. If words were once invisible to the participants, they now become mobilized as a set of phonic images that can be sorted and recombined to form new images. The use of phonic pieces as the image matrix of word formation would be, in Rancière's analysis, a type of syntactic parataxis of the "sentence-image" (Rancière 2007b, 54)—a juxtaposition of fragments within the "measureless common" (2007b, 45) that simultaneously joins and separates images from words and sense from sense.

The sentence-image is not simply the combination of word and image, the verbal and the visual. "By sentence-image," writes Rancière, "I intend the combination of two functions that are to be defined aesthetically—that is, by the way in which they undo the representative relationship between text and image. The text's part in the representative schema was the conceptual linking of actions, while the image's was the supplement of presence that imparted flesh and substance to it. The sentence-image overturns this logic" (2007b, 46). No longer does the image simply illustrate the word. In its materiality, the word is no longer seen simply as a transparent barer of meaning, and second, the image suddenly appears to have an active power to disrupt accepted narratives relying on cause and effect. Linkage and rupture are thus combined in the assemblage of the sentence-image. In Freirian literacy, we can actually see this process at work when the word becomes an image composed of phonic pieces, which, in turn, can be recombined through aesthetic montage to form other sentence-images in a never-ending chain. The space that makes Freirian literacy possible is the space opened by the aesthetic-arts, which begins with a new connection between the verbal and the visual, between the sentence and the image. If the eighth situation illustrates the generative power of the sentence-image for promoting literacy, then Freire's dialogical explication all too quickly chooses to bypass this insight in order to maintain a clear path from the illiteracy of images toward the literacy of the word. The immeasurable gap that separates and joins the two is mistaken for a myth of progressive territorialization of the image by the word.

This eighth image further complicates Freire's intended message which focuses on the difference between poetry and other forms of language and action. Recording his discussion with participants, Freire writes that they come to realize "that poetic expression, whose material is not the same [as other forms of aesthetic production], responds to a different necessity" (1973, 77). Freire uses the image of poetry to partition the sensible into discrete realms of expression, demonstrating different realms of action, each responding to their own specific set of interests and needs. Thus we see yet again the repetition of his simultaneous desire to make education an "aesthetic event" and his reluctance to fully embrace the relation between science and narration, word and image, theatre and pedagogy—each of which opens onto democracy through the uncertainties of conjunction or a relation to a nonrelation or expressivity and mute speech. In fact, it is the aesthetic event of his project—a project that hinges on the sentence-image—that blurs such distinctions in the first place, opening up the fundamental question concerning where such poetics "properly" reside.

Poetic production is not a specialization or a specifically denoted terrain of struggle—this assumption is nothing more than a return to the "representational regime" (Rancière 2006c, 22) of the arts which stipulated certain norms of production for certain subject matter. What Freire seems to miss is that this division between poetic production and other types of cultural, political, and economic activity is itself an *aesthetic partitioning* of the sensible connected to a specific artistic regime.

In short, the culture circle cannot simply remain within the causal paradigm of intention, codification, and reception without losing the key to the emancipatory potential of the pensive image—a (dis)sensual shift in the thought immanent to the sensible itself. Democracy makes an appearance between sense and sense, between production and reception, between image and word and thus is an *event* (not a pedagogical method leading to predetermined ends). The event of democratic dissensus therefore cannot be prefigured in the intensions of the artist or through dialogical narration but happens only momentarily when the silent speech of the image suddenly displaces the location of *aesthesis.*

From the Pensive Image to a Coming Community

Rather than a community united through solidarity (the consensus of beauty without the supplement of the sublime) that *prepares* participants for emancipation *through* literacy (the model of the teacher as sculptor where emancipation is temporally deferred), I am suggesting a new notion of an educational community that is inoperative yet simultaneously *embodies* democracy in its constituting disagreement. The sublime work of the educational community emerges through attentive curiosity toward the pensive quality of images and the dis-articulation of sense and sense that they perform. The pedagogical model of art can thus be retained but with a radically different meaning. Rather than a model of behavior to be emulated (a certain represented subject position waiting to be filled by the audience), the pedagogical function of art is an actual experience of the "efficacy of *dissensus*" of the community that emerges through the "conflict between *sense* and *sense*" (Rancière 2010c, 139). It is in this unfamiliar zone of ambiguity opened up through the image that new subjects can be invented that do not fit within predetermined allotments of activity and passivity, nature and culture, human and animal, etc. This is not to say that education collapses into art or art into education (see the Introduction to this book). Rather it is to suggest that art has a specific function in the educational community: the sensorial destabilization of any correspondence theory between intention and representation that opens the space for curiosity.

In this sense, the pedagogical function of art is radically different from the model proposed by educational theorists such as Maxine Greene. For Greene, art has the "unique power to release the imagination" (1995, 27) where the imagination is the "possibility of looking at things as if they could be otherwise" (16). In turn, releasing the imagination is important for Greene because it is the first step toward acting to change the world. In this sense, the imagination is necessary for producing new sensory worlds and new narratives that bridge sensation, reason, and action. Freire seems to agree with this assessment, arguing that the image opens up a space for imaginative narratives to rewrite histories of oppression. Yet, as I examined previously, it is curiosity which is the faculty most clearly linked with the dissensual politics of education precisely because curiosity is the sensorial rupture necessary for the staging of the theatrical will. The educational community is always a curious community whose ignorance is also an openness to the silence of the image which never has narrative closure and always interrupts the imaginative plots we, as students and teachers, write.

Chapter Seven:

Freire's Last Laugh

There is no better starting point for thought than laughter.
—*Walter Benjamin,* Understanding Brecht

The new is always laughable ...
—*Bonnie Honig,* Emergency Politics

Paulo Freire once described his pedagogy as a "bohemian pedagogy of happiness.... This will be a pedagogy of laughter, of questioning, of curiosity ..." (Gadotti 1994, 160). The inclusion of laughter along side problem-posing dialogue might strike some as an ambiguous gesture, considering that the global exploitation of the poor is no "laughing matter." And yet, laughter seems to be an important aspect of the pedagogy of the oppressed. For instance, in his dialogue with Myles Horton, Freire makes the strong claim, "It's necessary to laugh with the people because if we don't do that we cannot learn from the people, and in not learning from the people we cannot teach them" (1990, 247). In this quote Freire emphatically emphasizes that laughter is a *necessary* action within the pedagogy of the oppressed. Laughter is not sufficient for a critical compre-hension of the world, yet it does form an integral moment in breaking down hierarchical relations between teachers and students and thus challenging inequality. Finally, it is also important to note that those close to Freire—students and friends—repeatedly mention Freire's laugh as a constituent aspect of not only his personality but also of his methods. In her poem dedicated to the memory of Freire, it is "the childlike laughter" of Freire's eyes that Antonia Darder chose to emphasize (2002, xiii).

Given these comments, Freire offers us an *invitation* to reconceptualize the role of laughter in the critical pedagogy tradition. Recently, scholars such as Cris Mayo (2008) have argued that the transgressive politics of certain black humor traditions are integral to a critical pedagogy project, offering a critique of white dominance through a nonreciprocal actor-audience relationship. Also Joris Vlieghe, Maarten Simons, and Jan Masschelein (2010) have argued that the topic of humor and of laughter should be moved into the center of discussions concerning democracy and community in critical pedagogy classrooms. And yet, if Freire is to further our understanding of laughter and education, we have to ask what exactly Freire means by laughter. In particular, we have to ask a series of key questions that Freire's work poses. Are all forms of laughter equally emancipatory? Does the laugh of the cynic resound with the same hope for social transformation as that of the utopian dreamer? Certainly a revolutionary pedagogue *can* laugh, but *should* he or she, and what are the political (if not revolutionary) implications of this laughter?

In order to shed new light on Freire's enigmatic reflections on the necessary role of laughing in the pedagogy of the oppressed I will turn to contemporary theories of humor and jokes. From an analysis of laughter, this essay will then turn to an examination of the structural relationship between jokes and critical theory. Along the way, my argument will build a network of connections between Freire and a variety of philosophers who are, in some way, shape or, form, interested in democracy, education, and social activism. In particular, I turn to Rancière for his emphasis on the aesthetics of democracy and Paulo Virno who connects joke telling with critical theory. Overall, I argue that Freire was correct but that his comments need to be unpacked and rigorously theorized before we can begin to see the exact nature of the internal relationship between jokes, laughter, and educational emancipation. Through this analysis, joke telling and laughing emerge as integral parts of the aesthetics of universal teaching, redistributing the sensible that underlies educational relations between masters and pupils and sense and nonsense in the classroom.

Make'em laugh, Make'em laugh, Make'em laugh!

In a brilliant ethnography of a Catholic junior high school in Toronto, Canada, Peter McLaren argued that laughter in the classroom is a particular form of student resistance. "Laughter of resistance is unlike any other. It occurs when the entire class—or a significant number of students within the class—spontaneously turn against the teacher" (1999, 164). This laugh is unlike the laughter directed at the class clown or the laughter of merriment or the laughter of the saint. Rather, "the laughter of resistance serves to mock and denounce. It is a hostile act, an insurgent symbol, one which inscribes the *via culpa*" (McLaren 1999, 165). Such laughter "neutralizes" the power of the teacher (McLaren 1999, 165). The sacred authority of the teacher is shattered by the roar of resistance laughter that enables students to "reclaim their sense of collective identity" (McLaren 1999, 165) over and against the ritual performances of schooling. Such acts form the internally excluded, or liminal "antistructures" of the classroom— holes in the ritual authority of the school where students open up terrains of contestation. In the coda to this text, McLaren returns to the theme of laughter, this time imbuing it with a postmodern, ludic aura. Drawing on Derrida, Cixous, and others, McLaren argues that laughter "helps to counter totalizing discourses by writing through the body as a trans-gressive and recusant material act; it celebrates the multiplicity of narrative practices of the self and struggles against the givenness of the social world" (McLaren 1999, 288–9). Laughter is a type of embodied deconstruction where normalized discourses and power hierarchies demonstrate their artificial and thus fugitive natures. Thus in many ways McLaren agrees with Vlieghe, Simons, and Masschelein mentioned above in that laughter is an experiential democracy of the flesh that offers a radical restructuring of power relations in the classroom.

McLaren seems to give added ethnographic and philosophical weight to Freire's original contentions. Laughter emerges as a transgressive act against the ritual of schooling. Yet in the introduction to the third edition of *Schooling as a Ritual Performance*, McLaren retracts or at least heavily tempers his previous reflections on laughter. Here laughter becomes nothing more than a symptom of postmodernism's "giddy free-fall of infinite semiosis" (McLaren 1999, xxxviii). The rupture of laughter in the classroom is not a real rupture after all but rather a soft, ineffectual substitute for direct social action. Dismissively, McLaren argues that "such resistance does not aspire to the realm of critical practice and is not sufficient to free that aspect of agency subsumed to the larger determinations that position individuals in the world. Students are unable to invent the multiple strategies needed to overturn fixed ideological positions and reveal their anchorage in practice. Capitalism and its laws of motion quickly and effortlessly overwhelm this type of student (and sometimes teacher) resistance" (McLaren 1999, li–lii). Thus in the end, McLaren's introduction overwrites his previous, much more affirmative analysis of the laugh and of the critical capacity of classroom humor. In fact, this self-critique replays the ambivalent role of the comedian in Marxism as such. As Rancière points out, the role of Marxist science has been to safeguard the script of proletariat revolution from the comedians. "For the basic risk that menaces revolutionary action is not the threat of defeat or death in combat but the threat of comedy … as for the modern revolution, it is being attacked from within by the comedians who serve as its actors" (Rancière 2004c, 111). What Engels was to Marx, so too McLaren is to Freire: both attempt to prevent any comedian from coming on stage and corrupting the script that has been written for the proletariats of the world. Against the "backwards march" that is the "comedy of the *lumpen*" (Rancière 2004c, 107) who refuse to take up their world historical destiny in the struggle between opposing classes, Engels, according to Rancière, effects a displacement of the ambiguities of Marx's science and thus creates a humorless pedagogy that nevertheless relies on the very clowns and fools that it so ardently disapproves of.

Cultural critics such as Slavoj Žižek would agree with McLaren's more or less pessimistic reading of laughter. In his critique of Umberto Eco's popular novel *Name of the Rose*, Žižek argues that Eco's thesis is upside down. If Eco argues that the greatest threat to society is the totalitarian and dogmatic rejection of laughter, the truth is actually the opposite: the greatest form of totalitarianism today is not the lack of laughter but rather the persistence of laughter. Žižek argues "What is really disturbing about *The Name of the Rose*, however, is the underlying belief in the liberating, anti-totalitarian force of laughter, of ironic distance" (2001, 28). In this reading, laughter is internal to the cultural logic of late capitalism. If there is any transgression through laughter, it is a transgression that adheres to the structure of capitalism itself. The perfect examples seem to be "fake-news" anchors like John Stewart who insight laughter that is critical of contemporary politics yet without "anchorage in practice" (McLaren 1999, lii) beyond ironic stunts or subversions that are more for their entertainment value than for actual political transformation. In other words, if laughter was at one point resistant to being co-opted by capitalism and the culture industry, it is now fully integrated and anticipated ahead of time. Laughing transgressions are always already part of the internal power relations that constitute our postmodern condition. In this example, Žižek's critique of laughter is even more vehement than McLaren's, for if McLaren does not want to completely abandon laughter (just to demote it), then Žižek wants to link laughter with totalitarianism directly.

At this point, it would seem that McLaren has abandoned Freire's clarion call to laugh with the people. If he once championed laughter as resistive, now it would seem that laughter is at best a displacement of certain radical potentials into a gentrified cultural form and at worst a symptom of the very thing that laughter was supposed to resist: totalitarian excess. It is in other words part of the ritual performance of schooling as it is also part of the ritual of capitalism on a larger economic scale. In what follows, I want to argue against this claim and return to Freire's original thesis. But there is some truth to McLaren's and Žižek's warnings. In the next section of this chapter, I will outline a topography of laughter that will enable us to maintain both the critique of laughter as well as Freire's insistence on its necessary role in critical pedagogy. In other words, through this topography we will be able to qualify these critiques as regional critiques corresponding to specific modalities of laughter.

Modes of Laughter

The Happy Laugh

Herbert Marcuse once described the consciousness of the affluent society as a "happy consciousness." The happy consciousness, according to Marcuse, is a consciousness without a critical capacity to question/negate the present reality. In other words, "It reflects the belief that the real is rational, and that the established system, in spite of everything, delivers the goods" (Marcuse 1964, 79). Happiness is thus naïve because it takes reality at face value without problematizing claims of equality, freedom, and liberty despite the ongoing existence of inequality, exploitation, and subjugation. In other words, it accepts the distribution of the sensible that defines the given police order.

Likewise, the happy laugh becomes a pure positivity, laughing at that which is predetermined as acceptable "nonsense." It is yet another way of affirming the irrationality of the system and as such is part of what Freire would describe as the "magical" qualities of reality. Like magic, the happy laugh conjures away the pain of exploitation, and helps us "laugh it off" or "just relax" in the face of the growing human and environmental catastrophes that mark the present historical moment of late capitalism. In this sense, laughter plays the cathartic role assigned to it within the given order of things. Happy laughter is ultimately the laughter of the neoliberal, individualistic consumer who feels entitled to laugh in order to achieve personal gratification, stress relief, or as a reward for hard work ("I deserve a good laugh!"). In the classroom, the happy laugh is used regularly to dissipate tension, fight off the fatigue of testing, or act as a reward for a job well done. Such laughing is nothing more than crisis control, configured in advance by the specific needs of an institution to regulate and maintain the proper place of the improper (the nonsensical noise of laughter) and thereby make it function within an economy of prefabricated ends. Within this context Žižek's warning against the totalitarian nature of laughter rings true, for the happy laugh is the abandonment of reason to the irrationality of massification. The political ramifications of happy laughter become a form of symbolic violence unable to understand its own role in the reproduction of systemic crisis that its form masks.

The Cynical Laugh

Yet the happy laugh of contented naivety is only one side of the coin. As its obscene other, the janus face of happiness is cynicism. For Peter Sloterdijk, cynical reason is "enlightened false consciousness. It is that modernized, unhappy consciousness, on which enlightenment has labored both successfully and in vain. It has learned its lessons in enlightenment, but it has not, and probably was not able to, put them into practice" (1988, 5). Happy yet miserable simultaneously, the cynical laugh rebounds throughout the postmodern, affluent world. In the end, this critical distance from the pure positivity of happy consciousness does not result in collective action, does not challenge the authority that it pokes fun at. Rather it results in more isolation, or perhaps the illusion of individual liberation through new age spirituality, virtual reality gaming, or the occasional work-place/classroom transgression. The cynical postmodern laugh becomes a poor substitute for political action, a cathartic moment of release that simultaneously "affirms" one's superiority over the system while also indexing one's complacency with this modicum of reassurance. Stated differently, the cynic receives too much dirty pleasure from his/her privileged insider knowledge, and as such this pleasure sustains political inaction. In other words, if there is a critical dimension to this laugh, it has always already been co-opted by a cynical cultural logic that anticipates and feeds off of the very tendencies toward cynical pleasures that constitute the backdrop of the laugh. As argued in the introduction to this book, the paradox of critique is replayed through the symptom of the cynical laugh that subverts while also remaining dependent upon the very systems that it denounces. Perhaps it would not be too far-fetched to argue that the cynical laugh is an index of the "unhappy consciousness" (not in Hegel's sense of the term)—a consciousness that is negative without any of the liberating qualities that Marcuse once attributed to negation, or to critique more broadly. In sum, if such a laugh points out the absurdities of existence, it does not challenge these absurdities so much as maintain the cynical

the overwhelming reduction of educational outcomes to aggregated test scores indicates the statistical abstraction of the student body into a mere ensemble of parts to be counted. As Rancière would point out, this trend is part of a larger hatred of democracy where homogeneity of numbers (everyone can be counted in order to be corrected) replaces the heterogeneity of politics in schools. Contemporary, standardized education is a policing function of "archipolitics" (Rancière 1999, 70) that attempts to psychologize education through measurement of aptitudes via high-stakes testing. High-stakes testing in other words transforms a political wrong (the structural limits of national testing to account for systematic educational inequalities) into an administrative problem remedied through more scientific pedagogies, increasingly more rigorous accountability measures, and more authentic testing measurements. This affectless circulation of numbers and statistics where there once were embodied students and teachers also challenges traditional interpretations of education as a form of interpellation. As Rancière describes (2010c), the function of the police is no longer to hail a subject ("Hey, you there!") but is rather to organize the efficient circulation of objects, ideas, and people within a system in order to account for all movements and to calculate strategies of control. Applying this distinction to education, we can see that the classroom is no longer interested in the individual investment necessary to interpellate students but rather in the proper flow of grades through the policing mechanism of accelerated testing.

Curious laughing draws new lines of sensorial distribution that cut across the police order of standardization, introducing a surplus collectivity not necessarily reducible to predefined social roles within the structures that dominate standards of classroom behavior, etiquette, and notions of "appropriateness." Laughter as a political operator recomposes the perceptual organization of spaces marked for study versus play and private versus public, creating a paradoxical zone of indistinction or indetermination—an uncertain community where students and teachers face one another without the mediation of formal roles and standardized procedures, a space that is contingent, unpredictable, and thus open to the invention of new compositions of bodies, thoughts, and affects. Laughing in this schema is a return of the flesh and the voice into the immunizing powers of standardized curricula. By undoing the fundamental sensual and aesthetic divisions of the standardized classroom, the contagion and contamination of laughter demonstrates the artificiality of that order. While some classrooms might be full of laughter (the ludic postmodern classroom for instance), this cynical laughter is—as described above—already co-opted by the status quo as an internally acceptable dirty pleasure. Such a laugh exists within and thrives off of the logic, norms, and values of the preestablished police order and is thus already a consensus of opinions. Here McLaren might very well be right: such laughter is a distraction against confronting inequality and is thus a corporeal expression of yet another manifestation of the hatred of democracy. In such situations, the curious laugh is a laugh against laughing, an interruption of laughter within laughter, a joyful hope set against joyless cynicism and contempt.

Curious laughing is a violently *non-violent weapon* of democracy that opens a new space of dis-identification and dissensus with the given social allotment of roles and identities typified by educational standardization through a semiotic excess. The laugh is a threshold between sound and signification, between animal *phone* and human *logos*. Within the moment of laughing that destabilizes classroom etiquette (what kinds of interactions are legitimate) and power (who is qualified to speak) there exists an aesthetic kernel that creates, as Rancière puts it, "uncertain communities that contribute to the formation of enunciative collectives that call into question the distribution of roles, territories, and languages" (2006c, 40). Because the uncertain community is composed of subjects who do not coincide with the social division of parties (teacher as administrator of tests and students as abstracted/disembodied statistics), it cannot be measured by the preexisting police order. In another context, Rancière refers to these uncertain communities as existing in "atopia" or a zone of displacement where "we no longer know who we are" and that is "foreign to the system of places" that constitute a police order (2003c, 121–2). Atopia is not a utopia (a no-place that exists outside and over there) but is rather the democratic excess—an untamed and unnamed space that cannot be quantified by statistical measure—that always already exists here and now just waiting for a laugh to verify its existence. Curious laughter marks the contours of atopia within the classroom, creating an uncertain community that lasts for only a fleeting second before it dissipates. In this model, the laugh is transformative not because it raises consciousness and thus reveals a darker reality hidden behind the veil of appearances—as is suggested by Freire's original model of critical consciousness analyzed through the former chapters of this book—but rather because it introduces a new mixture or arrangement of the sensible according to the joy of a community without a name.

Rancière argues that a democratic dissensus names a wrong and thus inaugurates a disagreement between the count and the no-count. According to Rancière, politics is the staging of a dispute whereby the uncounted proclaim a wrong that divides the social against itself, breaking consensus. If politics concerns the redistribution of sense within a community through the staging of a new *logos*, then laughter is the redistribution of the nonsensical. The affective break of the curious laugh with the relation between sense and nonsense then becomes r(u/a)pture of joy. The joy of the curious laugh is the experience of an egalitarian community whose flesh has not yet been made into words, whose sense falls outside the parameters measuring the distance separating sense from nonsense. The laugh is therefore not so much the proclamation of a wrong (in the formal sense) but rather the affective verification of a surplus equality—it is the sensual pleasure of nonsensical redistribution. As an embodied democratic experiment, the curious laugh is a type of hypothesis testing in which the function, location, and mode of nonsensical humor is reorganized and repartitioned beyond "legitimate" uses.

Theorizing the politics of laughter is not an attempt to make the community coincide with itself in a moment of immanence, but rather an inaugural rupture of the flesh and word that, as my opening epigrams suggests, is the beginning place for thought/education. Here a comparison is called for. Antonio Negri argues that laughter, "is able to affirm a principle of existence for the immeasurable" by creating allusions "between different existential orders—nature and spirit, singular and collective, labor and non-labor" (2009, 59). Thus for Negri, laughter has an ontological power to expand being. What differs in my reading from Negri's is that for me laughter is more about division than ontological holism. For instance, one of the major criticisms lobbied against lyric poetry for Rancière is its attempt to identify the word and the flesh (2004a)—to transform words into an ontological power. A political analysis of the laugh is not simply championing the body/voice over the word, but rather is an inquiry into the particular disruption of curious laughter as a sensational splitting of the subject from the subject as well as the community from the community. The space of *atopia* is the space of a new sensory world suddenly appearing within the given world. Atopia is a space between word and flesh that speaks to a passionate redistribution of pleasure and pain.

And this is why the curious laugh is necessary for Freire as well as for Rancière. Laughter, as I am theorizing it here, emerges from a certain fissure in the relation between flesh and words, a certain disconnection between rules and applications, a certain ambiguity between sense and nonsense. Thus thinking the joy of laughter enables us to challenge Freire's tendency to want words to correspond to specific interests/bodies/ forms of consciousness/social positions. As opposed to this model, the joy of curious laughter emerges through the *heresy* of jokes that always happen out of turn and always act to disturb any logical ordering of social relations. And, while Rancière locates passion within the political possibilities of literature (2009f, 278), I would argue that education itself involves a passionate or affective rupture/disturbance in the organization of pleasure and pain, public and private, sense and nonsense. Combining Freire and Rancière, I would suggest that more than a distraction, the curious laugh is a particular passion: *joy* as a spontaneously sensual affirmation of a democratic excess that has yet to be named by words. The joy of leveling hierarchical divisions offers an affective lure for igniting a somatic curiosity that, in turn, focuses the will to translate the laugh into new forms of knowledge and new practices of staging and performing, new organizations of sense and nonsense.

Yet we must pause to return to possible criticism of this position—this time from the opposite direction from Negri's ontological reading. Echoing my description presented above, Mladen Dolar argues that the laugh is a "postlinguistic" (2006, 29) eruption of the material voice beyond mere signification. In the moment of the laugh, the voice emerges as a surplus of language, and excess of meaning. Turning to political theory, Dolar suggests that this precarious position of the laugh as surplus is structurally identical to the "state of exception" that also exists both inside yet outside the social order. The state of exception is a zone of radical indistinction between law and fact, public and private, nature and culture. The sovereign decides the state of exception by suspending the law (thus the law remains constitutive through its deactivation), yet ironically enough, it is precisely this suspension of the law that in the last instance *founds* the law (Agamben 1999). Just as the state of exception finds within the heart of the polis the radical exteriority of the lawless state of nature, so too the voice lies between nature and culture, constitutive of yet disavowed by the symbolic order. Because of this correspondence, Dolar is leery of the voice, linking it directly with the sovereign decision—an observation also made by Agamben who connects laughter with the enjoyment of the master (1991, 50). Dolar argues, "the voice is structurally in the same position as sovereignty, which means that it can suspend the validity of the law and inaugurate the state of emergency" (2006, 120). For instance, in Fascism, the irrational, violent, and vengeful voice of the leader corresponds with the letter of the law (i.e. nature and state coincide). Perhaps this coincidence of laughter and sovereign voice explains the importance of the maniacal laugh of the arch villain in Hollywood films—who, although outside the law, are more often than not those on the radical interiority of the law (politicians, business elites, etc.). As such, Dolar would seem to agree with Žižek's previous warning against the totalitarian nature of the laugh. In particular Dolar has discovered the structural relationship between voice and sovereignty that supports Žižek's cultural analysis. Read symptomatically, the laugh might not at all be a true rupture of the division of the sensible, instead merely revealing, if not reveling in, the state of exception within the heart of any given police order.

An interesting educational example of the connections between sovereign violence and laughter can be seen in the movie *Dead Poets Society* (1989). When the iconoclastic teacher, Mr. Keating instructs his students to rip out the preface to their poetry anthology, the students are doubtful at first. Mr. Keating insists, and the students proceed to tear out a scale used to rate the "perfection" of a poem. At first blush, this appears to overturn the logic of the police order of the school, rupturing the norms and values of precision, scientific rigor, and discipline that form the hallmarks of the Welton Academy for boys. The illusion of improvisational theatre, contingent disruption, and democratic equality appear to break the oppressive pedagogical consensus that dominates through the four pillars of tradition, honor, discipline, and excellence. Within the logic of the pillars, only the cynical laughter of the occasional schoolboy prank can be heard—a laugh that pokes fun at the curmudgeonly old teachers who have no idea what the boys are *really* up to behind their backs. And yet in Keating's English class, the relation between sense and nonsense is suddenly thrown into disorder. Students suddenly become curious about poetry precisely through his use of humor to effect a shift in perception of the world—most dramatically enacted when he has students stand upon his desk and "take a look around." Yet if the curious laugh is ignited briefly in the film, so too is the dangerous connection between the laugh and the power of the sovereign over his or her subjects. In the critical scene when students rip out the preface to their poetry readers, Keating temporarily withdraws into his office, purportedly to find a trashcan. In his absence students laugh, tear paper, and there is a general sense of freedom in the sudden cathartic release from the rituals of tradition, honor, discipline, and excellence. While passing by, the "pragmatic" teacher Mr. McAllister is shocked by what he sees in Keating's classroom. Intervening on Keating's behalf, McAllister steps in to play the role of the authority only to discover Keating emerging from within his office. Perplexed, McAllister proclaims, "Oh, I did not know you were here." To which Keating responds, "Yes, I am here." This brief exchange reveals the problematic that I am outlining in this chapter: the relation between sovereign voice and the laugh. If the sovereign withdraws his power in order for the "transgressive" laugh to emerge, then this sovereign power does not simply disappear. Rather it continues to function in its very withdrawal. In fact, the laugh of the students becomes a *proxy* for the sovereign, testifying to the presence of his *logos* in the voice of the students. His power thus emerges through a ventriloquism act. In other words, the laugh does not break with sovereign power over the boys (as represented by the rules and regulations of the school) but rather remains dependent on the (absent) sovereign for its verification and its circulation. Keating's romantic enchantment of the boys only grows stronger through their laugh; their interpellation into the cult of the dead poets is completed in his quiet retreat from the scene of laughter. Perhaps this point is nowhere more apparent then at the end of the film when Keating is fired from Welton Academy. As he is removing his personal belongings from his office, the timid boy Todd Anderson stands upon his desk and proclaims "Oh Captain, my captain!"—a final salute to their master whose laughter enchanted them.

Yet we cannot foreclose on laughter just yet. If the laugh exists as a surplus of language then it is not only an instantiation of the state of emergency declared by the sovereign but also of the state of emergency of the authentic revolution inaugurated by the people from the ground up—a non-sovereign laugh that knows itself to be fragile, ephemeral, powerless and yet for all these reasons, a great refusal of the logic of sovereignty (see Agamben 2005). If the state of exception is decided upon and sustained by the sovereign, then the authentic state of emergency is a separation from this decision—an interruption of the interruption of the decision. Thus the happy laugh, the cynical laugh, and the curious laugh all hold the same structural location as exceptions. It is the smallest of differences that shift us from the register of dystopia to utopia, from Žižek's totalitarianism to Rancière's uncertain community.

The Joke of Critical Theory

It is my contention that this difference lies in a particular fidelity to the *structure* of the joke. As Freire argues, to laugh with the people it is necessary to engage with a variety of popular acts of "subterfuge" including "parties, dances, jokes, legends ..." (cited in Roberts 2000, 129). But what is it about jokes as such that makes them spontaneously transgressive and thus can lead to curious laughter? For Italian political theorist Paulo Virno, the joke "resides in a no-man's land that separates a norm from its

realization in a particular case. The point of honor of the witty remark
lies in its ability to show how many different ways one can apply the same
rule" (2008, 119). Jokes exist in a state of exception that always questions
the rule of law. Because there is a disconnection between every rule and
its particular application, there is need for linguistic ingenuity on the part
of humans. Not only are jokes part of this creativity, but they are also, for
Virno, "the *diagram* of innovative action" (2008, 73). As model or diagram
for virtuosic performance, jokes are a form of praxis that "open up an
oblique path that links together heterogeneous semantic contents previously unrelated" (Virno 2008, 97). Wit is the faculty of creative exploration
through which the joke explores the openness/inherent difference that
exists between rules and particulars calling into question the order of
things. The emphasis on difference experienced through the joke exposes
the contingencies of judgments, and reveals that there is a residue of the
state of exception (the state of indistinction) within every application that
cannot be erased. The joke's ability to set into relation "heterogeneous
semantic contents" is a reorganization of what can and cannot be said
or heard or thought. In Rancière's language, I would argue that the joke
offers an opportunity to free words from standardized relations. The joke
is in other words a *democratic theatre* for (dis)connecting signs and bodies
that opens up the state of exception through which the curious laugh can
emerge.

   In order to safeguard his analysis against criticism, Virno is quick to
point out that the joke as a model of innovative action does not mean that
political praxis rests on illogical if not ridiculous premises. The absurdity
of the joke only appears as an absurdity within the framework of the
existing rules of application that attempt to deny the underlying state of
exception which all applications of rules harbor. Viewed from a slightly
different perspective, the erroneous appearance of the joke becomes the
"main ingredient of *counterfactual reasoning*" where jokes "contribute to
elaborating a hypothesis about what would happen if conditions other
than those at hand were to prevail, if certain empirical data were to vary,
if other *endoxa* [opinions and beliefs of a community] or other rules were
in place" (Virno 2008, 140). In fact, Virno finds surprising similarities
between the methodology of mathematicians formulating new theorems
and the "fallacies" of jokes. In both, the "logic of discovery" emerges as
totally distinct from "the logic of justification" because both jokes and
abstract mathematics must rely on "irresponsible tools" such as analogy to
explore the openness between rule and application. Thus the shockingly
"absurd" claims of string theory in quantum physics appear to be similar

to the witticism of Lewis Carroll who also speculated about alternative dimensions where new rules of physics and of logic apply. With jokes "we are dealing with *productive* fallacies, whose function is to vary a linguistic game or a lifestyle" (Virno 2008, 146). Extending Virno's analysis, I would argue that the joke of critical theory is that it is a joke, that it *is* a laughing matter, and this is precisely its powerless power to challenge the authority of a police order with the paradoxical ambiguity that lies within its own rules and procedures of justification.

If this is beginning to sound like the postmodern resistance or transgression that McLaren previously warned about, we must keep in mind Virno's critical distinction between entrepreneurial innovation and exodus. Rather than simply a condition of late capitalism where the entrepreneurial self is an educational and social norm unique to neoliberalism (Foucault 2008), for Virno, every linguistic animal is an entrepreneur who must inevitably play with the open polysemy of the symbolic order. Because of the no-man's land between rule and application, all linguistic animals must play with a combination of symbolic elements in order to form meaning. Virno's analysis in many ways coincides with Rancière's own analysis of joke telling. In a recent essay on the fate of aesthetics in contemporary art (2009b), Rancière makes the provocative claim that the critical confrontation of heterogeneous elements found in political art has been replaced by the innovative play of the joke. The dialectical clash of two competing politics of sensoriality once had the ability to shed light on class conflict and political dissensus, yet in the reconstruction of art as a joke, "the conjunction of the heterogeneous elements is still staged as a tension or polarity, pointing to some secret, but there is no more secret" (Rancière 2009b, 46). Art becomes devoid of political power and can no longer organize itself under the sign of dispute and disagreement, only playful innovation and ironic commentary. In other words, art as a joke remains within the strictures of the consensus of the police order. While these small innovations exist within the strictures of preexisting symbolic frameworks, there is another much more radical example of the joke that Rancière misses: the joke as a political praxis of exodus from any predefined relation between sense and nonsense existing within a police order. Rather than remain within the parameters set by a rule and its normative applications, exodus modifies or short-circuits the grammar that predetermines set choices and set applications. In other words, jokes can modify what Nicholas Holm refers to as "the distribution of the nonsensical" (2011) or the partitioning of that which does not make sense within consensus. Through joke telling, it is possible to redistribute the relation between sense and nonsense. Thus Rancière misses how joke telling can become a "a side road" (Virno 2008, 148), "a displacement" (149), or an "abrupt deviation in the axis of discourse" (149) that exposes the self and the collective to the open possibilities of the state of exception where the carefully policed boundaries between sense and nonsense are suddenly suspended. In short, by focusing on the counter-factual as a political operator (an uncertain utterance that short-circuits the safe boundaries designating the time and place of sense *and* nonsense), certain jokes become the enactment of dissensus. Thus the politics of joke telling verifies an underlying social equality: those who tell jokes express their deep understanding of the rules of the police by interrupting these rules. Nonsense is not a lack of sense but rather the examination of the state of exception between rule and application that the common sense of the police order attempts to contain and constrain. And it is this perplexing, strange, unfamiliar suspension of what we expect to find (the established ratio of sense to nonsense) that ignites our curiosity in the form of a laugh.

When Freire argues that it is necessary to laugh with the people, he is arguing for a fidelity to the counter-factual logic of the oppressed as expressed by telling jokes. What distinguishes the curious laugh from the happy or the cynical is that this laugh embodies the joy of joke telling as a sensual theatre of political exodus challenging all inequalities, all preconceived notions of what counts and what does not count as a "legitimate" philosophical, political, or social claim. In this sense, we can now fully appreciate Freire's description of his pedagogy as a "pedagogy of happiness, laughter, of questioning, of curiosity, of seeing the future through the present, a pedagogy that believes in the possibility of the transformation of the world." Existing in the open of the state of exception, laughing is a postlinguistic somatic excess for which we do not have a fully formed language, only a joyous voice. It is through the laugh that the irritant/affliction of curiosity becomes a certain joy in the collective exploration of this atopic space. The ignorant schoolmaster must therefore verify the will to explore the exception that suspends all claims to expertise and interrupts the conventional sensory distributions that define the standardized classroom. The laugh as a sensual disruption is the experience of a new horizon of the possible that has yet to find a name within the order of the police and thus a powerful moment of dissensus. Schematically we could say:

1) The joke is an utterance that opens the state of exception, a void or atopos within the portioning of *pathos* and *logos*.

2) The curious laugh in the classroom is the aesthetic pleasure of democracy erupting from within this atopic space of the joke—making the joke corporeal and collective.

3) The curious laugh is the lure that ignites the will to explore this strange no man's land of the joke between sense and nonsense.

Here I would like to give an example from my experience teaching Rancière's *The Ignorant Schoolmaster* in both undergraduate and graduate teacher education courses. When confronted with this strange text, with its parodic chapter headings ("The Blind Man and His Dog," "Everything is in Everything," "Of Brains and Leaves," "How to Rave Reasonably," Of Sheep and Men," and of course "The Emancipator and His Monkey" just to name a few), seemingly absurd if not downright bizarre pedagogical suggestions (including "the ignorant person will learn by himself what the master doesn't know if the master believes he can and obliges him to realize his capacity" [1991, 15]), and perplexing formal qualities (is it a "method" of instruction, a history, a novel?), students are at first confused but then often begin to laugh—tentatively, curiously. Their disbelieving snickers and chuckles seem to ask: "Is this for real? Am I to believe this?" The text suspends the exact ratio between sense and nonsense, provoking equal doses of unease and curiosity in pre-service teachers. As opposed to their other textbooks in the teacher education program, Rancière offers no clear advice, no clear pedagogical skill set, no clear, empirical data that quantitatively proves his claims (if he is making any). Laughter emerges in the curious space opened by the text, not filling the void of silence, but rather throwing it into relief, making us pay attention to our collective unrest when dealing with this book that seems to defy all categorization. These laughs that ripple through the classroom are not merely cynical responses (and thus dismissive), nor are they merely cathartic expressions of enjoyment, rather they are curious, ignorant of their own epistemological status. And although tentative, there is an unmistakable joy expressed through such a laugh: a momentary release from the taken-for-granted curriculum that defines so much of teacher education and a short voyage to a different kind of thought and experience.

This is why *The Ignorant Schoolmaster* is a joke: it breaks the operative logic defining the typical teacher's manual or educational handbook, repartitioning the relationship between sense and nonsense, what counts and what does not count as "legitimate" scholarship. In this sense, the laugh is radically different from that depicted in the film *Dead Poets Society*, where the laugh is reduced to a kind of violence sanctioned by the absent-presence of a sovereign. In relation to *The Ignorant Schoolmaster*, there is no secret master explication hiding behind our laughter, guaranteeing its legitimacy, offering a final punchline that will resolve the perplexing status of the text, interpellating us into a predefined subject position. If the sovereign laugh is one of power, then the curious laugh is a powerless power wedded to the aporia between rule and application. There is only this strange text, needing translation, parodically commanding us to transform our curiosity into a will to keep laughing. This is not a community of nonsense, but a community organized around the sensation of the suspension of fixed rules that enable us to identify sense from nonsense. As Freire suggests, the teacher should laugh with his or her students in such instances of suspension and rupture—not as a sovereign power but as an equal participant, exposing his or her own ignorance through the collective joy of the curious laugh.

Lights, Please!

Given these arguments we should not underestimate laughter in the classroom (as McLaren's analysis suggests), nor can we simply dismiss laughter in total (as with Žižek). Rather we must see within laughter a certain form of potential that is both aesthetic and political. As critical educators, the laugh is an opportunity for exodus and thus for entering into a zone of heterogeneous mixing and contamination that, as Rancière would argue, undermines the distribution of the sensible in order to introduce a democratic recount of the miscount that defines the order of things. This entrance into the state of exception for which there are no rules for the application of rules is a creative and innovative space. In this sense, it is a space that is no laughing matter that nevertheless must be laughed at! The space of atopic exodus is central to renewing the critical pedagogy tradition. As Mayo has recently argued, "These interventions [the laughter from black humor traditions] provide a way out of the stalled space of social justice pedagogy, because their humor is intentionally a vehicle for bending angry encounters into puzzlingly pleasurable encounters for speaker and audience as well" (2008, 251). In other words, the serious "earnestness" of the critical pedagogue, for Mayo, must be replaced by a return to a Freirian emphasis on the politics of laughter and its internal relationship with democratic education. The teacher should laugh with the oppressed in order to *verify* the counter-factual logic of democratic disruption even in the most "naïve" or "superstitious" consciousnesses.

One final thought. For those whose stoic, revolutionary sensibilities find this chapter too playful for its own good, we must remind ourselves that Marx once said "Hegel remarks somewhere that all facts and personages of great importance in world history occur as it were twice. He forgot to add: the first time as tragedy, the second as farce" (2001, 7). History returns or repeats itself as a humorous play with human subjects involved in increasingly ridiculous situations without a punchline. Thus Rancière's tragic theatre becomes a comedy full of the most untimely laughter. For education perhaps we can say that the first time is tragedy (see Burbules 1990 for an examination of the tragic sense of education) and the second time is parody.

Conclusion:

Death and Democracy in Education: Freire's Easter Revisited

There is an anxiety in Freirian scholarship that we will lose our immanent and personable connections with "the master," Paulo Freire himself. Thus collections like *Memories of Paulo* (2010) edited by Tom Wilson, Peter Park, and Anaida Colón-Muniz emphasize personal stories/encounters with Freire. In his open letter to Freire at the beginning of the book *Pedagogy of Indignation*, Balduino A. Andreola states, "On September 19, 1998, during the popular closing celebration for the First International Paulo Freire Colloquium, in Recife, Nita mentioned that she just couldn't think of you as being absent ... you remain our partner in the journey" (Freire 2004b, xxxv). Andreola continues, granting Freire a type of "permanent-presence" (Freire 2004b, xxxv) in the world that defies death—a message that his own posthumous letter to Freire seems to embody. Such work attempts to close the gap between Freire as a historical person and Freire as a discourse—his discourse must be supplemented by his permanent-presence as a historical person and likewise his historical person must be continually invoked through his discourse. As such, there is a movement within Freirian scholarship that fills space opened up by his death with a proliferation of memories, whose accuracy is "guaranteed" because of proximity to Freire "as he really was." Inspiration here is dependent on a certain avoidance of death in the form of memoirs as well as continual invocations of his bodily presence in the form of photographs on and within books by or about Freire. In other words, memory returns Freire to life, creating a continuity between his flesh and his words, and in the process denying any absence instituted by and through the event of death.

This radical critique of death is not simply the result of the longing induced by his passing. The pedagogy of the oppressed is itself an attempt to challenge death both physically (overcoming the pain and suffering of oppression) and also ideologically in the form of consciousness-raising. In

Pedagogy of the Oppressed, Freire observes that the pedagogy of oppression is necrophylic. Rather than biophylic or in love with life, banking education promotes a fetishization of death in the form of a nihilistic fatalism concerning social and individual transformation (2001b, 77). Banking education separates *bios* from politics, from language and action in the public sphere. For Freire the result is an untimely death, a passive existence in the order of things and a fatalistic outlook on social transformation. In order to define the parameters of necrophylic pedagogy Freire contrasts his utopian vision with banking education: "Revolutionary utopia tends to be dynamic rather than static; tends to life rather than death; to the future as a challenge to man's creativity rather than as a repetition of the present … to dialogue rather than mutism …" (1985a, 82). Death is here conceptualized as the negation of life in the form of mutism, repetition, passivity. Death is, in other words, a silenced existence lacking in words and deeds wherein students see themselves as passive rather than active agents in their lives. Furthermore, death is an "anesthesized curiosity" (as discussed in Chapter Four) stunting the student's inquiry into the way the world works. In sum, necrophylia is the educational logic of the morbidity of life, draining life of its creative potential. Freire argues that "In addition to the life-death cycle basic to nature, there is almost an unnatural *living death*: life that is denied its fullness" (2001b, 171). The living death of banking education is an existential death that separates life from itself from within life—a passive life devoid of the meaning and personal biography that defines *bios* as an active life in the polis. In short, for Freire, banking education is a form of pedagogy that ends up "terminating life" (1996, 165) while problem-posing education is fueled by a "love for life" (1996, 164). In fact, the radical fight today concerns the "*biophilic*" fight for "purity" (Freire 1997, 83). In this sense, biophilia is the purification of life from the contaminant of death that, for Freire, is always characterized as mutism and the end of history/ historical becoming. The new love for life is expressed in Freire's theory by a revivification of epistemological curiosity into the nature of reality (see Chapter Three). If banking education creates the fatalistic condition in which life becomes a form of symbolic death (wherein world and word are separated), then problem-posing revivifies life by reconnecting it with political activity and the active construction of knowledge through the proper naming of the world.

Existential death is a form of dehumanization for Freire. Even if the question of life is distinct from the question of becoming fully human, nevertheless Freire's characterization of death as a mute, passive existence recalls his discussion of the state of animal captivation. For Freire, animal

words of the poor). Rancière summarizes: "Positivist history [of the chroniclers] refuses to confront the absence of its object, that 'hidden' without which there is no science and that can't be reduced to the archive buried in its files" (1994, 64). Reformers on the other hand embrace death but only in the figure of ideological critique and denunciation of mystification (for Freire this would amount to critical consciousness raising). They fail to see how in their attempt to retrieve the silent witnesses of history, they demand a certain infallible correlation between speech and place, cognition and recognition that, like the chroniclers before them, ends up effacing the possibility of historical events. In both cases, death becomes the *heresy* that these discourses do not permit. Heresy is "life turned away from the word, turned away by the word" (Rancière 1994, 73) and thus a narrative predicated on the non-correspondence of flesh and word, on the glance of the actor on stage rather than the retrospective and belated gaze of the expert. Yet, as Rancière argues, "The difference proper to history is death; it is the power of death that attaches itself solely to the properties of the speaker, it is the disturbance that this power introduces into all positive knowledge. The historian can't stop effacing the line of death, but also can't stop tracing it anew. History has its own life in this alternative throbbing of death and knowledge. It is the science that becomes singular only by playing on its own condition of impossibility, but ceaselessly transforming it into a condition of possibility, but also by marking anew, as furtively, as discreetly as can be, the line of the impossible" (1994, 74–5). The line "of meaning and death" is precisely the line of "historiality and literariness, without which there would be no place to write history" (Rancière 1994, 76). In other words, death is the sublime beauty at the heart of historical science that is both the motor for knowledge and its stumbling block, the pensive detail that shapes the literary dimension of the aesthetics of knowledge. It is the detail that escapes memory and thus all sense of self-possession and self-recognition. If Freire's pedagogy of the oppressed is an attempt to create a beautiful, "pure" community of solidarity built out of shared class interests (a reformist approach to history wherein word and flesh, consciousness and class position are once again reunited so as to speak the truth of oppression sanctioned by the critical sociologist, philosopher, or critical pedagogue), then death is the ghost in the machine that prevents full presence while also generating the need for new translations and performances.

It is this accounting for death through new narratives that in turn must be accounted for. While death might introduce an excess between word and flesh, Rancière points out that death is also what sets in motion explication. In relation to Rossellini's film *Europa 51*, Rancière argues, "There is never a lack of deaths or explanations" (2003c, 111). In the film, the suicide of a young boy sends the mother, Irene, searching for answers. Her question was not "Why did he kill himself" (which conjures up psychological or socio-economic explanations) but rather "What did he say" right before he died. Although psychiatrists and socialists attempt to carve up her question, there is something in her original phrasing that remains impossible to answer completely. Drawing on Rancière's reading of this film, Mark Robson makes the following observation:

> Death is enough to set explanation going, but the explanation that answers one question may itself be a way of avoiding the posing of another, more disturbing question. The obscene question disappears from the scene. Or rather, it disappeared in the act of explanation, and this is attributable to 'the politicians.' So, then, there is a politics of the question, a politics of explanation, and, of course, a politics of death.... In particular, the explanations that are all too readily at hand—the usual thanatological suspects—are rounded up with such ease that they fail to explain anything. (2011, 185)

In this sense, death opens up to a flurry of explanations that erase the event of death—the introduction of a void into the order of things that cannot be explained away using the formulas and predictive theories of politicians, philosophers, or sociologists. As such, two alternatives must be avoided. First, denial of death leaves no room for historical difference to appear. Memory and recollection of "how Freire was" replace the void that attracts and stimulates curiosity. Here memory becomes a kind of self-reassurance that nothing has been lost, that the spirit of Freire remains as it always was, that he is "right here with us" and thus we do not have to act *on our own* within *our specific context* without his guarantee. Second, the quick proclamation of death in order to pass judgment on history equally dispenses with the pensiveness of death and thus the space of curiosity. The death of man, the death of history, the death of modernism, the death of politics, the death of Freire all become foundations for the emergence of a new explanatory paradigm, a new cultural logic that appears on the horizon through a series of "posts" (posthumanism, postmodernism, postcritical discourse, etc.) that claim the right to pass judgment over the dead and thus subsume the past within a totalized horizon of understanding. What is therefore missed in both cases is a sustained relation to death as a void in the partitioning of the sensible, a certain pensive detail that resists death in its dying and in turn resists giving life to yet another master discourse or explicating order.

Thus death is a dangerous figure that dialectically seems to oscillate in Rancière's work. As Michael Dillon argues (2005), death is essential for understanding Rancière's *kairological* understanding of emancipation. In this argument, death is neither a comforting memory nor simply a past needing to be explained away (thus denying the events of historical change). Instead, death becomes a type of messianic *mise-en-scene*, a staging for the event of translation that simultaneously destroys and creates. In Dillon's messianic reading, the messianic in Rancière's work has its own "sacrificial violence" where "any actualized possibility of egalitarian contingency is always the death of some other equality" (2005, 447). In other words, for equality to be verified, there must be a "making room" (2005, 447) through a sacrifice. Joseph Jacotot's teaching as not teaching is one prime example of this sacrificial logic at work in Rancière's writings. This is a pedagogy that exists in the *kairos* of emancipation where dis-identification with both the master and the slave is a certain form of existential death. Thus death is an essential component of both the arrival of history and the arrival of emancipation.

At this point we can bring together Rancière and Freire in terms of the shared interest in the messianic. While Rancière downplays the messianic in his work, it is this concept that helps solve the question of the relation between life and death which is always present but never fully elucidated in his reflections on history, film, and literature. Likewise, it is Freire's emphasis on Easter as a messianic event that can be used to rethink the positive role of death in his pedagogy (a function which many of his followers seem to have overlooked for the false purity of biophilia). Easter, he writes, is a praxis; "it is historical involvement" (Freire 1985a, 123) that is not simply biophilic or necrophilic but rather a paradoxical performance of an atopic zone between the two—a suspension of the dialectic of life and death, and thus a radical interruption of the logic of immunization. Easter enables us to thus rehabilitate death not as a necrophiliac love but as a form of "historical dynamism" (Freire 1985b, 123) that resists the reassuring sentimentality of memory or the expertise of the master's discourse. If passive viewing is living *death* that must be negated, then Easter is a celebration of *living* death—not as the immunization of life against death but rather a life that retains within itself the pensive muteness of death as a form of intelligence immanent to the aesthetic re-partitioning of the senses. Read in this light, Freire's reflection on Easter becomes a fulcrum for challenging the distribution of the sensible that separates the order of things into humans and animals, action and inaction, speech and mutism, life and death. Within the event of Easter, Freire is not returned to us as a full presence which lives forever but rather a reminder of the distance between words and things that *living* death produces. And in this final turn, we are able to move beyond anthropocentric and necrophobic tendencies that otherwise might haunt Freire's pedagogical practice. In this sense, Easter is never a return to life or a simple separation from death but rather a space of aporia, of the void, of the surplus detail that remains in excess of both memory and explanation. It is a miracle: the appearance of the impossible within the possible, a state of grace that remains curious. Such an event cannot be celebrated in memories so much as in theatrical performances that translate rather than explain. The danger in either denying death (via the self-possession of memory) or proclaiming death (through the master discourse of "post" that passes judgment over the past) is that the need for poetic production is lost. In this sense, critical pedagogies of the memoir or the eulogy miss the need for constant re-staging of the event of Freire's Easter.

If I began this book with one type of death (Rancière's "murder" of Althusser), I end with a messianic Easter that falls outside the dichotomy of birth and death and the hierarchies between sensation and intelligence upon which they are built. Easter induces an atopic space and time between Freire (the person and his aura) and Freire (as a collection of words and texts) to open—a space-time nexus where we can invent new roles to play and perceive new aleatory encounters between and across various translations of his work. It is not our closeness to Freire that is important but precisely our distance. It is not our proximity/intimacy to Freire's living person that enables us to write the weird fiction of democracy but precisely our departure from him. The utterance of the ignorant scholar is not "Remember Freire!" but rather the ignorant and curious question "Who was Freire?" This new departure enables us to see what remains pensive in his words and in turn is what stimulates curiosity to translate and thus create new stages for democratic dissensus. Only now, in the parodic moment of Easter where the distinction between life and death is held in suspension, can we finally laugh!

Bibliography

Agamben, Giorgio. 1991. *Language and Death: The Place of Negativity.* Minneapolis: University of Minnesota Press.

—1999. *Potentialities.* Stanford: Stanford University Press.

Althusser, Louis. 1969. *For Marx.* London: Verso.

—1990. *Philosophy and the Spontaneous Philosophy of the Scientists and Other Essays.* London: Verso.

—2001. *Lenin and Philosophy and Other Essays.* New York: Monthly Review Press.

—2006. *Philosophy of the Encounter: Later Writings, 1978-1987.* London: Verso.

Althusser, Louis and Étienne Balibar. 1979. *Reading Capital.* London: Verso.

Arendt, Hannah. 1998. *The Human Condition.* Chicago: University of Chicago Press.

—2003. *Responsibility and Judgment.* New York: Schocken Books.

Aristotle. 1941. *The Basic Works of Aristotle.* New York: Random House.

Arsenjuk, Luka and Michelle Koerner. 2009. "Study, Students, Universities: An Introduction." *Polygraph* 21: 1–13.

Badiou, Alain. 2005. *Metapolitics.* London: Verso.

Bal, Mieke. 1996. *Double Exposure.* New York: Routledge.

Baldacchino, John. 2008. *Education Beyond Education: Self and the Imaginary in Maxine Greene's Philosophy.* New York: Peter Lang.

Balibar, Étienne. 2009a. "Althusser and the Rue d'Ulm." *New Left Review* 58 (July–August): http://www.newleftreview.org/?view=2792.

—2009b. "Interview with Étienne Balibar." In *Communities of Sense: Rethinking Aesthetics and Politics*, edited by Beth Hinderliter, William Kaizen, Vered Maimon, Jaleh Mansoor, and Seth McCormick, 317–36.

Benjamin, Walter. 1968. *Illuminations: Essays and Reflections.* New York: Schocken Books.

Biesta, Gert. 2006. *Beyond Learning: Democratic Education for a Human Future.* Boulder: Paradigm Publishers.

—2007. "Democracy, Education and the Question of Inclusion." In *Proceedings of the 2007 Philosophy of Education of Great Britain Conference.* Retrieved February 5, 2008, from http://www.philosophy-of-education.org/conferences/pdfs/BIESTA%20PESGB%202007.pdf

—2008. "Toward a New 'Logic' of Emancipation: Foucault and Rancière." In *Philosophy of Education Society Yearbook, 2008*, edited by Ronald Glass, 169–77. Urbana: University of Urbana-Champaign.

—2010. "Learner, Student, Speaker: Why It Matters How We Call Those We Teach." *Educational Philosophy and Theory* 42 (5–6): 540–52.

—2011. "The Ignorant Citizen: Mouffe, Rancière, and the Subject of Democratic Education." *Studies in Philosophy of Education* 30 (2): 141–53.

Bingham, Charles. 2008. "The Pedagogical is not the Political: Jacques Rancière's Other Critical Theory." Paper presented at the annual AERA convention, March 24–28.

—2009. "Under the Name of Method: On Jacques Rancière's Presumptive Tautology." *Journal of Philosophy of Education* 43 (3): 405–20.

—2010. "Settling No Conflict in the Public Place: Truth in Education, and in Rancièrean Scholarship." *Educational Philosophy and Theory* 42 (5–6): 649–65.

Bingham, Charles, Gert Biesta, and Jacques Rancière. 2010. *Jacques Rancière: Education, Truth, Emancipation.* London: Continuum.

Boal, Augusto. 2002. *Theatre of the Oppressed.* New York: Theatre Communications Group.

Bogad, L. M. 2005. *Electoral Guerrilla Theatre: Radical Ridicule and Social Movements.* New York: Routledge.

Burbules, Nicholas. 1990. "The Tragic Sense of Education." *Teachers College Record* 91 (4): 469–79.

Cho, Daniel. 2005a. "Teaching Abjection: A Response to the War on Terror." *Teaching Education* 16 (2): 103–15.

—2005b. "Utopian Concerns in Pedagogy." *Pedagogy and Theatre of the Oppressed Newsletter2005* http://www.ptoweb.org/assets/files/newsletters/fall-2005.pdf

Citton, Yves. 2009. "Political Agency and the Ambivalence of the Sensible." In *Jacques Rancière: History, Politics, Aesthetics,* edited by Gabriel Rockhill and Philip Watts, 120–39. Durham: Duke University Press.

—2010. " 'The Ignorant Schoolmaster': Knowledge and Authority." In *Jacques Rancière: Key Concepts,* edited by Jean-Philippe Deranty, 25–37. Durham: Acumen.

Darder, Antonia. 2002. *Reinventing Paulo Freire.* Boulder: Westview Press.

Daston, Lorraine and Katherine Park. 2001. *Wonders and the Order of Nature, 1150–1750.* London: Zone Books.

Dean, Jodi. 2009. "Politics Without Politics." *Parallax* 15 (3): 20–36.

Dillon, Michael. 2005. "A Passion for the (Im)Possible: Jacques Rancière, Equality, Pedagogy, and the Messianic." *European Journal of Political Theory* 4 (4): 429–52.

Dolar, Mladen. 2006. *A Voice and Nothing More.* Cambridge: MIT Press.

Dunn, Kevin T. 1998. *Bright Colors Falsely Seen: Synaesthesia and the Search for Transcendental Knowledge.* Connecticut: Yale University Press.

Eagleton, Terry. 2009. *Trouble With Strangers: A Study of Ethics.* Malden: Wiley-Blackwell.

Ellsworth, Elizabeth. 1989. "Why Doesn't This Feel Empowering? Working Through the Repressive Myths of Critical Pedagogy." *Harvard Educational Review* 59 (3): 297–325.

Esposito, Roberto. 2008. *Bios: Biopolitics and Philosophy.* Minneapolis: University of Minnesota Press.

Foucault, Michel. 2008. *The Birth of Biopolitics: Lectures at the College de France, 1978–79.* New York: Palgrave MacMillan.

—2011. *The Government of the Self and Others: Lectures at the College de France, 1982–1983.* New York: Palgrave McMillan.

Freire, Paulo. 1972. *Cultural Action for Freedom.* Baltimore: Penguin.

—1973. *Education for Critical Consciousness.* London: Continuum.

—1985a. *The Politics of Education.* Massachusetts: Bergin & Garvey Publishers.

—1985b. "Reading the World and Reading the Word: An Interview With Paulo Freire." *Language Arts* 62 (1): 15–21.

—1996. *Letters to Cristina: Reflections on My Life and Work.* New York: Routledge.

—1997. *Pedagogy of the Heart.* London: Continuum.

—1998. *Teachers as Cultural Workers: Letters to Those Who Dare to Teach.* Boulder: Westview Press.

—2001a. *Pedagogy of Freedom: Ethics, Democracy, and Civic Courage.* Lanham: Rowman and Littlefield.

—2001b. *Pedagogy of the Oppressed.* London: Continuum.

—2004a. *Pedagogy of Hope.* London: Continuum.

—2004b. *Pedagogy of Indignation.* Boulder: Paradigm.

—2007. *Daring to Dream: Toward a Pedagogy of the Unfinished.* Boulder: Paradigm.

Freire, Paulo and Antonio Faundez. 1989. *Learning to Question: A Pedagogy of Liberation.* London: Continuum.

Friedrich, Daniel, Bryn Jaastad, and Thomas S. Popkewitz. 2010. "Democratic Education: An (Im)Possibility That Yet Remains to Come." *Educational Philosophy and Theory* 42 (5–6): 571–87.

Gadotti, Moacir. 1994. *Reading Paulo Freire.* New York: State University of New York Press.

—2002. "General Theme: The Possible Dream. Paulo Freire and the Future of Humanity." Paper presented at The Third International Paulo Freire Forum, Los Angeles, 18 to 20.

Galloway, Sarah. In press. "Reconsidering Emancipatory Education: Staging a Conversation between Paulo Freire and Jacques Rancière." *Educational Theory.*

Giroux, Henry. 2001. *Theory and Resistance in Education: Toward a Pedagogy for the Opposition.* Westport: Bergin & Garvey.

—2005. *Schooling and the Struggle for Public Life.* Boulder: Paradigm Press.

—2010. *The Mouse that Roared: Disney and the End of Innocence.* Lanham: Rowman and Littlefield.

Greene, Maxine. 1995. *Releasing the Imagination: Essays on Education, the Arts, and Social Change.* San Francisco: Jossey-Bass.

Guénoun, Solange. 2011. "Parody and Politics of Incarnation: Jacques Rancière's Aesthetics of Politics and Michel Journiac's Body Art." *Parallax* 17 (2): 8–20.

Hallward, Peter. 2006. "Staging Equality: On *Rancière*'s Theatrocracy." *New Left Review* 37: 109–29.

Halpern, Richard. 2011. "Theatre and Democratic Thought: Arendt to Rancière." Critical Inquiry 37 (3): 545–72.

Hardt, Michael. 2010. "The Common in Communism." In *The Idea of Communism,* edited by Costas Douzinas and Slavoj Žižek, 131–44. London: Verso.

Hardt, Michael and Antonio Negri. 2000. *Empire.* Cambridge: Harvard University Press.

—2005. *Multitude: War and Democracy in the Age of Empire.* London: Penguin Books.

Heidegger, Martin. 2008. *Being and Time.* New York: Harper Perennial.

Heller-Roazen, Daniel. 2009. *The Inner Touch: Archeology of a Sensation.* New York: Zone Books.

Hewitt, Andrew. 2005. *Social Choreography: Ideology as Performance in Dance and Everyday Movement.* Durham: Duke University Press.

Hill, Dave. 2005. "State Theory and the Neoliberal Reconstruction of Schooling and Teacher Education." In *Critical Theories, Radical Pedagogies, and Global*

Conflicts, edited by Gustavo E. Fischman, Peter McLaren, Heinz Sünker, and Colin Lankshear, 23–51. Lanham: Rowman and Littlefield.

Holm, Nicholas. 2011. "The Distribution of the Nonsensical and the Political Aesthetics of Humor." *Transformations* 19: n.p.

Horton, Miles and Paulo Freire. 1990. *We Make the Road by Walking: Conversations on Education and Social Change*. Philadelphia: Temple University Press.

Jameson, Fredric. 1971. *Marxism and Form*. Princeton: Princeton University Press.

—1994. *The Seeds of Time*. New York: Columbia University Press.

—2000. *Brecht and Method*. London: Verso.

Kant, Immanuel. 1977. *Prolegomena to Any Future Metaphysics*. Indianapolis: Hackett Publishing Company.

—2003. *On Education*. New York: Dover Press.

—2006. *Groundwork of the Metaphysics of Morals*. New York: Cambridge University Press.

Karatani, Kojin. 1995. *Architecture as Metaphor: Language, Number, Money*. Cambridge: MIT Press.

Lambert, Cath. 2011. "Psycho Classrooms: Teaching as a Work of Art." *Social & Cultural Geography* 12 (1): 27–45.

Lewis, Tyson E. 2006. "Critical Surveillance Literacy." *Cultural Studies↔Critical Methodologies* 6 (2): 263–81.

—2007. "Revolutionary Leadership↔Revolutionary Pedagogy: Reevaluating the Links and Disjunctions Between Lukacs and Freire." In *The Philosophy of Education Society's Yearbook, 2007*, edited by Nicholas Burbules, 289–93. Illinois: University of Urbana-Champaign.

—in press. "The Aesthetics of Education." *Journal of Aesthetic Education*.

Lewis, William. 2005. *Louis Althusser and the Traditions of French Marxism*. Lanham: Rowman and Littlefield.

Macherey, Pierre. 2009. "Althusser and the Concept of the Spontaneous Philosophy of Scientists." *Parrhesia* 6: 14–27.

Marcuse, Herbert. 1964. *One-Dimensional Man*. Boston: Beacon Press.

Marx, Karl. 2001. *The Eighteenth Brumaire of Louis Bonaparte*. London: Electronic Book.

Masschelein, Jan. in press. "Inciting an Alternative Experimental Ethos and Creating a Laboratory Setting: Philosophy of Education and the Transformation of Educational Institutions," *Zeitschrift für Pädagogik*.

Masschelein, Jan, and Maarten Simons. 2011. "The University: A Public Issue." In *The Future University: Ideas and Possibilities*, edited by Ronald Barnett, 165–77. New York: Routledge.

May, Todd. 2011. "Wrong, Disagreement, Subjectification." In *Jacques Rancière: Key Concepts*, edited by Jean-Philippe Deranty, 69–79. Durham: Acumen.

Mayo, Cris. 2008. "Being in on the Joke: Pedagogy, Race, Humor." In *Philosophy of Education Society Yearbook, 2008*, edited by Nicholas Burbules, 244–52. Urbana: University of Illinois.

Mayo, Peter. 2004. *Liberating Praxis: Paulo Freire's Legacy for Radical Education and Politics*. Rotterdam: Sense.

Mbembe, Achille. 2003. "Necropolitics." *Public Culture* 15 (1): 11–40.

McLaren, Peter. 1999. *Schooling as a Ritual Performance: Toward a Political Economy of Educational Symbols and Gestures*. Lanham: Rowman and Littlefield.

—2000. *Che Guevara, Paulo Freire, and the Pedagogy of Revolution.* Lanham: Rowman and Littlefield.

Meier, Deborah and George Wood, (eds) 2005. *Many Children Left Behind.* Boston: Beacon Press.

Mieville, China. 2009. *The City and the City.* New York: Del Rey.

Mitchell, W. J. T. 2006. *What Do Pictures Want?: The Lives and Loves of Images.* Chicago: University of Chicago Press.

Montag, Warren. 2003. *Louis Althusser.* New York: Palgrave MacMillan.

Morrell, Ernest, and Jeffery Duncan-Andrade. 2006. "Popular Culture and Critical Media Pedagogy in Secondary Literacy Classrooms." *International Journal of Learning* 12 (9): 273–80.

—2008. *The Art of Critical Pedagogy: Possibilities for Moving From Theory to Practice in Urban Schools.* New York: Peter Lang.

Morris, Christine B. 1998. "Paulo Freire: Community Based Arts Education." *Journal of Social Theory in Art Education* 18: 44–58.

Morrow, Raymond and Torres, Carlos. A. 2002. *Reading Freire and Habermas: Critical Pedagogy and Transformative Social Change.* New York: Teachers College Press.

Negri, Antonio. 2009. *The Labor of Job: The Biblical Text as a Parable of Human Labor.* Durham: Duke University Press.

—2011. *Art and Multitude.* Malden: Polity.

Neill, A. S. 1992. *Summerhill School: A New View of Childhood.* New York: St. Martin's Griffin.

Noguera, Pedro. 2009. *The Trouble With Black Boys: ... And Other Reflections on Race, Equity, and the Future of Public Education.* San Francisco: Josey-Bass.

Ostwald, Michael, J. 2008. "Rancière and the Metapolitical Framing of Architecture: Reconstructing Brodsky and Utkin's Voyage." *Interstices: A Journal of Architecture and Related Arts* 8: 9–20.

Ottey, Sherilyn. 1996. "Critical Pedagogical Theory and the Dance Educator." *Arts Education Policy Review* 98 (2): 31–9.

Panagia, Davide. 2006. *The Poetics of Political Thinking.* Durham: Duke University Press.

—2009. *The Politics of Sensation.* Durham: Duke University Press.

Pelletier, Caroline. 2009. "Emancipation, Equality and Education: Rancière's Critique of Bourdieu and the Question of Performativity." *Discourse: Studies in the Cultural Politics of Education* 30 (2): 137–50.

Plato. 2002. *Five Dialogues: Euthyphro, Apology, Crito, Meno, Phaedo.* Indianapolis: Hackett Publishing Company.

Rancière, Jacques. 1989. *The Nights of Labor: The Workers' Dreams in Nineteenth-Century France.* Philadelphia: Temple University Press.

—1991. *The Ignorant Schoolmaster: Five Lessons in Intellectual Emancipation.* Stanford: Stanford University Press.

—1994. *The Names of History.* Minneapolis: University of Minnesota Press.

—1997. "Democracy Means Equality." *Radical Philosophy* 82 (March/April): 29–36.

—1998. *La Parole Muette: Essai sur les Contradictions de la Littérature.* Paris: Hachette Littératures.

—1999. *Disagreement: Politics and Philosophy.* Minneapolis: University of Minnesota Press.

—2000a. "Jacques Rancière: Literature, Politics, Aesthetics: Approaches to Democratic Disagreement." Interviewed by Solange Guénoun, James Kavanagh, and Roxanne Lapidus. *SubStance* 92: 3–24.

—2000b. "What Aesthetics Can Mean." In *From an Aesthetic Point of View*, edited by Peter Osborn, 13–33. London: Serpent's Tail.

—2003a. "Comment and Responses." *Theory & Event* 6 (4): n.p.

—2003b. "Politics and Aesthetics: An Interview." Interviewed by Peter Hallward. *Angelaki* 8 (2): 191–211.

—2003c. *Short Voyages to the Land of the People*. Stanford: Stanford University Press.

—2004a. *The Flesh of Words: The Politics of Writing*. Stanford: Stanford University Press.

—2004b. "Introducing Disagreement." *Angelaki* 9 (3): 3–9.

—2004c. *The Philosopher and His Poor*. Durham: Duke University Press.

—2005. "Democracy, Dissensus and the Aesthetics of Class Struggle: An Exchange with Jacques Rancière." Interviewed by Max Blechman, Anita Chari, and Rafeeq Hasan. *Historical Materialism* 13 (4): 285–301.

—2006a. *Film Fables*. Oxford: Berg Press.

—2006b. *Hatred of Democracy*. London: Verso.

—2006c. *The Politics of Aesthetics*. London: Verso.

—2006d. "Thinking Between the Disciplines: An Aesthetics of Knowledge." *Parrhesia* 1 (1): 1–12.

—2007a. "Art of the Possible: Fulvia Carnevale and John Kelsey in Conversation with Jacques Rancière." Interviewed by Fulvia Carnevale and John Kelsey. *Artforum* 45 (7): 256–68.

—2007b. *The Future of the Image*. London: Verso.

—2007c. *On the Shores of Politics*. London: Verso.

—2008a. "Aesthetics Against Incarnation: An Interview by Anne Marie Oliver." *Critical Inquiry* 35 (1): 172–90.

—2008b. "You Can't Anticipate Explosions: Jacques Rancière in Conversation with Chto Delat." Interviewed by Artemy Magun, Dmitry Vilensky, and Alexandr Skidan. *Rethinking Marxism* 20 (3): 402–12.

—2009a. *Aesthetics and Its Discontents*. Malden: Polity.

—2009b. "Contemporary Art and the Politics of Aesthetics." In *Communities of Sense: Rethinking Aesthetics and Politics*, edited by Beth Hinderliter, William Kaizen, Vered Maimon, Jaleh Mansoor, and Seth McCormick, 31–50. Durham: Duke University Press.

—2009c. *The Emancipated Spectator*. London: Verso.

—2009d. *Et Tant Pis Pour les Gens Fatigués: Entretiens*. Amsterdam: Hors Collection Edition.

—2009e. "A Few Remarks on the Method of Jacques Rancière." *Parallax* 15 (3): 114–23.

—2009f. "The Method of Equality: An Answer to Some Questions." In *Jacques Rancière: History, Politics, Aesthetics*, edited by Gabriel Rockhill and Philip Watts, 273–88. Durham: Duke University Press.

—2010a. *Chronicles of Consensual Times*. London: Continuum.

—2010b. "Communism Without Communists?" In *The Idea of Communism*, edited by Costas Douzinas and Slavoj Žižek, 155–66. London: Verso.

—2010c. *Dissensus: On Politics and Aesthetics*. London: Continuum.

—2011a. "Against the Ebbing Tide: An Interview with Jacques Rancière." In *Reading Rancière: Critical Dissensus*, edited by Paul Bowman and Richard Stamp, 238–51. London: Continuum.

—2011b. *Althusser's Lesson*. London: Continuum.

—2011c. *The Politics of Literature*. Malden: Polity.

—2011d. *Staging the People: The Proletarian and His Double*. London: Verso.

Rancière, Jacques, and Alain Badiou, (eds) 1992. *La Politique de Poètes: Pourquoi des Poètes En Temps de Détresse?* Paris: Albin Michel.

Roberts, Peter. 2000. *Education, Literacy, and Humanization: Exploring the Work of Paulo Freire*. Westport: Bergin & Garvey.

Robson, Mark. 2011. "Film, Fall, Fable: Rancière, Rossellini, Flaubert, Haneke." In *Reading Rancière: Critical Dissensus*, edited by Paul Bowman and Richard Stamp, 185–99. London: Continuum.

Ross, Alison. 2011. "Expressivity, Literarity, Mute Speech." In *Jacques Rancière: Key Concepts*, edited by Jean-Philippe Deranty, 133–50. Durham: Acumen.

Ross, Kristin. 2009. "Historicizing Untimeliness." In *Jacques Rancière: History, Politics, Aesthetics*, edited by Gabriel Rockhill and Philip Watts, 15–29. Durham: Duke University Press.

Rousseau, Jean-Jacques. 1979. *Emile or On Education*. New York: Basic Books.

Ruitenberg, Claudia. 2010. "Distance and Defamiliarization: Translation as a Philosophical Method." In *What Do Philosophers of Education Do?* edited by Claudia Ruitenberg, 103–17. Malden: Blackwell.

Sadovnik, Alan R., Jennifer A. O'Day, George W. Bohrnstedt, and Kathryn M. Borman, (eds) 2007. *No Child Left Behind and the Reduction of the Achievement Gap*. New York: Routledge.

Shor, Ira, and Paulo Freire. 1987. *A Pedagogy for Liberation: Dialogues on Transforming Education*. Massachusetts: Bergin & Garvey.

Simons, Marteen, and Jan Masschelein. 2008. "The Governmentalization of Learning and the Assemblage of a Learning Apparatus." *Educational Theory* 58 (4): 391–415.

—2010. "Governmental, Political and Pedagogic Subjectivation: Foucault *With* Rancière." *Educational Philosophy and Theory* 42 (5–6): 588–605.

Sloterdijk, Peter. 1988. *Critique of Cynical Reason*. Minneapolis: University of Minnesota Press.

Smith, Jason. 2011. "The Master in His Place: Jacques Rancière and the Politics of the Will." In *Everything is Everything: Jacques Rancière between Intellectual Emancipation and Aesthetic Education* edited by Jason E. Smith and Annette Weisser, 89–100. New York: Art Center Graduate Press.

Sullivan, Shannon and Nancy Tuana, (eds) 2007. *Race and Epistemologies of Ignorance*. New York: SUNY.

Swanger, David. 1983. "The Future of Aesthetic Education." *Journal of Aesthetic Education* 17 (1): 15–30.

Tanke, Joseph. 2011. *Jacques Rancière: An Introduction*. London: Continuum.

Taylor, Paul. 1993. *The Texts of Paulo Freire*. New York: Open University.

Toscano, Alberto. 2011. "Anti-Sociology and Its Limits." In *Reading Rancière: Critical Dissensus*, edited by Paul Bowman and Richard Stamp, 217–37. London: Continuum.

Vallury, Raji. 2009. "Politicizing Art in Rancière and Deleuze: The Case of Postcolonial Literature." In *Jacques Rancière: History, Politics, Aesthetics*, edited by Gabriel Rockhill and Philip Watts, 229–48. Durham: Duke University Press.

Virno, Paulo. 2008. *Multitude: Between Innovation and Negation*. Los Angeles: Semiotext(e).

Vlastos, Gregory. 1991. *Socrates: Ironist and Moral Philosopher*. Ithaca: Cornell University Press.

Vlieghe, Joris, Maarten Simons, and Jan Masschelein. 2010. "The Educational Meaning of Communal Laughter: On the Experience of Corporeal Democracy." *Educational Theory* 60 (6): 719–34.

Voelker, Jan. 2011. "Communist Education." In *Everything is Everything: Jacques Rancière* between *Intellectual Emancipation* and *Aesthetic Education* edited by Jason E. Smith and Annette Weisser, 64–78. New York: Art Center Graduate Press.

Willett, John (ed.) 1964. *Brecht on Theatre: The Development of an Aesthetic*. London: Hill and Wang.

Wilson, Tom, Peter Park, and Anaida Colón-Muñiz, (eds) 2010. *Memories of Paulo*. Rotterdam: Sense.

Wolfe, Katharine. 2006. "From Aesthetics to Politics: Rancière, Kant and Deleuze," *Contemporary Aesthetics* 4: n.p. http://www.contempaesthetics.org/newvolume/pages/article.php?articleID=382

Žižek, Slavoj. 2001. *The Sublime Object of Ideology*. London: Verso.

Index